William Temple

An Archbishop for All Seasons

William Ebor: 1935

WILLIAM TEMPLE
An Archbishop for All Seasons

By
Charles W. Lowry
D.Phil.(Oxon.),D.D.

With a Foreword by
The Most Rev. Robert Runcie
Archbishop of Canterbury

i

TO
MY SONS

Charles Wesley Lowry, III
Atherton Clark Lowry
James Meredith Price Lowry

A hundred little things make likenesses
In brethren born, and show the father's blood.
> Euripides, *Electra*
> (Translated by Sir Gilbert Murray)

Illustrations

CONTENTS

FOREWORD

William Temple was a prophet of controversial views but he was never strident or ungracious, and maintained a wide range of friendships with the most diverse characters.

The final chapter in Dr. Lowry's book is entitled The Friend, and this seems to me to be very appropriate. I am still constantly meeting people whose lives were never the same after they had met and enjoyed the friendship of William Temple.

I hope that this timely book, produced in the centenary year of Temple's birth, will serve to introduce this notable 20th century Christian prophet to a wide circle of new friends.

† Robert Cantuar.

Lambeth Palace
London
8/81

PREFACE

William Temple, Archbishop of York and then of Canterbury, became a legend in his own time.

In the middle and late 1930s he was the acknowledged leader of the Ecumenical Movement, in its non-Roman Catholic phase. No other Churchman, probably in all Christendom, compared with him in all-round stature — as an ecclesiastical statesman, a Christian person, a social prophet, a devotional master, an Apostle to the universities, and a profound, systematic philosopher-theologian.

It was the destiny of William as priest and prelate to be in the fore-front of the Church Militant as spokesman and symbol in two World Wars. It is not the least of his accomplishments in the Spirit that in the inferno of war he remained the simple yet exalted follower of the Lord Christ, serene and fearless, refusing to make harsh or final judgments, yet with utter trust in God expecting victory and prophesying faithfully with respect to the world and the will of God beyond the war.

It was as Archbishop of Canterbury in World War II that the Temple legend achieved its consummate expression. It says a great deal for the British people as well as for him that a spokesman with his purity of conscience and loftiness of Christian vision was able to catch the ear of all classes and conditions. It was stated more than once after his untimely death on October 26, 1944 that his hold on the nation as a whole was exceeded only by that of the great war-chieftain, Sir Winston Churchill.

A third of a century has passed. In the first and even the second decade after his death there was a considerable Temple literature. Even today doctoral theses in universities and theological seminaries continue to be written on him. There is still a wide if shrinking circle of persons who knew him and will never lose the memory of the man and his influence.

But in the churches generally and in theological seminaries and colleges, it is clear that the young both on faculties and in student bodies know not Temple. It was, I think, in 1976 that a pupil of mine, a son and grandson of Bishops and now a theological professor, said to me: "Temple is in danger of being forgotten; you ought to write a book on him and try to revive his influence."

This conversation stirred an uneasy conscience, for my personal debt to William *Ebor. et Cantuar.* is inestimable. I determined to do what I could in the direction indicated by my friend and pupil, the Rev. Charles Lawrence. This book, aimed at the Centenary of William Temple's birth but for various reasons delayed in publication, is the fruit of conscience, labor, and precious memory.

What I have tried to do is to write, not for the specialized scholar, but for the average parson, seminarian, and lay person. I have sought to present a study of Temple the man — his mind, character, and spirituality — as well as to provide a concise biography, one which comes in between the voluminous official Life of Dean Iremonger and the numerous short sketches which have accompanied various anthologies of Temple's writings or scholarly studies of his thought.

I believe that this remarkable man merits and will find a secure place in the annals of Christian and religious biography. Today especially he has much to teach us. We are living in a very religious age. I was bold enough, writing in 1952 in my book *Communism and Christ*, to declare that we had entered "a new historical period. The dominant motives are not, as in the past 600 years, reason and scientific knowledge. Instead they are religious, mystical, personal. The great aim of man in the new age is not to win mastery by knowledge but to find personal well-being through union with forces and powers greater than himself. This is the meaning of *religious* in its broadest sense."

I was, it appears, even more prophetic than I realized. Everywhere today religion is on the move; some form of salvation is the universal quest. It is very much as it was in the world into which Jesus the Christ was born.

In America it is said, on the basis of polls, that two out of every three persons professing religion claim to be "born again." Our last two Presidents are included in this category. The "revival of revivalism" (a phenomenon I commented on in 1952) has reached phenomenal proportions. Fundamentalism is having a field day not only in the Americas, but, as the whole world knows, throughout the length and breadth of Islam.

This situation is in truth amazing. It puzzles and confounds many people. It is particularly paradoxical since we are living also in a very dissolute time. Ours is an age of disorder and denial, of lawlessness, immorality, and apostasy.

Actually this is the reason for the recrudescence of revivalism and fundamentalism. It explains the fantastic incidence of conversion, born-again experience, radical turning to faith. God fulfills himself in many ways; never does he leave himself without witness. As St. Paul wrote in his celebrated account of the moral or immoral enormities of the culture of the Roman Empire, "For all that may be known of God by men lies plain before their eyes; indeed God himself has disclosed it to them." (Romans 1:19. NEB)

The living God, always both hidden and revealed (Isaiah 45:15), breathes continuously upon the world by his Spirit, and sends his winds whipping ceaselessly down the farthest corridors of time. Thus it comes about that men who defy the most High and flout his laws find themselves strangely turned around or at least forced to look with astonishment at the wonders of grace and the vitality and durability of Religion.

William James, Harvard psychologist and pragmatic philosopher of a century ago, was impressed by the range and "varieties of religious experience." But he detected alongside twice-born persons others whose lives seemed to be of one piece. He called them once-born as religious types.

William Temple is a classic example of this latter type. His life was remarkable in its wholeness and unity. It suggests the seamless robe of our Lord, emphasized by St. John in his Gospel. Temple is comparable here to Origen of ancient Alexandria and St. Thomas Aquinas in the 13th century. Yet he was profoundly aware, as the Saints invariably are, of "the exceeding sinfulness of sin" and stressed constantly the reality of original sin. He had a strong sense of grace and opined on more than one occasion that Pelagianism was the only damnable heresy.

This Titan of his age and of the whole Christian Church, who was yet a person of such simplicity and warm friendliness, has a message, alike in his life and in his thinking, for our troubled time. Great and relevant in so many departments, he is indeed an Archbishop for all seasons.

It was my immeasurable privilege to call William Temple my Friend and to enjoy a privileged relationship with him from 1935 till his death. During this period he wrote me 30 letters, all but four in his own hand-writing. When he became Archbishop of Canterbury he invited me to write one of a series of Lent books which he immediately planned in advance. (He had begun the series while still Archbishop of York.) He gave me the title of the book he desired, *The Trinity and Christian Devotion;* and I produced the book, though he did not live to read it.

In the last chapter of the work which follows I have written of Temple as Friend and have drawn on an experience which seemed then and still seems like a chapter from an improbable romance. For now it is enough to say that of all the great Archbishop's gifts and graces, none was more marked or more distinctive or sweeter than his genius for friendship. I loved His Grace for this (who could have helped it?) but also for all that he was as a man, a scholar, a Churchman, and a Saint.

One feature of the book which follows necessitates a short, further note. It presents as a kind of overture a short essay called "Two Stout Theologians." I am calling this *Prologue,* thinking of St. John and of William's deep love for this Gospel. On this Gospel more than on any-thing else his life from his youth up was founded. In the *Preface* to *Readings in St. John's Gospel* he tells us that for as long as he can re-member he has had more love for this Gospel than for any other book.

The idea of this "Prologue" came to me as a kind of brainstorm after a re-reading of G.K. Chesterton's creative and exciting volume, *Thomas Aquinas.* I had however in 1942, at the time of Temple's enthronement at Canterbury, been led to institute a comparison of his physique, tem-perament, and spiritual wholeness with those of the Angelical Doctor. (See *Christendom,* New York, Winter 1943. I was asked at that time to write the principal American article on the new Archbishop of Can-terbury.)

It is believed that most educated readers, particularly those interested in history in its broad sweep and in theology will appreciate the overture to this book. It is however entirely possible to skip this scholarly *bonus* and plunge at once into Temple's Life, beginning with Chapter I. The grand aim of this work, after all, is to introduce or re-introduce con-temporary persons of all ages to one of the supreme figures of this cen-tury and of English religious history.

Charles W. Lowry

October
1981

TO WILLIAM TEMPLE

A Sonnet

Temple! thou art sore needed at this hour.
The world and England are in danger grave;
The order that for long the Empire gave
Is shattered, while amidst rank chaos cower
The righteous forces that once brought to flower
A Kingdom strong. Yet they were used to save
God's people from the maw and fiery cave
Of churning passions raging to devour.

Thy faith was like a rock; thy dauntless hope
A beacon that gave courage to the weak.
Above all, thou wast captive to the love
Of God in Christ, whose Kingdom of the meek
Once turned the world around, reversed the slope
And tide of things, and gave mankind the Dove.

Charles W. Lowry

September 1979

PROLOGUE

TWO STOUT THEOLOGIANS

This is the story of two men who were separated by many centuries—more than six and a half to be precise. Nevertheless, they were much alike in many ways.

They were both fat men: stout or "tubby" is a better description, for there was nothing gross about them and both men lived abstemious lives. In fact they were both Saints, the older one acknowledged as such by canonization in the manner of the great Catholic Church of the West, the later one recognized as such by the general consent of all who knew him and observed him carefully.

What is more important than their girth or stature: both men had the temperament that seems to go with the glandular equipment that decrees *avoirdupois* in physique. The point can be better put by illustration than by attempted abstraction.

G.K. Chesterton was himself a fat man. In one of his inimitable studies, dealing with the first of our theological worthies, he speculates on the fact that he was called the Angelical Doctor and says, "Unfortunately, good temper is sometimes more irritating than bad temper."

We have now given away the identity of our first theologian. He is of course Thomas Aquinas. It has been said of him that there was never a single occasion on which he indulged in a sneer.

This is true also of our latter-day theologian whose identity is evident — William Temple. Temple, I believe, did not know how to sneer. And there is a charming story about his temper and temperament which illustrates perfectly the Chestertonian remark quoted above.

One day Temple was walking down Victoria Street, London with his good friend and greatly loved mentor, Bishop Charles Gore. They had just left a difficult meeting at which Gore, an irascible type, had lost his temper. The younger man, Temple, had of course kept his and as usual was beaming.

Gore, gloomy and penitent, said, "It is a terrible thing to have a bad temper." Then, glancing at the sunny face of his younger friend, he burst out: "But it's not so bad as having a good temper."

Our theologians, separated by the centuries and by the differences of their times, are astonishingly alike in background, in preparation for their task, and in their conception of what needed to be done. There is, curiously, a sharp drop-off in the optimistic situation that in each case appeared to exist and that had called forth a gigantic effort of mind and will in our two thinkers.

Both men died young and suddenly. Thomas was 49, William 63. They were in their prime, their work unfinished, Yet in a larger perspective, there is a completeness about both lives and the sense of a mighty task appropriately accomplished.

Thomas was born just as Chartres, foremost Cathedral of Christendom, was rebuilt following the dread fire of 1194. Two great Gothic Cathedrals, at Amiens and Salisbury, were begun about 1220, five years before his birth. The latter, Salisbury, was finished about the time of Thomas' death. The Protestant Cathedral in Lausanne, Switzerland, also duplicates almost exactly the dates of Salisbury.

1

It was a tremendous period, the 13th century. It was a time of *kairos* — of fulfillment in a unique and most eminent manner. Chartres, the *Summa Theologica* of Thomas, and Dante's *Divine Comedy* typify this time.

Dante, to be sure, did not do the actual writing of his immortal masterpiece until the first years of the new century — the 14th. But it belongs with Chartres and the *Summa* inasmuch as Thomas supplied the doctrinal framework of the *Divine Comedy* and the poet chose the theologian to guide him on the stairway to the highest heaven.

Thomas with startling acumen and extraordinary energy mapped the universe of being and of duty. He leaned heavily for his rational foundations on Aristotle but his outreach was wider and higher, his method of analysis and argumentation more intensive and ingenious. But it is the Aristotelian logic which he employs.

Thomas is first of all a philosopher. To reason and what it yields — he believes autonomously and independently — the Angelical Doctor adds doctrine derived from revelation given directly by God and not accessible to the unaided reason, though in no manner contrary to it. Thus he wove together in his gigantic fabric both philospohy and theology.

The Thomistic synthesis, as this system is often called, is in many ways the counterpart of a great Gothic Cathedral. It is an architectonic marvel with its totality arrived at by the addition of numerous harmonious units rather than through the composition of a single organic whole.

Still the Thomistic construction stands for all time as a wonder of the world of mind and spirit. Albert the Great, the teacher of Thomas, proved a true prophet when he said that his pupil for all that he appeared like a Dumb Ox would one day bellow so loud that his bellowing would fill the world.

The mass and extent of his writings stand, too, unmatched in the annals of thought. They include the topics on which the master Aristotle wrote besides others and many commentaries. The *Summa contra Gentiles* is in 4 volumes, the *Summa Theologica* in 21. Thomas' published writings in all fill 10,000 double-column folio pages. William Temple was not a Thomas Aquinas, obviously, but there are many parallels both as to time and talents.

William was never called a Dumb Ox, for one thing because he was never noted for keeping silent. His stature however made him an easy mark. There are famous lines about Temple from the pen of one of the wittiest of Oxford men, Ronald Knox, then Chaplain of Trinity College, later a Roman Catholic Monsignor. They begin thus:

> First, from the Public Schools — Lernean Bog —
> No paltry Bulwark, stood the Form of OG.
> A man so broad, to some he seem'd to be
> Not one, but all Mankind in Effigy.

This young stalwart, after opening himself eagerly to all that Rugby had to offer and more that he seized hold of on his own initiative, came up to Balliol College, Oxford as an Exhibitioner in 1900. He was just under 19 years old. Balliol was the College of Benjamin Jowett, translator of Plato. Jowett had been the intimate friend of Frederick Temple, the father of William, at Balliol. The Master in Temple's time was the Scottish Hegelian, Edward Caird.

Plato came in strong as young Temple laid the foundations of his thinking together with the emotional overtones that are never absent from basic cogitation and speculation. This philosopher remained forever after a master influence on William Temple. One of his early books, published in 1916, was on *Plato and Christianity.*

The Plato of Temple's studies was however different from the restricted and copied Plato of tradition at the time of Aquinas. In the Oxford Schools all his dialogues were laid open, and the study of this philosopher was of his infinite range and variety.

Furthermore, we are in the period of the reign of idealism in philosophy. Temple entered Oxford in 1900. The great, expansive, optimistic 19th century did not end really until 1914. It was closed off and the new, destructive 20th century inaugurated by the First World War.

This fact must be kept in mind in understanding the mind of William Temple. And there is a real and instructive parallel at this point with Thomas Aquinas.

G.K. Chesterton in interpreting the latter emphasizes his essential optimism. Thomas, he says, stands out as the great orthodox theologian who reminded men of the creed of Creaton. He remains the enemy of all "atmospheric pessimisms." For "he did, with a most solid and colossal conviction, believe in Life; and in something like what Stevenson called the great theorem of the livableness of life."

This is equally and quintessentially William Temple. And the atmosphere of the 19th century is crucial. It was a time of growth and expansion in every way. Synthesis was in the air philosophically. It was the hour of Hegel, the third great system-builder (after Aristotle and Aquinas), and his Anglo-American epigoni (Bradley, Bosanquet, and Josiah Royce).

Edward Caird became the mentor of Temple. The latter will dedicate his magnum opus, *Nature, Man and God,* to the memory of Caird and he always attributed to Caird such mastery of dialect as he possessed. This meant dialectic in the Platonic manner as method but synthesis a la Hegel in the end result aimed at. Truth lies in noting, accepting, and overcoming contradictions.

We are ready now to generalize with respect to Temple as a theologian. He was trained, as he always realized, primarily as a philosopher. He never really studied systematic theology, as the Germans viewed and expounded it. Paul Tillich thought that Temple once indicated to him that he understood what he, Tillich, was about in his three-volume *Systematic Theology,* and was very pleased. But Temple's understanding was far from being the same as the German's.

As a person steeped in Church and Christianity as far back as he could remember, and as a Believer always consciously committed and dedicated to Christ as the Incarnate Son of God, the eternal Word made flesh, William never doubted the centrality of the Incarnation. Here was the key to everything.

But as a trained philosopher he had to begin without dogmatic assumptions. He had to set out from the circumference of the circle and

3

move in to the center. Once attained, the center made it possible to look back and retrace the mind's steps in the full light of Divine Revelation.

Thus it seemed possible to map the world of being from the Christian point of view. Writing in November 1929, shortly after the outbreak of World War II, Temple says that in an earlier day that is what he and his contemporaries sought to do. "We tried, so to speak, to make a map of the world as seen from the standpoint of Christian Faith."

This as a matter of fact describes very well what the mature Archbishop Temple attempted to do in his magisterial Gifford lectures delivered at Glasgow during the academic years 1932-33 and 1933-34. He gave 20 lectures under the title *Nature, Man and God.* They were published immediately in 1934.

Reversing the approach of modern European philosophy from Descartes on, Temple begins not with man and mind but with nature as science examines and reports on it, including man. With empirical man however he is obliged to consider the nature of mind, value, and freedom. This leads up to the reality of Transcendence. The immanent God is seen to be transcendent.

The argument now shifts in accordance with a major dialectical transition. There are four of these transitions in all. They are vintage Temple, and his masterly handling of them must have delighted the soul of Edward Caird if he was permitted to overhear in Paradise the words of his devoted and illustrious pupil.

The Archbishop entitles Part I of his work (the first 10 lectures) "The Transcendence of the Immanent." Part II is "The Immanence of the Transcendent" and is of course a sustained overview of reality in the light of the existence of Transcendent Mind and Personhood.

The great themes here are Revelation, Spiritual Authority, Finitude and Evil, Divine Grace, The Commonwealth of Value, the Meaning of History, Eternal Life, and the Sacramental Universe. In expounding them the Scholar-Archbishop rises to great heights.

The whole weight in these dicussions is on synthesis, harmony, fulfillment, and the Divine satisfaction in Eternal Perfection. The structure is not only brilliant; it is brilliant in an architectonic way. It is not too much to say that it is worthy of comparison with the system of the *Summa Theologica* of St. Thomas.

The scale of Temple's construct is less massive. The unity and integration are more marked. If the system of St. Thomas is comparable to a Gothic Cathedral, Temple's edifice of thought is more like St. Paul's Cathedral, London, dominated and unified by its magnificent dome.

These analogies prove out when we note a point of principal difference in the thought of our two theologians, namely, the relations of reason and revelation. Both men are devoutly rational, if one may so express a profound commitment to reason. They stand together at the antipodes of fideists such as Tertullian, St. Bernard of Clairvaux, the foe of Abelard, and Martin Luther.

At the same time both of our theologians are equally convinced that Revelation is real and paramount. God, being of the kind of God He is, was bound to reveal Himself.

Wherein then is the difference between Thomas and William? It is in the division of territory.

4

Thomas divides the realm of our religious knowledge into two spheres. One is controlled by reason, the other revelation. This becomes the classical theological position.

The Gifford Lectures are supposed to be on this basis. Lord Gifford in founding them directed that the Lecturers were to treat their subject, that of Infinite Being, as a strictly natural science, without reference to any supposed revelation.

Temple was at an advantage, for he rejected as irrelevant abstraction the traditional division of theology into territorial spheres. Instead he put forward the fertile thesis that the distinction between Natural and Reveales Theology is not really concerned with the subject matter discussed, but with the method of discussion.

Thus, as the Archbishop said, we are today vividly conscious that the Bible, whatever it may contain of Divine self-disclosure, is also the record of a very rich and significant human experience. Modern Biblical scholarship has enlarged our understanding of the humanity of the Bible.

Likewise the Comparative Study of Religions, so popular today in American colleges and universities as well as among lay people, is grist for the mill of the Natural Theologian. At the same time the Buddha remains sacred to the Buddhists and Muhammad abides for the faithful of Islam as the ultimate Messenger of God, completing but not repudiating Moses and Jesus.

And of course for the Christian the ultimate authority is Jesus the Christ. The issue from the point of view of study is one of method.

As Temple sums up the matter, "So far as any doctrine is accepted on authority only, such acceptance lies beyond the frontier of Natural Theology....But the fact that a doctrine forms part of a dogmatic system, which is itself based on utterances regarded in some quarters as beyond all criticism, cannot exclude that doctrine from the purview of the Natural Theologian, provided that he considers it, or proposes it for acceptance, independently of such authority."

This acute analysis constitutes the presupposition of Temple's whole construction in *Nature, Man and God*. What he presents in this sustained and magnificent work is an essay in philosophical theology, but no idea *per se* is excluded from consideration by the author.

We have still to consider an important point, highly relevant to the difficult times in which we live and labor.

Thomas was scarcely in his grave, when enemies of his ideas attacked him vehemently. The quarrel reached up to the Papacy itself. In 1277 the Bishop of Paris, directed by Pope John XXI, issued a decree in which 219 propositions were branded as heresies. Three of these were attributed expressly to "Brother Thomas." They were, that angels have no body and therefore must be individually separate species; that matter is the principle of individuation; and that God cannot multiply individuals in a species without matter.

A point that particularly aroused opposition was Thomas' bold and very modern doctrine of the unity of soul and body in man. This was in opposition to the received Platonic doctrine of the soul. Teachers often illustrated this doctrine by saying that it, the soul, was in the body as a sailor in a ship.

Thomas did not hesitate to break at this point with the Platonizers, following instead Aristotle and Scripture. He declared, in a notable saying which rises to a great height of humanism, that though the soul is nobler than the body, the whole man, soul and body, is nobler than the soul.

For this and other views, Thomas was denounced at Oxford as well as in Paris.

The battle was not one-sided. Thomas' teacher, Albert, at 76 left the quiet of retirement to do battle for his pupil and Aristotle. The Dominicans in general were with their brother; the Franciscans, no longer brothers of the poor, were against him. In any event Pope John XXII became convinced that he was a saint and authorized in 1323 his canonization.

This action did not arrest the downslide of theology or society or Church influence. Thomas would in time stage a comeback and his doctrinal synthesis would virtually become canonical.

At the Council of Trent (1545-63) Thomas' *Summa Theologica* was put on the altar with the Bible and the conciliar Decrees.

It is most important to realize however that the main trend of Catholic theology after Thomas was against his central standpoint and was so powerful that it persisted in influence down to *and through* the Reformation. G.K. Chesterton's book on St. Thomas is vitiated by his apparent ignorance of this fact, and he is led into a great build-up of Luther as an Anti-hero that is as unjust as it is unhistorical.

Luther was a Fideist, he did turn savagely against scholastic theology which however at one period he had taught; he did call reason "that pretty harlot." But he did not arise like Melchizedek, the shadowy priest forever, in the Old Testament, without father or mother. He had a lineage in scholastic thought in its main line after Thomas Aquinas.

Thomas, it is clear, was to a considerable degree a rationalist. He believed in reason as a reflection of the Divine Light which was the perfect Union of Truth and Goodness. He labored to use reason and to have it take the mind as far as it could.

Nor was reason set aside when man was confronted by saving knowledge that could come only with God's revelation of self-disclosure through the prophets and perfectly in His Son Jesus Christ. Such knowledge was not, and could not be, on Thomas' view contrary to reason.

Unfortunately a storm was blowing up in the high Middle Ages over the subject of the will in relation to reason. The Scriptures tell us that man never continues long in one stay. This is profoundly true. There is always action and reaction, a swinging of the pendulum from side to side.

Thomas' moderate rationalism inspired by Aristotle was destined to make a strong comeback and remain the basis of post-Reformation Roman Catholic theology down to our time. But it did not satisfy for long in the heated atmosphere of the University of Paris in the late 13th and early 14th centuries. To Paris scholars flocked from all over Christendom. From Oxford brilliant Franciscans came, such as Duns Scotus and William of Occam, who magnified the will in the being of man and of God.

These men and their successors stressed the independence and arbitrary freedom of the will. With man this created problems, for the power of God had to be reckoned with. But an arbitrary infinite will is indeed a fearsome concept. It is something that is bound to be extreme and overwhelming.

For one thing universals such as justice went by the board. Realism rooted in the ideas or eternal forms of Plato was rejected, and common unitive qualities that had been seen as the basis of classes, species, and genera were dismissed as mere names (nominalism).

Thus it came about that the theological atmosphere that conditioned the Protestant Reformation was one dominated by extreme volitionalism and nominalism. This really means that the tools of basic reasoning and thinking are absent.

The way is paved for an exclusive reliance upon Scripture, an extreme emphasis upon such doctrines as total depravity, justification by faith alone, and double predestination and — what is relevant to our discussion — the rejection of the natural law and the elevation of kingly authority above Law and Right. A new and a-moral version of the divine right of kings came into play. It not only fortified the tyranny of Henry VIII, and wrecked the Stuarts, but spilled over into the claims of the Catholic monarchs as well.

William Temple was a Platonist and an idealist in his sense of reason or the "sentiment of rationality." For him faith and reason were even more intimately coordinated than for Thomas Aquinas.

If there are four distinct positions in the manner of the relations of faith and reason, namely, fideism, the *credo ut intelligam*[1] of St. Augustine and St. Anselm, the Thomistic division of territory, and the *logos* doctrine of the Stoic Platonists and St. John, it is the last which attracted Temple.

The Archbishop knew of course that faith was a powerful and necessary thing and that reason had its limits. Nevertheless he found no real tension between them. They were, it seemed, different aspects of the mind and soul of man contemplating the world, experience, and God. At the very least they were full partners and compatible teammates.

Coming into maturity as he did in the essential 19th century (through 1913), Temple was grasped by two goals. He thought that the time was ripe for mapping the world from a Christian standpoint. And he saw no reason not to claim the actual world of human beings and human relationships for God in the spirit and meaning of the religion of the Incarnation.

These were the two keys to William Temple. As the philosopher became more and more submerged in the affairs of Church and Nation, he saw his dream of possibly forging a mighty synthesis of Christian thought recede. But when the opportunity and challenge of the Gifford Lectures came, he moved boldly to undertake a synoptic view of Reality — Nature, Man and God — working by reason in the light of the religious vision.

Even as a philosopher, the young Temple put a strong emphasis upon

---

[1] I believe in order to understand.

7

action. As a Churchman, he was inspired and guided by what was in effect a "transformational theology." The time for doing the will of God was now. The field was not the Church merely, but the Nation and the World.

St. John did not stop with the gift of eternal life to the individual believer. "For God sent not his Son into the world to condemn the world, but that the world through him might be saved." And even John 3:16 begins: "For God so loved the *world.*"

The First World War does not seem to have disturbed Temple in his basic, optimistic outlook. He went ahead steadfastly with his certain conviction that the Gospel of the Kingdom was a total Gospel.

The 1930's however were a difficult period. The Great Depression gave the Totalitarian experiments a new lease on thought and life. Democracy was thrown on the defensive. In theology pessimism replaced optimism. Barth, Brunner, Kierkegaard, Niebuhr were the great names. In England among the younger men Neo-Thomism was a strong force.

By the late 30's a doctrinal gale was blowing and Temple, ever open and sensitive to others, felt its force. His own outlook was hardly changed, but he was ready to acknowledge the radical shift in climate and outlook.

Miss Dorothy Emmet, who corresponded with the Archbishop in 1942 on this whole matter, has quoted extensively from a comprehensive letter written to her. The quotation is in her chapter on "The Philosopher," contributed to the official Temple biography by F.A. Iremonger.

Temple thinks that the modification in his thinking that is demanded is substantial but not important. "It is a much clearer perception of what is worked out in the Gifford Lectures about process and value."

> What we must completely get away from, he continues, is the notion that the world as it now exists is a rational whole; we must think of its unity not by the analogy of a picture, of which all the parts exist at once, but by the analogy of a drama where, if it is good enough, the full meaning of the first scene only becomes apparent with the final curtain; and we are in the middle of this. Consequently the world as we see it is strictly unintelligible. We can only have faith that it will become intelligible when the divine purpose, which is the explanation of it, is accomplished. [1]

When Temple, now Archbishop of Canterbury, wrote this letter to Miss Emmet, he was at work on a small book, but one that he regarded as all-important — *Christianity and Social Order*. It is indeed characteristic of the man that, with world war fiercely raging, and with all the vast range of his new and exacting responsibilities, he should focus his full attention on what England should try to be, and should be, as a Nation and Society.

We can see here, as in a flash, the mind of Temple as a theologian and its contrast with the characteristic thrust of theology across the centuries.

Professor H.L. Goudge, the father of the well-known novelist, once declared that there are only two doctrines in the Bible: God and the

[1] pp. 537-8.

Church. Temple knew and valued this epigram. I have heard him quote it in a lecture. Nevertheless, he was far from accepting it as the fundament of his outlook and basic theological construct.

St. Paul, it seems to me, agreed with Goudge, or vice versa. The same general standpoint was controlling for St. Augustine. He worked it out with transcendent genius in his *City of God.*

In the Augustinian scheme however, as in the Bible, there is a strongly dualistic element. It is provisional not ultimate. "Christianity is a proximate pessimism but an ultimate optimism."

In the end God is victorious; his purpose is achieved. This is the meaning of eschatology. But the outcome is not monistic. Evil is defeated and expelled, as well as transmuted. Hell is a reality, as well as Heaven, in the final transcendental situation.

This scheme, in which election and predestination play a critical part, is fundamental in Christian orthodoxy. Aquinas accepts it and at the Reformation it received a new lease on life and a long run of consummate influence.

The 18th century marked a division point. It was the era in which reason was canonized. The 19th, though far more expansive, reaching out to embrace feeling and romanticism, did not turn away from reason. In fact, it gave birth to monism, something new in the history of thought.

This expansive outlook, typified by Hegel, the third great system builder, took into account and indeed was dominated by the new sense of history. Temple, to some extent the child of this time, received a permanent impress from the monistic impulse. At the same time he held on to a transcendent God and the Incarnation. These remained his supreme guidelines as he confronted history, past, present and future. It is fair to say that he ends up, not with a block universe in the mode of absolute idealism but with transformational theology with an acceptance of process as well as a bias toward optimism.

Back in 1944 it was hard to accept the death of Temple. He was only 63 and at the height of his powers which were so magnificent. By common consent he was the greatest Christian churchman of his time. In Britain he was seen as the voice of conscience, a spokesman for the country's inner, better self. A book would shortly be written on him as "The People's Archbishop."

Notwithstanding, it may well be that there was something providential in his leaving the scene at the moment when victory was in sight and he was on top of things in point of influence and leadership. The sudden fall of Churchill after VE Day warns us of the fickleness of popular opinion and the never-ceasing oscillation of fortune in the political order. Temple to be sure was anchored by his office in the spiritual order — in the Church. But the Church has as a visible organization a political aspect. Moreover, Temple as a thinker and a leader was uniquely astride both orders, and therefore doubly vulnerable.

The example of Abraham Lincoln is relevant to such a reverent speculation as this. His outlook was so right from the standpoint of North and South in the post-war period. He was born to be a reconciler. But the passions of war are a harsh reality, and they do not subside readily with the cessation of hostilities. They seem to demand not only an outlet but an object on which to vent anger and hostility. This is probably more true of popular war in the era of Democracy than it was in the situation of limited war prior to the French Revolution and Napoleon. Anyway as we look back on history, it seems doubtful that Lincoln could have become the transfigured person he became and remains had it been his destiny to fight the political battles of Reconstruction.

Thus we are brought up against the ways of God in relation to time and history, which are not as our ways. And we are confronted by the role of influence — moral and spiritual influence — exerted from beyond the grave by saints and seers, heroes and martyred leaders, in the ongoing history of mankind. From this point of view we see that a figure such as William Temple, far from being exhausted in his meaning for life by contemporary biographers, requires scrutiny and study from generation to generation. History, it has been said, is mainly biography, and the lives of the saints are the lifeblood of the Church.

There is therefore no impropriety in adding to the studies that have been made, the portraits that have been drawn, of this tremendous man who will loom larger as we see him in perspective and are able to compare him with his peers in the gallery of the immortals in the things of the Spirit. Four men were ranked by the Middle Ages as Doctors of the Church: Jerome, Ambrose, Augustine, and Gregory the Great. It has been well suggested by Professor Joseph Fletcher, doubtless with this precedent in mind, that William Temple was the last of Anglicanism's "Four Great Doctors", standing in the succession of Richard Hooker, Joseph Butler, and F.D. Maurice.

Of all these however it is William Temple who, alike in personality and in the range and sweep of his philosophico-theological system, most resembles St. Thomas, the giant of the Middle Ages and the Angelical Doctor of Western Catholicism.

CHAPTER ONE

BACKGROUND AND BOYHOOD

A great English poet wrote — at the beginning of the 19th century:
The Child is father of the Man;
And I could wish my days to be
Bound each to each by natural piety.

These lines assuredly describe the development of the subject of
this sketch, William Temple, and the linkage of all his days. Of course
in the end he was himself, and the form of his life and being was freedom. At the same time he was to a phenomenal degree the product
of his background, early home and church life, and childhood and
boyhood. To an extent truly extraordinary his life and career were of a
single piece.

William was the younger of two sons born late in life to a remarkable
scholar of Oxford, headmaster, and prelate — Frederick Temple.

Frederick did not marry until after he was Bishop of Exeter. As long
as his mother, to whom he owed much and was deeply bound, lived, he
had her with him and did not marry. At the age of 55 he married a lady
20 years his junior, Beatrice Blanche Lascelles. She was the niece of
three Dukes and the blood that flowed in her veins was as blue as any
in England. Her father, the Rt. Hon. William Saunders Sebright
Lascelles, was a younger son of the Earl of Harewood and Lady Caroline
Howard, daughter of the Sixth Earl of Carlisle.

Beatrice was born in 1845 and at that time standards for the education of women were very different from those of the 20th century.
William has a note about this that has especially interested me. In one
of his letters, written at the time of his mother's death in 1915, he wrote:

> There was a spaciousness of mind about her and others of her gen-
> eration which I don't think modern methods and girls' colleges tend
> to produce. She was never **taught** anything. She got rid of her gover-
> ness when 11 years old; but she lived in houses where most of the
> leading folk assembled from time to time. No doubt Girton or Somer-
> ville is better than home for most. But to be about the place from
> childhood on, while Gladstone, Dizzy, Harcourt, Mat Arnold, Bal-
> four, talked at large, must be better still.

Like his father, William lived with his mother during her last years.
After he became a Fellow of Queen's and a philosophy don she moved
to Oxford. Her house was a gathering for kindred spirits. William was
not backward in making known his ideas and views, and the story is
that once after he had pontificated away at a great rate, his mother
said, "Willie, you know more than I do, but I know best."

William inherited from his mother, according to his nephew, the
Right Reverend Frederick Stephen Temple, Bishop of Malmesbury

with whom I talked in 1977, his tendency to stoutness. I particularly queried him about this, for Professor Joseph Fletcher in his book *William Temple, Modern Churchman* asserts that William Temple resembled in stature and other ways his parental grandfather, Major Octavius Temple. Bishop Frederick Temple said that this was not so.

William was close to his mother but the great influence on his life and thought was his father Frederick. The father was himself an Archbishop of Canterbury. This is unique in history and is in itself a notable coincidence.

The older Archbishop is no longer well known. Were it not for his son William it is doubtful if he would be remembered late in the 20th century at all. Yet Frederick Temple was in his own right a man and a churchman of marked distinction. It is not too much to say that alike in character and in intellect he was a giant in his day.

The Temples were a well known family in the 17th and 18th centuries. William Johnston Temple, the grandfather of Frederick, was a contemporary of Samuel Johnson and James Boswell and an intimate of the latter. Temple and Boswell had known one another at the University of Edinburgh. When Temple in 1763 entered Trinity Hall, Cambridge, he loaned his rooms in the Inner Temple to Boswell. The latter wrote: "I found them particularly convenient for me, as they were so near Dr. Johnson's."

This Temple's father was also a William and he was a substantial man. Over the Town Hall of Berwick-on-Tweed one can still see the inscription: "Finished 1754. William Temple, Esq. Mayor."

This William and his father George were Presbyterians and were Trustees of the Low Meeting-House, the chapel of the Scottish Presbyterians who were regarded in Berwick as Dissenters.

Frederick's father Major Octavius Temple was an Army man and a minor imperial civil servant. He was Resident or Commandant of Santa Maura, one of the Ionian Islands, and it was here that Frederick was born on St. Andrew's Day, November 30, 1821.

At the age of nine Frederick moved with his family back to England, to a farm near Culmstock in Devon which Major Temple had purchased. Three years later Octavius accepted an appointment as Lieutenant Governor of Sierra Leone in Africa. He lived however less than a year following his departure for the Dark Continent.

It is evident that this family was not well off and indeed suffered acutely from poverty after the death of Major Temple, Frederick's father. His mother, Dorcas Carveth Temple, was left with many mouths to feed and also heavy educational responsibilities.

Dorcas belongs in the select company of exceptional Mothers whose influence on the world through their children is incalculable. This Cornish Mother accepted heroically a role for which she was ill-prepared, that of schoolmistress as well as Mother. Alike in her ingenuity and conscientiousness she reminds us of Susannah, the Mother of the Wesleys.

There was a particularly close relationship between Dorcas and her 13th child, Frederick. There were 15 in all, of whom eight "grew up." It is worthy of note that Octavius was the 8th and youngest child of

William Johnston Temple, clergyman and literary light, Boswell's friend.

A sister of Frederick, Jennetta Octavia, two and a half years his senior, dictated many years later memoranda of her Mother to Archdeacon J.M. Wilson at Cannes. "My mother" she wrote, "was considered a beautiful woman, with gentle manners, knowing no language but her own, not clever in the sense of brilliant at all, but thoughtful, with excellent judgment, great sense of personal dignity, governing her family without any effort, without severity. Her word was unquestioned law. Her children were obedient, without feeling the possibility of being otherwise. In the usual daily life and in sickness, tender and loving; but if her children did wrong, regarding them with surprised anger at the possibility of doing it; so that while grave faults would be confessed to my father, they would not be confessed to her — from no fear of punishment, but from fear of the look of horror in her eyes."

Dorcas was the only teacher her children had at the elementary level. She taught them to read and write. Arithmetic was taught by steady repetition, since she knew little herself. She used a key to the sums in the arithmetic book. If an answer was wrong, the exercise had to be repeated the next day, and if necessary the next.

She taught her boys Latin in a similar way, by rote and repetition. When Frederick was 12 and went to school, he knew his grammar perfectly, as no other boy knew it. But he could not pronounce a word of Latin and therefore was at first put at the bottom of his class. Euclid he had been taught the same way by his Mother. Algebra he had learned so far as he was able himself.

Books were scarce on the Island of Santa Maura but when Frederick was 7, we are told, he had read Duncan's *Caesar,* Dryden's *Virgil,* Pope's *Homer, Evenings at Home* (whatever that was), and much of Watkin's *Encyclopedia.* Not bad for a start.

Dorcas also read daily with her family without comment the appointed Psalms and Lessons. This in lieu of a chaplain and regular Services. The Catechism was taught in the same way, systematically but without comment.

At the age of 12 Frederick entered Blundell's School, Tiverton and was a student there for 4 years. The quality of the boy and of the educational influences of the school can be gauged from the fact that Frederick read "nearly the whole of Euripides in my spare time out of school" and that he got hold of Brand's *Algebraical Problems,* a standard textbook, and "worked entirely through it in my playtime, and found that it gave me a mastery of the lower parts of algebra which I doubt if I could have obtained from any teacher whatever. I must confess, therefore, that I have a love for the old Grammar School system."

It was thus that Frederick wrote when he was nearly 50 years old and had been consecrated Bishop of Exeter, having given up the Headmastership of Rugby for the Episcopate. At Rugby he had encouraged a system that gave boys the opportunity to do independent work and the freedom to do or not to do it. His son William at Rugby 25 years after the speech quoted above would make superb use of such freedom, though primarily in reading greedily the English poets and philosophers modern and ancient rather than mathematics.

In the summer of 1838, before he was 17, Frederick won a Blundell's Scholarship to Balliol College, Oxford. It tells a great deal about this boy when one realizes that, despite his unskilled early schooling, he rose in three years from the bottom of the school to the position of monitor, and then went on to capture the Oxford Scholarship.

This event was a turning-point in the life and career of Frederick Temple. At Oxford in spite of poverty and acute privation, when he skimped and saved in order to send money home to his Mother, Frederick blossomed and flowered, intellectually and in every other way.

His character was well formed, and he kept his feet on the ground in a period of intense ferment in the University, religiously and intellectually. The Oxford Movement had begun in 1833. It was the day of Newman, Keble, and Pusey, and of Hurrell Froude and W.G. Ward. It was also the Oxford of Benjamin Jowett, just four years Frederick's senior, and of Matthew Arnold, Arthur Hugh Clough, Lord Coleridge (John Duke), J.C. Shairp, F.T. Palgrave, Arthur Stanley (later Dean of Westminster), and A.C. Tait (Temple's Tutor, Later Headmaster of Rugby and Archbishop of Canterbury) — all friends of Frederick.

When Frederick arrived at Oxford, he was consciously a Tory and very conservative. He was but 17, fresh from his simple farmstead background and the studies of a provincial Grammar School. Unavoidably he was thrust into the very vortex of the Oxford Movement. Soon he is writing home about the *Tracts for the Times,* which he is reading. Newman was still in the Pulpit at St. Mary's. Frederick writes home about a sermon by Pusey, "one of the most beautiful" he ever heard. He became very friendly with W.G. Ward and writes of a long walk and talk with him about the Church of Rome and of England. Ward gave him the 4th and 5th volumes of Newman's Sermons, after finding that he knew the 1st and 3rd.

All this was very heady, but Frederick it is clear kept his feet. He was never tempted to go off on a tangent. Part of the reason was the supremacy in him of the moral being. He was by nature and training a Wordsworthian and a Kantian. This was ever more fundamental in his being than a trend in doctrine or churchmanship. Like William in the next generation he was firmly anchored in the central tradition of Anglicanism and was never tempted to become a "party" churchman.

Another factor was the enormous diligence of this boy — acquired in childhood and ever characteristic of the man. As Bishop of London at 75 he will be working 14 and 15 hours a day. From 76 to 81 he will spend himself without stint in the awesome position of Archbishop of Canterbury. Duty and work were uppermost in the undergraduate and the man. Deep in his being was the reiterated admonition of his Mother.

"Freddy, don't argue; do your work."

We cannot do better than quote here a few excerpts from a remarkable letter written in February, 1889 by the great Benjamin Jowett, then Master of Balliol, in which he gives his reminiscences of Frederick

14

Temple.

Temple was now Bishop of London and his older sister, Miss Jennetta Octavia Temple, had written the Master of Balliol asking for some reminiscences of her brother's Oxford days. Dr. Jowett wrote:

> *I have always thought him the finest young man we ever had at Balliol. He was so good and simple; he had such uncommon force of mind and power of acquiring knowledge. I have seldom, if ever, known any one like him....His perserverence and self-denial were extraordinary. That he might not be a burden to his friends, he used to practice a rather severe economy. He would sit without a fire in the depth of winter...He was always liberal and generous, as he continued to be through life. It could not be said of him that he had not got the chill of poverty out of his bones, for he never had it in him. He had a loud and hearty laugh, and was quite free from shyness. The high spirits of youth made him at times a little uproarious. When he became a College tutor, he was a tower of strength....Almost immediately after he took his degree (a double first in classics and mathematics) he became mathematical tutor at Balliol College. During the five years which succeeded he read a good deal of German philosophy, and was one of the few Englishmen who understood what he read. In those days he and I were much together; he was one of the kindest friends, and though he was four years younger than myself, I learnt a great deal from him. He had thought more than most of us, and had great powers of influencing his contemporaries at Balliol who had more cleverness and more originality; but in none of them was there the same interpenetration of moral and intellectual qualities, or the same simple-minded desire to do good, under the control of good sense.*

It is worth noting that Frederick Temple was the first person at Oxford for many years who obtained a first-class degree without the help of a private tutor. He wrote his mother that this had saved him L50. Frederick was only 20 when he took this distinguished degree.

He was a natural mathemetician, with a singular power of visualizing space relations and numbers. He was able, too, to see without counting comparatively large numbers.

An amusing example given by Archdeacon J.M. Wilson of the latter faculty was his discovery as Bishop of Exeter that boys were in the habit (presumably it was a game) of coming to be confirmed a second time. The clergyman would bring the list for the vestry with, say, 40 names on it. "But there were 43," said the Bishop. "No, my Lord, only 40," was the reply. "Did your Lordship count them?" "No, I saw them," and it turned out that he was right.

Another side of young Frederick Temple — this was before he was ordained — was his habit at Balliol of inviting, on the evening before the monthly administration of Holy Communion, to his rooms any undergraduates who chose to come, to hear a short address. The room, a moderate-sized lecture room," was generally full. The addresses, which he read, were of a devotional character — never controversial — simple, earnest, affectionate, full of sympathy with young men in their trials and difficulties, sometimes delivered with marked emotion." (Recollection of Dr. Hornby, Provost of Eton, many years later.)

Frederick Temple left Oxford in 1848 (after nine years residence as a student and tutor) to devote himself to the education of the English poor under Government auspices. Plans had been made for establishing a Normal School for training teachers for Workhouse Schools, and Temple was to be head of it.

Thus in 1850 he became Principal of Kneller Hall where for five years he gave himself with burning energy and rare consecration to what was for him an especially sacred task. The project was experimental and in the end failed — the victim of inherent problems in the Workhouse set-up and denominational jealousies.

From the testimony of a pupil who had been under Temple at Kneller Hall, it is clear that the latter made an enormous impression on the students under him. It is also fascinating to read again of his friends.

"The most constant visitor whom I can recall was Mr. Jowett. We recognized also his (Temple's) extraordinary power, and we took it as quite in the natural order of things that men like Macaulay, Tennyson, and others, whose fame was already widespread, should be among his ordinary visitors."

It is evident that there was no little interest in this bold educational venture on behalf of the poor. After it was decided to close Kneller Hall, Temple was made and served two years as Inspector of Church of England Male Training Colleges. In 1857 he was called to be Headmaster of Rugby School and accepted.

Among the chorus of testimonials commending Temple for this position, that of Matthew Arnold, son of Thomas Arnold, the famed former Headmaster of Rugby , is the most arresting. He wrote:

> In the most important qualities of a headmaster, in the union of piety, energy, and cheerfulness, in the faculty of governing the young, in the power of commanding at once the respect and the affection of those under his charge, Mr. Temple, more than any other man I have ever known, resembles, to the best of my observation and judgment, my late father.

Frederick Temple was a great success as Headmaster of this key school. From there he went on step by step to the highest office in the Church of England, and one with many State overtones. It is no part of our purpose to pursue his career further save as his son William was affected by it. It is important that we know what manner of man the father was, for he was the master influence on his son.

In the case of Frederick, the influence of his mother was primary and premier. With William the reverse is true. The father exerts the dominant influence.

For one thing William knew his father only as a great prelate and a ruler of men. William was born in the Palace of Exeter. Before he was four, Frederick had been translated to London with the family installed in Fulham Palace.

This was home till William was fifteen, when his father was made Archbishop of Canterbury. By this time the boy had been for more than a year a Scholar of Rugby.

It would be hard to imagine a more ideal home, from the angle alike of Christian nurture and family solidarity, than the Temple household.

Frederick the Bishop and Archbishop was at once an authoritarian figure, strong, rugged, fiery, yet a man of deep feeling, with a natural love fortified and deepened by the conscious love of Christ. The relation of husband and wife was a close one, exalted and spiritual as well as affectionate.

This was the atmosphere, the penumbra, in which the boy William lived from birth and to it was added the physical and sensuous associations of chapel, church, and religious ceremonial.

There is a memorable description in Iremonger's *Life* of the daily order of things devotional and ecclesiological at Fulham Palace, London. The day began with prayers in the Palace Chapel.

> *For this there was a well-established ceremonial. The boys (William and his older brother Frederick) waited in the vestry, which was separated from the chapel by a stone-flagged passage. The butler also waited, with the Bishop's surplice over his arm.*
>
> *Mrs. Temple and other ladies would come hurrying down the passage, followed by the Bishop. He never stopped, but kissed each of his sons as he walked on; and the butler put his surplice over the Bishop's arms extended backwards, and on to his shoulders. The boys fell in beside their father, who put his arms around them, looking (as was remarked) like a large angel with wings as he entered the chapel. He turned into his stall, and William stepped over his mother's feet to take his place on her left.*
>
> *Going out, the boys chased after their father, who dropped his surplice just outside the door, without looking round, into the hands of the pursuing butler, and again put his arms over the shoulders of his sons.*

These impressions could not help being formative and powerful, as was the tenor and content of the chapel services. More than fifty years later Temple wrote of this to a friend:

> *I am constantly thinking of the enormous difference that it must have made to you and me that from a date before we could clearly remember things, we heard some verses of the Bible read every day; probably three times out of five we did not directly attend to it; but it was flowing over our growing minds, even when attention wandered, and must have been producing a great effect in making natural and spontaneous that whole outlook upon life which the Bible expresses. Whereas one of our great troubles now is that the predominant outlook upon life is formed by scientific and not by religious categories. Causation is much more prominent in men's thoughts than purpose and judgment.*

This is a prophetic passage of singular importance, not only because of what it tells us about the life and mind of William Temple, but because of its penetrating clarity as an analysis of the predicament of man in a scientific and technical age.

In an article written for the publication *The Blessings of Liberty* (January 1977), I put forward the thesis that the eclipse of spirituality in our time even in the great organized churches is due to the general loss of a religious view of the world. This view has been swamped by a naturalistic outlook based on science and regarded mistakenly, as the philosopher Whitehead has cogently shown, as more concrete and experiential, than that of the poets, the seers, and the saints of our race.

17

CHAPTER TWO

EDUCATION

William Temple was the son of a great educator and natural teacher. He was in every way worthy of his father. In receptivity and ability the son left nothing to be desired, or perhaps even dreamed of, by either of his parents.

Not surprisingly, William received and achieved a first-class education — the best that England had to give at the time when classics were still the order of the day. To this foundation the boy and young man added, out of innate aptitude and abounding energy, a splendid grounding both in English poetry and in philosophy.

William was privileged to have both a "Nana" and a Governess. And he was lucky in the character and devotion of both.

His "Nana" was Ellen Langdon, a native of Devon as William was and the daughter of a country station-master who was a distinguished amateur astronomer. She became a fixture in the household and stayed with William until his marriage. She read all his books as they came out and died in a home for the blind after bequeathing to him nearly all her savings.

A second influence was that of a Governess, Edith Maskell, who began on 31 May 1886 "to teach Freddy and William (to read) at Fulham Palace." William was then four and a half years old.

He spoke often in later years of what he owed to his Governess. He congratulated her on his Balliol Exhibition: "A great part of the credit certainly belongs to you." On her death he wrote that she was "one of the most simply good and self-denying people that I have ever known."

Lessons went on in the Palace until William was nearly 10. In the summer of 1891 he was entered in a new day-school under Mr. James Brewster — Colet Court, Hammersmith. Here he began the study of Greek and eventually mathematics.

By the end of 1893 he was head of the school in classics and class-list. To this was added mathematics in his last term. On 25 July 1894 he records: "Yesterday I brought home my ninth and last prize from Colet Court."

William was quite musical and during this period learned to play on the piano. Then he went on to the organ. He seems from an early date to have found Church choirs fascinating.

He was confirmed in June 1894 (at 12) and made his first Communion a week later. A month before that he had an attack of what was to be his bane for the next half century — gout. He had his first attack when he was only two years old.

I remember as yesterday a bad attack William, then Archbishop of York, had in the middle of the Edinburgh World Conference in 1937.

He was President of the Conference and normally wore his Archbishop's clericals and gaiters. But while enduring and wearing out his gout, he shed clericals and limped about with a stick.

William told me then with a burst of his inimitable, explosive laughter that the doctors told him he was one of the few people who had the original, old-fashioned variety of gout. He was, in fact, unusually abstemious. He drank no hard liquor and only a little wine on occasion. Between 1935 and 1937 he started dieting and at Bishopthorpe in 1937 he took only coffee and fruit for breakfast. At Tea it was only tea.

In September 1894, less than a month before his 13th birthday, William entered Rugby. There was no other school for a Temple. Here it was given to him to strive and thrive. During his six years at Arnold's and his father's school, he continued building and perfecting the foundations of his superb education.

Rugby, Temple was to write later, was the most strenuous of schools. "It makes everyone work." He adds that there is very little free time except for boys quick enough to make extra time. Thus he "had two hours' preparation on end for two consecutive hours in School: I could nearly always do this in ½ hour and so got an hour and a half free. It was in time so made that I read the whole of 7 English poets before I left School."

In this way also William was able to read all of the *Phaedo* of Plato and the *De Rerum Natura* of Lucretius. Enamored early of philosophy, he found the time in addition to start reading modern European philosophers in earnest.

This process was facilitated by the fact that by the time he was fifteen and a half — the earliest permissible age — he had reached the sixth form. Here he remained until 1900, studying hard and largely following his native bent. In 1900 at 18 he went up to Oxford.

At Rugby William finished third of the 22 boys on the Upper Bench. He was never a raving grammarian. He aspired to master the works of great thinkers rather than to excel in textual criticism or prosody. Even so the Headmaster wrote of the boy to Frederick Temple: "I think *anything* is possible to him."

One of the first philosophers he tackled was Kant. At seventeen when on holiday in the Lakes, while others fished, he would sit in a boat all afternoon absorbed in the *Critique of Pure Reason*. Many years later in his magnum opus, *Nature, Man and God,* he says that when as a boy he read Kant's *Critique of Pure Reason,* never having heard of Descartes or Berkeley, he got the impression that Kant meant what he afterwards learnt was the meaning of Berkeley. At Oxford he would hear his philosophical mentor and college Master, Edward Caird, say: "Kant started from both ends of the road at once, but he never met himself."

Other philosophers or theologians he read, in addition to Plato, were Aristotle and Bishop Butler, Coleridge and Bacon. He was reading regularly the Greek New Testament and was already grappling with the problem of the will and its freedom. We know all this from William's correspondence with his father, whom he wrote once a week.

He plied the Archbishop with all manner of queries. His father answered them meticulously but on occasion found the opportunity gently but firmly to guide and even admonish the precocious young philosopher. On one occasion he wrote: "The danger of your speculation is that if you do not take care you will lower your idea of God."

This is one thing that William never did — as a student, an Oxford don, a churchman, a prelate, a man among men, a Christian statesman in peace and war. He never lowered his idea of God. The God whom he served was in his mind always "the God and Father of our Lord Jesus Christ," the supreme Being, truly the *summa res*, who was perfect goodness and perfect love. By this God his whole life — of mind, will, and affection — was directed.

This is the key to Temple the man. He lived his whole life as under the eye of God — but a God of love and goodness — the God reflected in the face of Christ. Inevitably his own character was an expression, consciously and unconsciously, of the character of God.

Prior to his Final Examinations and taking his Honors B.A. in June 1904, William was elected to the only office he ever coveted in his entire life. During the Lent Term of 1904 he was President of the Oxford Union.

The Union exists for speaking and debate on the issues of the day. It is a kind of embryonic Parliament. William distinguished himself from the start as a speaker and debater in the Union. "He had already," his Tutor wrote, "an unusual gift of ready and lucid speech." During 1903 he had been successively Secretary and Librarian at the Union. He was not to be denied the presidency, though being from Balliol was perhaps at that time a handicap in being elected to this supreme office.

There is no end to extracurricular interests and activities at Oxford. William seems to have been open to all the winds that were blowing in his time. One of his particular interests was music. This ranked next to the Union. He became an officer of the College Musical Society with responsibility for the Sunday evening concerts in Balliol Hall.

There is a striking letter, written to his mother soon after his 21st birthday, in which he gives impressions and arresting characterizations of favorite composers. He finds in them, Mozart excepted, struggle of some kind. "In Bach it is over — he is the Musician of attainment; his atmosphere is that of St. John in his First Epistle; they are both in Heaven — (or Paradise if you like). Beethoven is climbing the Mount of Purgatory; he is as far from this world as Bach, but is undergoing purification 'so as by fire'." Handel, on the other hand is "the musician of victory in battles, but the campaign is not over; he is altogether on earth, and the most human of them all, with his floods of tears and triumphant shouts." Mozart he calls the musician of innocence, free from spiritual struggle, "a sort of musical Ariel."

Later on, after he becomes a Fellow of Queen's, William will become a member of the Bach Choir under Sir Hugh Allen and at a time when it performed such things as the Beethoven *Mass in D,* the Bach *Mass in B Minor,* the *St. Matthew Passion,* and Brahm's *Requiem.* Despite all this Wagner was at this stage the master for whom he conceived his greatest musical passion.

20

All of this was doubtless of immense importance in the development of young Temple. By all odds however the most momentous thing that happened to him as an undergraduate was his contact with Edward Caird.

Caird at Balliol lectured on philosophy and William at a very formative phase of his development attended his lectures. A profound relationship resulted. Caird became Temple's special mentor. The Scotsman influenced the English youth deeply and permanently by his personal example and total commitment to philosophy.

Many years later as Archbishop of York Temple will dedicate his Gifford Lectures, *Nature, Man and God* to the memory of Edward Caird. In his Preface he writes, "such method in thought as I possess, and especially such grasp of the principles of Dialectic as I have acquired, I believe myself to owe to my Master at Balliol, Edward Caird."

The heart of Caird's faith and practice as a metaphysician was his dedication to dialectic. His basic idea is derived from Hegel, though it is modified by British moderation and the intensive study of the dialogues of Plato. Nevertheless, anyone who has gone through, as I have more than once, the tortuous volumes of Caird entitled *The Evolution of Theology in the Greek Philosophers*, cannot doubt the seriousness of the Scotman's commitment to the philosophic faith of Hegel.

He believed that the backward dualism of the Greeks before and after Plato, and including the latter together with his Master Socrates, could be transcended by the patient application of Hegel's grasp of dialectic. And it must not be forgotten that the German had laid out the basic lines of the most ambitious and comprehensive philosophical system which the world has seen and perhaps will ever see.

Like Hegel, Caird was confident that truth is, and is dialectical. He believed that reality is monistic. It is ultimately mental and is a perfect unity. It is the thinking of God that is determinative of truth and reality.

This thinking however, in its essential structure and method, is dialectical. It has the character of a complex process. It involves subject and object and the overcoming of all contradictions. We know that the latter exist because nature and history are constituted by the Divine thinking and clearly opposition and struggle are a large ingredient in both.

In the created world seen as process we behold finite forms evolving and rising through conflict and suffering to higher and higher modes of Spirit. Thus the abstract Infinite Idea by making itself finite and successive realizes its fullness and richness and as the climax of the trinitarian process knows itself as concrete Spirit, infinite and eternal.

The English mind is not, at base, very metaphysical. The Scottish is perhaps more so. Both had an instinct, I believe, to shy away from the murkiest depths of Teutonic speculation. In Temple, as we shall see, idealism is always muted and in the end transcended. Men like Caird and T.H. Green were very much concerned with life and practice, and tended to exit, as their pupil, Temple, did, in emphasis on Christian social ethics and what needed to be done.

Nonetheless, idealism as a philosophy had a long and strong run in

England and especially at Oxford. At a famous and most unusual dinner given in 1932 for me, an Oxonian and not quite yet a graduate and a doctor, by Dr. J.F. Bethume-Baker, Lady Margaret Professor at Cambridge, I met the doughty Cambridge philosophical theologian, F.R. Tennant. He was tactless enough to spring on me a joke that by this time was probably sterile and shopworn but that contained undoubted truth.

What is the definition of Oxford? quoth Dr. Tennant. He then with relish provided the answer: "The place where old, worn-out German philosophies go, to die."

I did not tell him, I believe, that the same was true of Harvard. There Royce had flourished, sending out pupils all over America. And under one of them, William Ernest Hocking, I had sat for a year taking "Metaphysics" at the very moment when the bright star of Whiteheadian realism was rising, also from Harvard.

Temple took his degree in 1904 and soon thereafter was elected a Fellow and Lecturer of the Queen's College, Oxford. He was just under 23 years of age.

What manner of man was young Temple, full of laurels, a scholar and undergraduate leader — on the threshold of adult life and still unknown career, even in probable outline?

As a speaker he was gifted to an outstanding degree. This talent had propelled him to the Union presidency. But nothing human is perfectly simple, and there was a drawback in this superb distinction.

His tutor, Dr. A.W. Pickard-Cambridge, said of him, as we noted above, that he "had already an unusual gift of ready and lucid speech." but added that this "led him at times to think that he had found a solution, when he had found a phrase." William's father used to say to him according to the former's official biographer, Dean Iremonger, that the boy was extremely difficult to teach because he expressed himself so clearly as to give his teacher the impression of knowing more than he did.

This same Tutor, Dr. Pickard-Cambridge, was in the congregation many years later when as Archbishop of York Temple came to preach on the thousandth anniversary of Rotterdam Church. Looking back on his now illustrious pupil, the tutor wrote:

> He was already the man that he was later, and when I look over the list of my old pupils with whom I have still kept acquaintance, I can think of none who changed less in every essential...he was entirely void of priggishness and pretence.

This is a remarkable tribute and should be spread on the record. There was however another view of young Temple that was less favorable.

The English are trained to be uninhibited in being critical. The atmosphere of Oxford was never one of hesitancy or restraint at this point, especially in the Junior Common Rooms. It was therefore not exceptional that William was portrayed as an "Isis Idol" in the weekly undergraduate newspaper at the height of his prominence. There were those who described him as "bumptious" and as one who was more anxious to collect followers than to make friends.

G.M. Young, a contemporary of William at Balliol, commented not entirely favorably on Temple's confession in his Gifford Lectures that of two ways of reaching conclusions — one by considering the evidence, the other by intuition, he tended to the second, so that he often found himself propounding as certain a proposition he had only just thought of.

Young notes, apparently ironically, that he was very familiar with such propositions, e.g., "Browning never wrote a line that was not poetry" and "Aristotle had the mind of a churchwarden." Young then comments, "His exuberant self-confidence in action took, in thinking, the form of an equally exuberant certitude."

I believe, in general, and shall elaborate the point in due course, that William Temple as a man and a Christian stands in contrast to the goodly company of saints who at some point in their lives had to be turned around sharply and to experience a radical conversion. We speak of these classical examples of the work of grace as twice-born men.

William, on the other hand, is a classic example of the thesis of Horace Bushnell in the 19th century that wise and steadfast Christian nurture may and should produce persons who have no need of a crisis conversion. He exemplifies, along with such men as Origen in the third century and Thomas Aquinas in the 13th, what we may with William James call the once-born type in religious experience.

This does not mean that such a distinction is hard-and-fast or absolute. It does not rule out a strong sense of sin and the weightiest emphasis on Divine grace. Temple had both and stresses them emphatically. He is among Anglican theologians notably anti-Pelagian. We find him in his prime after he has become an Archbishop putting great weight on the virtue of humility and defining and delineating it with originality and profundity.

This unquestionably is something that welled up out of this great man's experience. This experience was not, one is sure, that of an Augustine or a Paul. It was not that of more intermediate characters in their experience of crisis like Francis of Assisi and John Wesley.

Most probably it was William's recollection of pride and excess in self-confidence as a youth and a don that directed his later thinking about sin and grace, repentence and conversion, humility and self-forgetfulness.

After Oxford, Temple remained at Oxford. This is one of the great possibilities and benefits of the English educational system at the post-graduate level. "The brightest and the best" are elected immediately to college fellowships, to supervise the education of the generations under them and to continue their own education in the priceless opportunity of association with dons who constitute generally a ladder of older generations.

William in being elected immediately to a fellowship at Queens entered into this heritage. He seems to have handled it independently, perhaps a trifle individualistically. But in this there was more than pride, for in 1905, his first year as a Fellow, he joined the Worker's Educational Association, of which he was President from 1908 to 1924 and President of the North-Western section from 1924 to 1929 — the period of his Manchester Episcopate.

Temple's identification with working people and with the poor and under-privileged is one of the notable aspects of his character, and it was deeply rooted in the man. Probably it was expressive both of his temperament (always partly conditioned by training) and his Christian faith.

As a child of six William was staying with his parents on holiday at the Lakes and was about to enjoy a favorite dish, roast chicken, for lunch when he learned that the servants were not allowed chicken. At this he put down his knife and fork and burst into tears.

In this event we see a telling illustration of Wordsworth's contention, "The child is father of the man."

Of course William never knew when he was not a Christian or when God was not thought of as a Father and all human beings as his children. His experience from first to last had the character of a seamless robe.

Temple the man and the theologian is best understood if we keep in mind the Christian boy imbibing and becoming grasped by philosophy. His thought all along the even course of his life may be described as a marraige between the Christian faith and the impulse to philosophize.

In addition to teaching and lecturing during his period as a Fellow, William was enabled to make two visits to Germany. He studied at both Jena, then known as the Athens of Germany, and Berlin. At Jena he worked with Eucken and Hans Wendt; at Berlin he encountered Simmel, Von Harnack, and Pfleiderer.

This was the period of decision for William with respect to the Church and Ordination. It affords a useful mirror for inspecting the mind and outlook of the young Temple. He was attracted to the Church as a vocation: this had been the case, he said or wrote repeatedly, for as long as he could remember.

When, however, William approached the Bishop of Oxford, Dr. Francis Paget, about ordination, the latter found reason to doubt that he was ready for this step. The young Don was going through a period of being extremely critical of the working, "existential" Church of England. In addition, he was in a liberal phase respecting the doctrines of the Virgin Birth and the Bodily Resurrection, and the good Bishop was less than pleased with Temple's honest hesitancy at this point.

It thus came about that a wise Archbishop of Canterbury, Dr. Randall Davidson, got hold of the young Don in all of the pride of his intellectual armor and shepherded him through the shoals, to the glory of God and the lasting benefit of the Church of England. The irony of it all is that after he was duly ordained — Deacon in 1908 and Priest in 1909 — Temple speedily shed all his liberal reservations and stood out among theologians as one who felt no difficulty whatever about either the Virgin Birth or the Bodily Ressurection.

I myself heard him say as Archbishop of York in 1935, at the College of Preachers in Washington, that he was the one person of his acquaintance who had no difficulty whatever with the doctrine of the Virgin Birth of our Lord. Then almost before he had got out this remark he exploded, as only Temple could, with laughter.

I cannot resist commenting here, as in a postscript, on an Oxford contemporary of William who was one of my teachers and a good friend, in Cambridge, U.S.A.

I refer to Willard L. Sperry, a Michigan lad who went over to England and Oxford in 1904 with the first contingent of Rhodes Scholars. Sperry was not as fortunate as William Temple. When on returning to the United States he approached the Episcopal Bishop of Connecticut regarding ordination in the Episcopal Church, he likewise stumbled over creedal hesitation. But Willard had no Archbishop to reach out a hand when the Bishop of Connecticut said, "Too bad!"

The result was that Sperry remained in the Congregational Church, though his heart and aesthetic soul was elsewhere. I have heard him say more than once, with the look and voice of profound melancholy that seemed so characteristic of him, that the modernist movement in the Church of Rome appealed to him more than any other version of Christianity. Unfortunately, he would add, it never found ecclesiastical standing ground.

25

CHAPTER THREE

THE PRIEST—PROPHET

The relationship in the Old Testament between priests and prophets is one of exceptional interest and importance. It receives in our plural, secular world far too little emphasis. Not enough is known about it.

The Hebrew prophets have been much honored in the modern period, and justly so. They represent one of the most astounding and singular phenomena in the history of religion. It cannot be doubted that their role and significance in the story of Israel, the Chosen People, is providential.

Indeed the prophets of the Old Testament can only be explained as a very special work of the Spirit of God, the Holy Spirit. It is just and appropriate that the Niceno-Constantinopolitan Creed, commonly called and used as the Nicene Creed[1], should include in its third basic paragraph, devoted to the Holy Spirit the Lord, and Giver of life, the phrase, "He has spoken through the prophets."[2]

The special significance of the Hebrew prophets is their loyalty and fidelity as spokesmen of Yahweh, the God of Israel. They refused to be the yes-men of the Kings or Queens under whom they lived and served. Indeed they did not hesitate to speak against their rulers if the Spirit of the Lord so prompted them.

This took enormous courage. One can realize how much if one thinks of Henry VIII and his ministers, both ecclesiastical and lay; or of James I, whose homosexuality was the avenue to favor in his court. This was a terrible if submerged scandal that was particularly searing to the Jacobean bishops.

Archbishop Abbot refused to knuckle under. But poor Bishop Andrewes (whose Private Devotions both in English translation and in the original Greek and Latin is one of my most cherished possessions) was less fortunate. In the words of Dr. Alexander Whyte of Edinburgh,

> Shall I, to please King James and to shelter and satisfy his vile favorites, — shall I send my soul to hell! shouted Archbishop Abbot to one of the King's emissaries. No! I will not do it. But Bishop Andrews did it. And Bishop Andrews' soul is still in hell to the end of his life, and a hundred times in his remorseful Devotions, because he did it. There is no other word for it.

The Hebrew prophets were made of sterner stuff. But we must not in our minds, as I fear many modern people do in and out of the Churches, cut them off from the cult religion of Israel and of Judah.

At all times vital religions have required priests, for religion has always

---

[1] The original Nicene Creed of A.D. 325 concludes with the phrase, "And in the Holy Spirit."

[2] "Who spake through the prophets" in the better known, older Prayer Book version.

meant worship. The classic example is the call of the 8th century B.C. aristocrat, Isaiah, as reported so marvelously in the 6th chapter of the Book bearing his name. Reading this, one is transported almost magically to worship of the First Temple in Jerusalem.

Coming on to one of the greatest of "the goodly fellowship of the prophets," Jeremiah, he was called to his arduous mission, he tells us, in the 13th year of King Josiah (626 B.C.) and he lived until after the fall of Jerusalem in 586. Thus like his great predecessor, Isaiah, a century earlier, his career spanned a period of 40 years and embraced many stirring events.

Jeremiah was the scion of a priestly family from Anathoth, to the north of Jerusalem a few miles. He was probably descended from Abiathar, David's priest, whom Solomon deposed in favor of Zadok.

Ezekiel was himself a priest of Jerusalem who was carried off to Babylonia with King Jehoiachin in the deportation of 597 B.C. Interestingly he belonged to the priestly family of the Zadokites whom the Deuteronomic reform had established definitively as the official sacerdotal hierarchy of Judah. He never mentions Jeremiah but it is believed that as a young prophet he knew the older man and was influenced by his teaching and his courage.

There is a great deal more that might be said about the relations of priest and prophet in Israel's history. Samuel, who played an outstanding role in this history, was raised up providentially and was trained by the priest Eli in the temple at Shiloh. He seems to have been both priest and prophet. He is called a prophet and later a seer; also he was the last of the Judges. It would appear that he was a kind of national priest and the last theocratic ruler of Israel prior to its becoming a Kingdom.

We have dwelled on the relationship of priest and prophet, prophet and priest, in ancient Israel because it seems to provide a useful analogy to the career of William Temple. There was a prophetic side certainly, to the young Temple. Nor did he ever lose this side of his vocation. He was from first to last a social thinker, concerned with the Kingdom or rule of God in all the life of man.

At the same time William like the boy Samuel had been brought up in the temple and dedicated to the service of God in His Church. He said more than once that he could not remember when he had not expected to be ordained.

All his life William was a churchman. It was in his bones. In his prime, worship was supreme in his set of spiritual priorities. He saw the Church as divinely established and ordered — at once a Kingdom of priests and the extension of the Incarnation.

The purpose of the Church like the purpose of Christ was the transformation of the world. *For God sent not his Son into the world to condemn the world; but that the world through him might be saved.*

(John 3:17)

From this Biblical and Johannine point of view, as well as from a careful consideration of the man and his career, it seems that the very best way to view and treat William Temple as his professional life unfolded is as a priest-prophet.

Here, as in his personal and spiritual life, the best metaphor is that of the seamless robe. In him unity, not division, was forever uppermost. It was as a priest and theologian that he was a social thinker; and it was as a social thinker — a philosopher — that he valued the Church in the fulness of its life and rejoiced in it.

First however there was an interlude of gestation and preparation that must be noted.

In 1910 at the age of 28 Temple left Oxford to become Headmaster of Repton. He had tried to remove himself from consideration for this post and was on his way to Australia when a cablegram reached him saying that the Governors of the School had elected him.

Temple's official biographer, Dean Iremonger, says, in connection with a call to Clifton that did not materialize, that it is doubtful whether he was entirely convinced that it was his vocation to be headmaster — "which makes it hard to understand why he felt a definite call to Repton less than a year later." Probably the daemon of his father, ever present in memory and being as a living force, influenced him. And he had been told, earlier, apropos of Repton, that "they want, confessedly, an intellectual revival." This, I believe, was a lure and he was attracted, I suspect, by the prospect of a close pastoral ministry to young men along with the certainty of exerting a strong intellectual influence.

There is on record a very personal word about William's decision to accept this call. This account tells us a good deal about Temple the man — as he was in 1910 and as he remained 20 years later when he had become Archbishop of York.

During the great Oxford Mission at St. Mary's, which it was my privilege to attend for eight nights running, the Archbishop recalled a difficult decision he had once had to make. This was his witness to undergraduates in a context of openness to the Will of God:

> I was much interested in the work I was doing, believing it to be of some value. I was asked to take up another post which certainly was more conspicuous in the eyes of the world. I tried to avoid it. I asked all the friends of whom I could think, and they all said that I had better stay where I was. I had to make a decision in time to write a letter by a certain post, and having weighed the question as carefully as I could — and we must always do that — and having come to no conclusion at all, I began at eight o'clock in the evening to say my prayers, and for three hours, without a pause, I tried to concentrate all my desires on knowing clearly what was God's will for me. I do not know how those three hours went; they did not seem very long; but when eleven o'clock struck I knew perfectly well what I had got to do, and that was to accept; and I have never had a shadow of doubt since that it was right.[1]

Among the scores of congratulations that were sent mostly to his mother, since William was in Australia, one stands out. Michael Sadler (whom I knew later as Sir Michael Sadler, Master of University College, Oxford) wrote: "He is a very great power, with growing force in the national life. Hundreds of thousands of young people will watch his work and be helped by his courage and plainness of mind, and by his moral force....His influence is wonderful, and the most varied characters and the most critical minds respond to it."

[1]*Christian Faith and Life*, p.51.

28

This was a pretty high expectation and it can hardly be said that Temple's four years at Repton fulfilled such a prophecy. He did well in many respects; he was excellent in some; here and there some weakness was manifest. It would be fair to say that William was not a born head-master and I believe he found this out at Repton.

What he did do was infuse the school with his own intellectual and spiritual vitality. One tribute when he left was, "He made the whole school think." A colleague said that he put "Repton" on the map.[1] The best boys in his Sixth Form class got a great deal — better value, some thought, than any other school boys in England. Other boys in the top Form were bewildered or left far behind.

William was not good at discipline, which is not good for a head-master. He probably underestimated the bad in boys and it was consti-tutionally difficult for him to inflict pain on any human being. But un—questionably the goodness of the man — his faith, love, optimism, good humor, made an enormous impression. All of this, incidentally, was prophetic of things to come.

In 1914 Temple became Rector of St. James', Piccadilly. His Rector-ship coincided with the first World War and St. James' in the heart of London was a strategic place for William to be during the ordeal of this long-drawn struggle. Few men were as well qualified spiritually, intel-lectually, and theologically as he to preach, write, and guide at the na-tional level.

He was at once free of chauvinism and a convinced non-pacifist. He was able to deal with the inevitable tendency to hate the German people and all things German. He had a vision of Great Britian as a Christian nation even in wartime and he was not afraid to declare this vision and to strive to keep the path open for a better future.

Temple was wonderfully qualified to deal, too, with the vexing ques-tions raised for Christians and other thoughtful people by the horror and suffering of the war. How can such madness and such carnage be reconciled with a God whose name is Love?

The Rector of St. James' was one of the few Church leaders who was ready for just such an hour, and for the hardest questions. His long meditation, going back to school days and his father, on the character of God stood him in good stead. This was the rock on which he ever stood.

He was able to handle trenchantly and worthily the reality of Judge-ment, so often invoked and abused from the pulpit. He would have no truck with the idea of God's deliberately punishing people for sins by unleashing war and its suffering.

> We can trace the actual causes of war, and we know quite well that
> its causes were in human wills, and we are not at liberty to say that
> God intervened in the history of the world to inflict anguish and
> pain by means of the war as punishment for certain sins that have
> no relation to it. How could the war grow out of drunkenness? All
> the way through the Gospel of St. John we are taught that a judge-

[1] In Howard Spring's novel, *All the Day Long,* the heroine Maria Legassick asks her brother-in-law, Hugo Oldham, Vicar of St. Tudno, Cornwall, about his son John. Hugo replies, "Yes. Sixteen. He's at Repton. I admire William Temple, the headmaster. That's why I sent him there." This boy John is killed in World War I.

ment of God is not a deliberate act of His intervening in the world to make guilty people suffer, but an automatic product of His Presence and Revelation.

So shall we think of this war. It is, indeed, a judgement upon the world of sin, a judgement of the sin from which it arises — the sin of selfishness, individual and national, of which in various degrees all men and nations throughout the world are guilty. The sin which led immediately to the outbreak of the war we may believe to be mainly in one nation, but the root is to be found among all peoples, and not only among those who are fighting, but neutral peoples just as much. The punishment for that sin comes through the moral order which God has set up in the world, an order which reacts upon those who break it.

Temple had occasion from time to time to speak to the crisis of the war and to the soul-struggle of persons in wartime. But he could hardly build up the devotional life of his congregation just on this spiritual food, so he turned to the book of the Bible he loved best and relied on most for the Bread of Life, St. John's Gospel.

Thus to his congregation at St. James', in the midst of war, he gave on Sunday mornings what he was to give later to ordinands at Manchester, York, and Canterbury, the fruit of his study and meditation on St. John. Eventually this would be given to the world in the two-volume work, *Readings in St. John's Gospel,* which has been called the greatest devotional treatise in English since William Law's *Serious Call.*

William sent me these volumes as they came off the press, and I value them immensely for this reason as well as for their insight and excellence. In them we have the ripe fruit of a lifetime of meditation and dedication in love. They give us the essence of the inner life married to strenuous thinking of a great modern saint.

The late Canon B. H. Streeter, I believe it is, has suggested that the redactor or final author of the Fourth Gospel, whom we shall always call John, was a Christian prophet. This became a distinct order in the Apostolic Church. As there is certainly a great deal of the priestly in this Gospel — the high priestly prayer for example of Chapter 17 — it may not be fanciful to see in John the prototype of the union of priest and prophet which I have taken as a fundamental key to William Temple.

Reaching the nation during the war and preparing it for a better and more Christian way after the war, was on the mind of our priest-prophet from its start. The first action taken by him with a view to a larger ministry was to accept in July 1915 an invitation to edit the *Challenge.*

This was a Church of England weekly newspaper, a new entry in a somewhat crowded field. It had only begun publication on 1 May 1914. The war of course had intervened meantime, and by the summer of 1915 the *Challenge* as an enterprise was coming apart.

There were four other papers in this particular field: the Anglo-Catholic *Church Times,* with a circulation larger than all of the others put together; the ultra-Protestant *Record,* with a small circulation; the *Church Family Newspaper* — in time to turn into the *Church of England Newspaper* — an inoffensive organ, homely in tone, unpleasing in appearance, but *read* in the country, the suburbs, and the market towns: and, finally, the substantial and influential (out of proportion to its circulation) *Guardian.*

As an example of its quality, C. S. Lewis wrote for the *Guardian* week by week *The Screwtape Letters* before their publication in book form. Dr. W.R. Matthews produced in the same way his *Essays in Construction* (published in the U.S.A. under the title *God and This Troubled World.*).

Anyway, to the relief of its Board of Editors and its promoters, William Temple accepted the Editorship of *Challenge,* a position he continued to hold until 1918. While it would be excessive to call the paper during this period his organ, he did pull it together, dominated it in his quiet, inclusive way, and found in it a stimulating outlet for his views on issues of every sort.

Inevitably the war and its problems figured prominently in its columns, editorially and otherwise. Here, as we have seen, Temple was unique as a Christian leader. He had wisdom, balance, profundity — and he was articulate.

All manner of questions were up and were treated in the paper: theological issues like the Love of God and His Power, why does God not stop the war?, conscience and conscription and war service, ethical and social duty in wartime, and, looking beyond the war to peace, national reconstruction and international order.

In one important communication growing out of a book review, Temple dealt with H.G. Wells' doctrine of a finite God — Deity within Nature and Necessity. He was constantly opposing the rising tide of bitterness and hatred toward the Germans. A third issue was that of conscientious objectors — much more an area of agitation and abuse of individuals than in World War II. Temple as in everything was clear and cogent on this question. He was a reasoned non-pacifist, but he respected the rights of conscience and he understood the Christian case for pacifism even while rejecting it. He once said to me, The pacifists are wrong, but they err in the right direction. This was characteristic of the man and the thinker.

With respect to social policy, the paper tended to sympathize, as did Temple, with the ideas and positions of the Labor Movement. It criticised excessive drinking and its effect on the war effort and advocated editorially what Temple had in a sermon on his return from America in 1915, total prohibition. It was vigorous on educational issues, attacking all proposed reductions in education grants and criticising the paltry war bonus offered its teachers by the London County Council. Here William was always his father's son.

On ecclesiastical position and issues, *Challenge* was a useful forum for Temple. In its columns he was able to develop what was to be his special line and track. It was a church position at once authentically Catholic and Evangelical, with a liberal ingredient that stopped short of Liberalism or Modernism.

Cannon Spencer Leeson, a member of the paper's editorial Board, thought that it reflected the spirit and feeling expressed in the book *Lux Mundi* (1889), edited by Charles Gore. The stance of this work was essentially conservative, committed to Tradition, but aware of the intellectual isolation of the Faith in the modern world and the need for

31

bridges of communication across to it, philosophically and sociologically.

William himself took an important position on Eucharistic Doctrine in connection with the controversial issue of the Reservation of the Sacrament. Two Bishops from opposing sides, Gore of Oxford on the Catholic side and Watts-Ditchfield of Chelmsford on the Protestant side, had developed a compromise or *eirenicon*. Between them, they influenced wide sectors of opinion and to an important degree pulled the Church of England toward the center.

Temple came down strongly in support of the two Bishops and their *eirenicon*. He stated clearly his own doctrinal position.

With regard to the Blessed Sacrament...we most fully and absolutely believe in the real and objective presence of our Lord in the sacramental elements for the purpose of sustaining the souls of the faithful in Communion, but we have no warrant for believing any presence for any other purpose."

Thus our priest-prophet displayed the breadth of his interests and espoused a sacramental position close to that of the founders of the Oxford Movement, Keble, Pusey, and Newman. But it did not satisfy the extreme Anglo-Catholics in the second decade of the 20th century or thereafter. I am reminded of a remark William made to me as we walked up the courtyard of Bishopthorpe in 1937: "They say that I am becoming more Catholic, but the spikes — they don't say so." The Archbishop then exploded with laughter.

This episode had a certain significance for me. Up to that point I had never used the word "spike" or any other term that I thought might be offensive, ecclesiastically or racially. I won't say that the Archbishop's frankness worked any revolution in my usage, but it did make me feel freer about such matters. It was also an instructive example of the Englishman's independence and individualism in speech.

We in America are much more tender and conformist.

The *Challenge* episode in Temple's life during the St. James' years, which were the war years, was sufficiently demanding as a sideline or even a main line for most men. But not for William Temple. There was no end and no limit to his energy and versatility.

Temple had hardly more than got well into editing the *Challenge* when he was drawn into the center of a national church movement. It was the spiritual enterprise known as the "National Mission of Repentance and Hope." Essentially it was the baby of the Archbishop of Canterbury, Randall Davidson, who sold it to the Bench of Bishops as a whole. Thus it had a strong and lofty sponsorship, but conceiving such an enterprise was one thing, getting it operative and effective in a vital way was another.

It was this "National Mission" to which William gave himself without stint and with unreserved dedication through most of the year 1916. The idea of such a Mission was a natural one, given a National Church and given the agony of England in protracted war. But it was from laymen that first initiatives had come — a particular group of laymen who went to Lambeth and put with urgency their conviction of need before the Archbishop.

Slow to act, but thoughtful and prudent, the Archbishop was impressed. His actions were wise. He chose twelve men, of whom William was one, laying on them the responsibility of prayer for guidance that the Church might be led by the Spirit and find the right course. The twelve prayed for three months, then went into retreat, out of which a common mind and plan emerged.

This plan was laid before the whole Bench by the Archbishop. Thus it was decided that there was to be a "National Mission of Repentance and Hope," and that it was to begin in the autumn of 1916. Randall Davidson then appointed, taking a leaf out of the Gospel of Luke, "seventy others also" to form the Central Council of the Mission.

William was one of the five secretaries appointed by the two Archbishops and was responsible for the Literature Committee, one of seven committees of the Mission and one of the most important. He edited a series of pamphlets on behalf of his Committee and wrote some of them himself. One, *The Call of the Kingdom,* was notable and enjoyed a wide reading. Here we see the prophet in the Church at his best and most characteristic; and this was to be the case always, in all the great posts he held, up to the end of his life.

This man was so many things. There was no end to his gifts. He was priest, preacher, prophet, evangelist, pastor, teacher, scholar, philosopher, statesman, author. The National Mission found him ceaselessly active and many of these roles in play.

His schedule during many months has to be seen to be believed. Here is one sample, from a letter written in October.

> *The Mission makes life a perfect whirl just now. Last week I was at Bournemouth on Wednesday; London (all day committees) Thursday; three committees in London and then a sermon in Ipswich on Friday; meeting in Norwich Saturday. Two sermons here (S. James's) yesterday. This week will be worse. But there is no doubt that an immense amount that is very hopeful has happened.*

In another letter to his brother he tells of taking the Mission to Eton College — that most prestigious of English public schools and the most snobbish.

> *Last night we went down to Eton, where I preached this morning I never had such a tussle with an audience. I was on the Mission, and very keen to get it home, and at the start the Eton listlessness lay on the chapel like a blight. But I fairly pumped out the energy, and after 10 to 12 minutes had them listening like anything. Rather a triumph.*

Toward the end of the year, at the tenth meeting of the Council on December 7, Temple presented the Secretaries' Report. A good many things that had happened were highly encouraging. On the negative side, Church Services generally had drawn people who were already churched, not outsiders or the unchurched. Meetings however had been better attended than Church Services — in many instances had large crowds. The Report of the Secretaries ended on a high note:

> *Prayer has been abundantly answered, the love of the Father to His children has once more been revealed, new gifts through His Spirit have been bestowed, and the Church, more conscious than she has been before of her union with the Risen and Triumphant Lord,*

can advance to all that lies before her with humble gratitude and strengthened courage and hope.

Altogether 1916 was a strenuous year, but a great one for William. It found him in high gear and was one of tremendous achievement.

The year had had an interlude of pleasure and deep happiness. From the time of taking up his Fellowship at the Queen's College, Oxford, his mother had taken a house and made a home for him. She went to Repton with him, and thence to the Rectory of St. James', London. In this William was following in the exact footsteps of his father, Frederick, who had kept his mother with him and had not married until after her death.

William's mother, Beatrice Blanche Lascelles Temple, died on April 2, 1915, at the age of 70. This left a big hole in his life at a time of special need because of pressures from the war and the extraordinary calls his position in London gave rise to.

This gap, as English English would have it, was filled in the Spring and Summer of 1916 by his engagement to Miss Frances Anson and their marriage on June 24 with Randall Davidson, Archbishop of Canterbury, officiating. It was characteristic of William that he sat up late on the eve of his wedding in order to finish his first major book, *Mens Creatrix*. It was no less characteristic that in the evenings of his honeymoon he read aloud to his bride his favorite poems by Robert Browning.

The match was a suitable one in every way. The families had been connected over many years and Frances and Mrs. Frederick Temple had been friends. Frances knew William and his work and temperament well and beyond a doubt realized what she was getting into. They were not blessed with children and one had the feeling, when in their home or seeing them about at a great Conference, that they were in the best sense colleagues and friends.

It was at Bishopthorpe that I visited the Temples. Their predecessor in the Palace there, Cosmo Lang, was a bachelor. The quality of Mrs. Temple and of her contribution to Church and village at Bishopthorpe can be gauged by this tribute from a friend fully qualified — we are told — to judge: "Mrs. Temple was the best neighbor that Bishopthorpe could ever have had in an Archbishop's wife."

The National Mission had a sequel — for the Church of England and for William Temple. It might have seemed that William had done enough for the moment along the way of extraordinary action and exertion, off the beaten paths of conventional endeavor. There were those in high places who thought so, not only the highest prelates in the Church but men like Viscount Haldane and Lord Asquith in public life.

Undoubtedly William at 35 was a marked man and many eyes were on him, It was only a matter of time until important positions would open up and he would be tapped for preferment, just as it had been with his father Frederick before him. All he needed to do was sit and wait.

Any who expected that did not know William Temple the man and the follower of Christ. Ahead of him was the most venturesome act of his life and one of his finest hours.

34

In the autumn of 1917 he left his port of safety, resigned his living at St. James' of more than L2,000 a year, and went out like Abraham of old, with faith only for a guide, not knowing whither he went. In taking this action he was influenced undoubtedly by the realization that men of his age (36) were fighting and dying like flies in France. Sacrifice was the order of the day in the world, and why should it not be so in the life of the Church?

But above all William believed that the Spirit was speaking to the Church in England and calling it reform its life and in the liberty of Christ go forward to fulfill its mission in the world that lay beyond war and war's desolation. He was answering the work of the Spirit that in a Pentecostal vein had found utterance through him at a great meeting in Queen's Hall, London the night of July 16, 1917: "Come out from your safety and comfort; come out from your habits and conventions. Listen to the voice of the wind as it sweeps over the world, and stand where you may be caught in its onward rush."

The Life and Liberty Movement which Temple gave up the Rectorship of St. James' to head had its origin in a conversation between two parsons of the English Church — two men as different as could well be imagined, except for one point, dedication to the will of God and openness to the Spirit. These two men were H.R.L. ("Dick") Sheppard, Vicar of St. Martin-in-the-Fields, and William Temple, Rector of St. James'.

The igniting word came from Dick Sheppard. It was characteristic of him. The story has been oft told.

The two men were together in Temple's Rectory study talking, no doubt about various things, but certainly about England beyond the war and the Church's opportunity and call. Suddenly Dick said: he was a spirited chap and given to spontaneity — "Don't you think, William dear, that there ought to be a 'ginger' group in the Church?"

This was the beginning of the Life and Liberty movement in the Church of England. William Temple, priest and prophet, was to be its leader and was to give himself to this venture of the Spirit with rare abandon and, of course, the balanced intelligence and reasoned eloquence that were his special trademark. These were the gifts that made him the great and incomparable leader of all Christendom in the interregnum between the World Wars.

The background of the Life and Liberty movement, which must be kept in mind if it is to be understood, was the Anglican Establishment. This is entirely alien to Americans, being a thing proscribed in the First Amendment of our Federal Constitution. For the Englishman anything else is scarcely conceivable, though from time to time discontent has welled up and there has been negative talk and agitation for Disestablishment.

This was true as World War I wound down, and it seemed to have been true following World War II. I shall never forget the evening I met for the first time T.S. Eliot. It was in 1946 or 1947 and he was giving an address to the Men of St. Thomas' Church, Washington — the Church of which Franklin D. Roosevelt had been a member. The head of this men's organization was a Harvard classmate of Eliot and a great friend of mine, Bill Castle. (Bill was a protege of Herbert Hoover and had served as Under Secretary of State in the Hoover Administration.) He was a staunch Churchman, like Eliot an Anglo-Catholic, and he had invited his distinguished house guest to speak.

I don't remember much about Eliot's speech, except that in the manner of many Englishmen he rather droned on. In the question period, I asked him whether he thought it likely that the Church of England would be disestablished. His answer was wary and sharp in one brilliant sentence. "The answer to that depends upon events that have not yet taken place."

The Life and Liberty Movement was not aimed at Disestablishment. It was triggered by discontent with the secular confinement of the Church and its inability because of dependence on Parliament to order its life and reform its ways. Sheppard and Temple and the forces that gathered round them wanted fuller life and power for the Church and they demanded liberty in order to take the steps necessary for renewal.

It was impossible, for example, to do anything about extreme anomalies and inequalities in the system of livings for different parishes — set up for the most part centuries ago in a rural England without any thought of a coming industrial and urban civilization. Only Parliament could do anything about this aspect of the system or any other reform worth the mention. And Parliament had not shown any disposition either to act or to delegate its power.

There was also the problem of worship and the received Prayer Book, last revised in 1662. To many the impotence of the Church at this point was a scandal too grievous to be borne. Then there was the arbitrary manner of appointing Vicars or Pastors. Congregations were entirely passive so far as power was concerned. And the Parson's Freehold gave him complete protection but only added to the bankruptcy of the system so far as democracy and the local parish or congregation were concerned.

Such issues gave vitality to the movement for reform, which is essentially what the Life and Liberty Movement was all about. Dr. A.A. David, Headmaster of Rugby and later a Bishop, put it this way in a lucid statement on the first circulars of the Movement:

> The Life and Liberty Movement aims at securing for the Church without delay Liberty in the sense of full power to control its own life and organization. It does this in the belief that a unique opportunity is before the Church, which existing conditions prevent it from claiming to the full. The rising tide within the Church demands Liberty, because Liberty is indispensable to the fullness of Life and its practical expression. It must no longer be necessary to wait for the convenience of Parliament before adaptations can be made and reforms effected. **The opportunity is now, when our whole civilization has to be rebuilt.**

The italicized sentence is important for understanding the sense and mood which were responsible for the emergence of the Movement and which in turn it fostered and propagated. The time seemed ripe for great advance. Men and women felt in their bones that some mighty fulfillment was at hand.

It was this way in England in 1917 and following years. It was the same in Germany at least for a few years. The late Professor Paul

36

Tillich has testified to the high expectations held by many Germans including himself. The Movement into which he threw himself, religious socialism, was a monument to what Tillich calls *Kairos* or the right time as distinct from *Chronos* or formal time — clock time. He believed that the period following "the Great War" was a time of *Kairos*.

The great example of *Kairos* is the sense of time we find in the New Testament. "The time is fulfilled and the Kingdom of God is at hand." "But when the fullness of the time has come, God sent forth his Son, born of woman."

Tillich had a completely different feeling about the Second World War and its aftermath. He thought *Kairos* was not present and took no interest in politics. What counted mainly was concentration on Spirit or the Spiritual Presence that is always a reality. Cultural activity, intellectual work were the main thing. It had always seemed to me that the so-called Grey Book, entitled *The Kingdom the Power and the Glory*, published in 1924 and originally prepared as part of a new prayer book, was a powerful witness to the sense of *Kairos* at the end of and following World War I. This book became very popular in America and in 1933 a special American edition was published.

There is something fresh and ingenuous, expectant and triumphant, about this book. One might speak of it as conveying some of the spirit of a Francis of Assisi and probably of his older contemporary, Joachim of Floris, the eschatological monk. The tone of the book is a far remove from all previous English Prayer Books, and it seems unlikely today that such a tome will or should make its way in any fullness into a Book of Common Prayer.

I have not been able to find who the authors and compilers of the Grey Book were, or whether Temple had any hand in this experimental, supplementary prayer book. But it illustrates well the mind behind the Life and Liberty Movement and the motives of Sheppard, Temple, and hundreds, even thousands of keen Christians who to a certain extent wanted to take the Kingdom of Heaven by violence.

They met considerable resistance from the Archbishop of Canterbury, Randall Davidson, and from such leaders as B.H. Streeter and Dean H. Henley Henson. Streeter represented a faction that considered the Movement to be topsy-turvey: it was starting from the wrong end, the physical body of the Church, to the neglect of its soul. Henley Henson, a self-made type in contrast to Temple the child of privilege, and a sardonic hard-hitting intellectual, was a representative of conservatism, as was Archbishop Davidson. These men sincerely thought it better to hold on to the good you have and treasure it than to strike out over unknown ways and perilous seas. They instinctively took refuge in the need of deliberation and the appointment of more committees.

Some witty cleric got off this one about the Archbishop of Canterbury. If Randall Davidson, he said, happened to be at Lambeth when the last trump sounds, his reaction would be to appoint a committee to consider and report whether it was the last trump or the last but one.

Men like Dick Sheppard were understandably impatient with this mentality in the Church. William Temple at this stage was heart and soul with the young, the generous, the adventurous. He could and did answer with a thunderous voice, addressing England through the press on behalf of the Life and Liberty Council.

We are weary of perpetual deliberations. A disturbance would be better than a continuance of inactivity. Need we calculate much longer? We are clear that the Church just now has her greatest and

37

possibly her last opportunity of vindicating her Catholic and national character. But this can only be achieved by a struggle fierce and sustained, by a purging thorough and sincere, and by a summons such as many had hoped might be issued during these days of war to dare anything, that the Will of God might be done, as in Heaven, so on earth.

This was William in authentic prophetic vein. He never lost this as an element in the total mix of his mind and statesmanship. But he did change in tone and even in substance when the chips were down over the Prayer Book and Parliament, and after he had become Bishop of Manchester.

The issue was Disestablishment. He had not, nor had the Life and Liberty Movement, advocated such a radical step. But the leaders of the nascent Movement, with Temple as Chairman, had said in a signed letter to the Times of 20 June 1917: "Those who are promoting this Movement are convinced that we must win for the Church full power to control its own life, even at the cost, if necessary, of disestablishment and of whatever consequences that may possibly involve."

Prior to this — I believe in 1915 — William had expressed doubt that he ought to accept appointment by the Archbishops to serve on the Church and State Commission recommended by the Representative Church Council, because — he said — "I did not believe that there was any means of release from our difficulties except by way of disestablishment." Ten years later, in 1925, in a Manchester Visitation Charge he declared: "The question (of disestablishment) is one in which the Church need take no interest at all. It is a question for the State only."

Temple's biographer, Dean Iremonger, calls this indeed a "hard saying" and indicates that he possibly shared the disappointment in "the lost leader" felt by many devotees of the gallant movement of yesteryear for Life and Liberty in the Church. The truth would seem to be that Temple was by temperament a conservative rather than a radical, an institutionalist rather than an individualist, and was wise enough and normal enough to let age and experience temper the venturesomeness of youth.

The matter could be put another way by saying that he remained the priest even while surrendering to and voicing the ecstasy of prophetic passion in the power of the Divine Breath. The true priest is bound to be an institutional man, feeling as a matter of existential knowledge the strength and staying power of the sacred institution.

Temple was ever the philosopher and the statesman — as aware of the nation as of the Church — and these aspects of his being were not shed and lost when the mantle of the prophet was placed upon him. Possibly because he was so thoroughly trained in dialectic, he was less troubled than most thoughtful men by inconsistency. It is the American Emerson however who opined, "A foolish consistency is the hobgoblin of little minds / Adored by little statesmen and philosophers and divines."

The Life and Liberty Movement had one concrete result, which was relatively a triumph and greatly pleased Temple and his colleagues in the leadership of the movement. An Enabling Act was passed through three Readings in both Houses of Parliament and thus became law, in December 1919.

This Act represented a somewhat round-about way of recognizing the existence of the National Church Assembly as the central representative Council of the Church of England and enabling it to do its work. The new feature and great virtue of this Assembly was that it gave the laity of the Church for the first time a recognized, constitutional position in the management of the affairs of the Church.

It was no small achievement — and one in which Temple had a large and determined part — that women won an equal right to sit in the Assembly. When debate on this issue first began in 1918 at a session of the Grand Committee of the Representative Church Council he wrote his wife that "the Committee has adhered to its vile decision about women." This recommendation of the Committee, excluding women, went before the full Council. An amendment, reversing this effect, was seconded by Temple and hotly debated. Temple spoke in a masterly way on the current position of women, the ethical and psychological importance of the issue, and the importance for the future of recognizing at this critical time that women were in a full sense members of the laity of the Church.

By a substantial majority the amendment was carried.

Temple was gratified by the passage of the Enabling Act and wrote his brother that "the chief thing I have worked for since Christmas 1917 is the coming off, and that at the time we set which all the wiseacres said was impossible." He then quoted a sentence from Neville Talbot, "The Church is out of the ditch and on the road."

Subsequent events were to show that this gratifying development was not as decisive as the leaders of "Life and Liberty" had hoped. But it was still a notable milestone. In particular it was able expeditiously to effect reforms in Church administration and finances that might well have taken two generations to accomplish under the old order where all Church Bills had to be passed by Parliament.

Meanwhile the personal and economic situation of the Temples was precarious. William was not without offers. In the early Spring of 1919 he was invited to be Master of University College, Durham and a few weeks later his old College of Balliol, Oxford asked him to come back as Chaplain. Taking advice as well as following his own best judgment and guidance, he declined both offers.

Finally, the break that Charles Gore and other friends hoped for came. In June the Archbishop sent for William to tell him that he could become a Canon of Westminster Abbey if he desired. The special appeal of this was the need of peace and some leisure after the frenzied pace of the past three years as well as a return to convention and normalcy in the hierarchy of Church positions.

At Westminster there was no danger that William would find himself fenced off in an isolated pocket and out of the main stream. At the same time he would have, with his wife, a perfect opportunity for "recollection in tranquillity" and the recharging of his mental and spiritual batteries, with the pressure off at least relatively and temporarily.

CHAPTER FOUR

BISHOP AND ARCHBISHOP

It was in the cards that William Temple, under the English selection and appointment system, would be made a Bishop.

The predictable came to pass in early 1921. On January 25, 1921 he was consecrated as Bishop of Manchester. He was 39 years of age, in the prime of life and at the height of his powers, physical and mental. He was, to be sure, still in the act of growth mentally and spiritually.

The pivotal letter from D. Lloyd George, Prime Minister came on November 26, 1920. It was headed, under the salutation, "Dear Canon Temple," SEE OF MANCHESTER, and contained this sentence: "The Diocese is one of great importance, situated as it is in the center of a large business community and comprising a great industrial population."

Manchester as a place and area was a natural for Temple. There could have been little doubt about his acceptance. He had however been at the Abbey only 16 months and the Prime Minister's letter was very sudden. William and Frances had apparently had no warning. Their instinct, proper in every way, was to ask the Prime Minister for a few days in which to consider his proposal. Meanwhile there were four persons to be consulted: the two Archbishops, Charles Gore — intimate friend and counsellor, and the Dean of Westminster.

Randall Davidson put a quietus on this leisurely plan. When William phoned him after dinner, he came to the phone himself and counseled him to accept without delay. He could be sure that the other Archbishop knew and approved. Temple's duty was clear.

The next morning he saw the Dean, who proved also to be in the know, and had no doubt as to his duty. He called Gore on the phone. The latter replied definitively, "I know. Go. And of course I'll come to supper."

That evening (the 27th) William wrote two letters, to the Prime Minister and the Archbishop of York, Cosmo Lang. Two days later he had beautiful letters from both Archbishops. Randall Davidson's is brilliant, affectionate, moving — a measure surely of this great man. It is a testimonial, too, to the power of Christian friendship. The two men, one old, the other young, had been in the recent past adversaries. It had made no difference in their friendship, rooted in Christ.

So Randall Cantuar. wrote, "God be with you, my dear Son in Christ" and signed himself "Yours affecly." The letter assuredly was in his own hand. (I have 26 such from William Ebor. et Cantuar.) The Archbishop calls the vacant post "one of the greatest in the Church of England or perhaps in the whole Church of Christ, alike in the possibilities and in the weight of its burden." He imparts the information that he had been "anxious for the past fortnight, as things seemed to have hung fire and I feared some hitch."

The Archbishop of York's letter is cordial and affectionate also but less personal — perhaps paternal is the word. It contains an important diagnostic sentence. "It is only right to say that there are few places in England where Churchmanship and Conservatism go more closely together than Manchester, and I have long felt that there was need of some one who would make a more effective appeal to the new power of Labour than has been made in the past."

Temple's appointment to Manchester was popular in the Diocese and acclaimed throughout the Church of England. Seldom can a Bishop have entered upon a field of labor under more glowing and promising auspices. The note struck by the Dean, Temple's friend and coworker in national endeavor, in addressing the new Bishop following the enthronement, was typical of the general happiness and enthusiasm. "The measure of our welcome may be gauged by this fact — that out of the whole orbit of the English Church we would freely have chosen you first to guide the destinies of this great diocese."

The new Bishop was bound to do anything he undertook well. But he was suited by temperament to the Episcopal office and all his life up to the time of his consecration was a perfect preparation for great leadership. From the beginning William took to the life and work of a Bishop and was as happy in it as he was successful, in the best and truest sense of that word.

The office challenged him and as always he was invigorated by a challenge. He wrote a friend, after he had been 15 months in the new position, that it was "far the most invigorating job that I have had." There was great variety in his new life, but it was all within a pattern. It was stamped with a certain order derived from the fact that an institution was involved. Temple was intuitively an institutional man.

True, he was, on one side, of the race of prophets. He could never be just a mass priest, a ritual figure. But he knew as a historian and as a philosopher that institutions inhere in the social nature of men and are indispensable.

Bishops are the custodians, leaders, and symbol figures of the greatest of all institutions —the Church of God which has as its foundation and chief cornerstone the incarnate Son of God, Jesus Christ. Nor is this office, especially in England, a private, local proposition. "The office of a Bishop in the Church of England is not a local one," said Archbishop Benson. Much time is required for the corporate work of the Bishops, including since the Enabling Act legislation by consent, and for central Church meetings such as Convocation and those of the Church Assembly.

At the same time the Bishop is the Diocesan. He is within his jurisdiction the chief Pastor and Teacher and he is charged with the supreme administrative responsibility and leadership. He cannot in the last role be simply an administrator in the manner of a business executive, for the Church is a voluntary society. Cracking the whip is likely to be counter-productive. He must be a leader who can win men and women to follow him.

41

William Temple filled all these roles with distinction and marked effectiveness. His first outstanding test was the division of his diocese. It had long been realized that the See of Manchester was too vast for effective administration and spiritual cultivation. It had a population of 3½ million people, and it contained over 600 parishes. The city and its Cathedral moreover were at its extreme southerly end, so that the situation was an unwieldy one, especially for the Bishop.

Nevertheless, Temple's predecessor, Bishop Knox, had vehemently opposed the idea of dividing the Diocese. This was effectual in dampening enthusiasm for what was bound to seem a formidable change. In addition, there was a problem of choosing the best town for the see city of the second diocese. And there was the built-in, increased financial load.

So there were problems and statesmanship was required, if the creation of a new diocese was to be carried through with expedition and general stisfaction. In this Temple was eminently successful. The Diocese of Blackburn came into being and on February 28, 1927 the enthronement of its first Bishop took place. That summer Bishop E.A. Knox, Temple's predecessor, wrote him a handsome letter, congratulating him on "the extraordinary achievements of the early years of your episcopacy." Particularly impressive to Knox was the widespread increase in the value of the lower-level livings and thus the income of the incumbent clergy.

As a note of interest, even after the division of the diocese, Temple still had the second largest diocese in England, with nearly 2 million people and 400 parishes. But now he was within an hour's drive of every one of his churches.

The new Bishop's gifts of leadership and his moral force and concern were felt in manifold directions in Manchester — the Diocese and the City. It is not too much to say that during William's Episcopate the intersection of the Kingdom of God and the life of man in his jurisdiction was notably extended and intensified. The Will of God — ever this man's primary quest and standard — was more nearly done in Manchester, as it is in heaven.

Temple championed the cause of women and women's work and recognition in the Church. He was steadfast in encouraging missions and missionary work at home and abroad. He took a special interest in the University of Manchester, where now in the the University Library his papers have found a permanent home. (Formerly they were in the William Temple College, Rugby, an institution no longer in existence.) He received from this University an Honorary Doctorate as an expression of the esteem and respect in which he was held.

In outreach to other Christians and the whole range of united Christian witness and of good works bearing no denominational or even religious name, Bishop Temple knew no limits save those imposed by time and energy, and these often seemed in this man limitless. How tireless he was, how selfless, how willing always to take on more and more! There was the Student Christian Movement, Toc H, and the Worker's Educational Association. And there were the numerous bodies, of employers and employed, responsible and prominent in the ongoing life of a mighty industrial center, which he was ever ready to address and help in any way he could.

Nor was the outreach of this man, now a bishop in the Church of God, confined to his city or to the ecclesiastical jurisdiction for which he was peculiarly responsible — the Diocese of Manchester. There can be no limit to the concern of the Christian. The new American Prayer Book (Proposed in 1976, finally adopted in 1979) is right in altering the bidding of the general intercession in the Eucharist, Rite I to read: "Let us pray for the whole state of Christ's Church and the World."

But we are also finite; we are not God. Therefore there must be when we come to act some sobriety and realism. As great a man as Temple must consider reality when he feels the call to act. It is arguable that at times he erred on the side of too much idealism. But he believed that Christian concern and zeal for the Kingdom of God must embrace the nation. His faith and hope, and his resolute commitment, were the same as that other William's — William Blake.

I will not cease from mental fight
Nor shall my sword sleep in my hand,
Till we have built Jerusalem
In England's green and pleasant land.

It was this emotional but also reasoned, deeply rooted conviction that took Temple in April 1924 to a unique Conference in Birmingham, England. One is always coming across references to COPEC. That is the shorthand for "Conference on Christian Politics, Economics, and Citizenship."

The very theme is controversial. It is possible for Christians to doubt whether there can be such a thing as Christian politics or Christian economics. Dr. W.R. Inge, Dean of St. Paul's, a liberal in religion but a conservative in about everything else, wrote Temple a note in 1920 about a monthly magazine, the *Pilgrim* which he had undertaken to edit on the invitation of R.G. Longman the publisher. It had as a sub-title, "A Review of Christian Politics and Religion."

The Dean said in his note: "I think you must admit that 'Christian Politics,' in the *Pilgrim* and elsewhere, are tinged with roseate hues of early dawn. I should never call my brand of Whiggery Christian Politics, though they are the politics of one Christian."

Temple, of course, was unmoved by this criticism. He made a firm distinction — clearer as he got older — between ideas, values, truths, on the one hand, and a party politically organized to advance through laws a particular set of objectives. But he felt that the Lord's Prayer had to embrace all life — and certainly areas as important as politics and economics.

To put the matter another way, William felt strongly that society should be organized on the basis of freedom and fellowship. Any movement that sought to promote such a Christian objective ought to have the sympathy of the Church. But the Church as a whole ought never to be attached to any political party. At one time, be it remembered, there were those who defined the Church of England as the Tory Party at prayer.

Temple was wont to say in discussing COPEC that its origin was a

43

Student Christian Movement Conference in 1909, at Matlock, of which he had been chairman. The theme was "Christianity and Social Problems." There was at the close of the Conference unanimous agreement on three propositions: that large numbers of church people, in particular the clergy, were largely ignorant of the elements of the social problem; that education must precede conviction; and that an organization was needed to prepare textbooks for social study on lines paralleling those already available on missions.

COPEC came out of SCM by way of a small, informal, interdenominational fellowship that called itself *Collegium,* of which Temple was Chairman and Miss Lucy Gardner was Secretary. The aim of this dedicated group was prayer and thought in fellowship directed to social problems. To this end it took and maintained a house where meetings and small conferences could be held.

This was the background of COPEC, a very ambitious enterprise which was four years in the planning and preparing. The Conference brought together 1,500 delgates, of which 80 came from outside the British Isles. Six European countries together with Japan and China were represented. The King, Prime Minister Ramsay MacDonald, and former Prime Ministers Asquith and Baldwin sent messages.

Temple, a Bishop now but the same Temple, sounded a characteristic keynote. "With the steadily growing sense that Machiavellian statecraft is bankrupt there is an increasing readiness to give heed to the claims of Jesus Christ that He is the Way, the Truth, and the Life. We represent here today the consequence of a spiritual movement in the Church prompted by loyalty and hope, and a spiritual movement in the world prompted by disillusion and despair."

Temple earned golden opinions not only as a presiding chairman but as a guiding president able by his presence and magnetism to influence the spirit of an assembly. At Edinburgh in 1937 I was to have the opportunity to observe the mature Archbishop exercise the same gifts with comparable results in a much more complicated and diversified setting. COPEC had a considerable impact on the Ecumenical Movement within the Churches both by its example in planning and its emphasis on the practical application of Christian principles.

Two World Conferences in particular were in the COPEC tradition: the Stockholm "Life and Work" Conference of 1925 and the Oxford Conference on "Church, Community and State" in July 1937.

Two other events essentially national in which Temple was deeply involved must be mentioned. The first was the stoppage in the coal industry in the spring of 1926 which led to the General Strike. The latter did not last long but the coal mines were shut down for seven months. Temple and other Christian leaders intervened in trying to mediate between the owners and the miners, and there is evidence that not all they did was entirely prudent. Heavy criticism descended on them, but Temple was characteristically impenitent and good-natured under fire. His superb gift of clarity likewise stood him in good stead. "We never imagined," he said, in a *Times* letter, "either that we should suggest satisfactory terms of our own or that economic facts can be modified by humane sentiments. But we felt a responsibility for trying to secure that the settlement should not only be economically sound in itself, but reached with the minimum of bitterness or resentment and the maximum of good will."

The other happening seems far away now. But it came as a bombshell. The proposed 1928 Prayer Book on which so much pain, prayer, effort, and ability had been lavished was brutally turned down by Parliament. The crisis for the Church of England was grave. Many feared that Disestablishment would be the result. That this did not happen, and that the Church was able to muddle through the emergency without either grave organic disruption or loss of soul, was due to the cool sagacity of the Archbishops and their colleagues on the Bench and to the political genius of the English people — a genius rooted in moderation and the sentiment of compromise. We have already seen that Temple accepted *ex animo* this solution and ate his earlier and fierier words about Disestablishment.

It remains to take note of perhaps the most important aspect of any episcopate — the work of the Bishop as Pastor, Teacher, Father-in-God. Here by all accounts we see William at his best — and we find him developing patterns that will be with him in York and after that in Canterbury. The key to everything here is the God-consciousness of the Bishop and its glorious fruit in the man William Temple — the manner in which it emptied him of self-consciousness, — his utter selflessness.

With this rare spirituality went a commanding intellect, and this combination is always present in Temple — in his preaching and teaching, his charges and meditations, and in all his books. But the spiritual note rooted above all in worship of the Most Highest and irradiated by the love of God in the face of Jesus Christ is ever the dominant element, the *leitmotiv*. In retreats for clergy and for ordinands before ordination, his outreach for all beginning with himself was a holy aspiration in the presence of the Holy and utter dedication to the Divine Will.

This never abolished humor, fellowship, relaxation at proper times in the sense of a common humanity — here Temple the Bishop and Archbishop was in all Church groups the heart and soul of everything that made for happiness and joy — but prayer and worship and communion with God were at the top of his priorities.

Temple was a true Father-in-God especially to his clergy and the young men whom he ordained continued to have a special place in his heart and his prayers. His thoughtfulness often took the form of taking one of the younger curates in the Diocese with him to a commission meeting at Oxford or Cambridge, or to some town of special interest where he might have business. He and Mrs. Temple were especially gratified when, on their leaving Manchester for York, the men whom he had ordained gave them a handsome household gift — an armchair and a fender stool.

Temple's presidential addresses at the annual Diocesan Conferences were used by him especially as a vehicle of teaching and here too he excelled, as he did at everything. These occasions were felt to be out of the ordinary and would be listened to by a thousand persons jamming

45

the galleries and seated on the floor, anxious not to miss a word, while the Bishop spoke from 40 minutes to an hour. Quite a contrast, one must say, to what Diocesan Conventions in the American Church at least have come to be!

Nor should it be assumed that Temple intended or allowed his Conferences to be one-man shows. He encouraged the idea of conferring, or letting each man speak his piece freely. He was essentially a patient man, but there was something of his father in him too. Once when asked how he managed to be so patient with bores, he replies: "By prolonged bouts of inattention."

He could take control — if he seldom did with any acerbity. As was said by one of his clergy, "Bishop Temple had the punch, but no man ever used it so sparingly." On one occasion however a speaker who had gone on and on still did not want to stop. "But your revered father said," he insisted; whereupon Temple cut him off, "I do not know whether my revered father said it or not, but if he did I disagree entirely with what my revered father said." At this the Conference applauded loudly, and the speaker sat down.

Temple's episcopate in Manchester was of eight years duration. It is strictly accurate to say that it was a great period, for the Bishop and for his clergy and people and for the not yet so secular city. There are, according to Temple's official biographer, on paper a good many attempts by parsons and laymen of Lancashire to give an estimate of Temple's episcopate. The reports are consistent in speaking of spiritual advance, ever-increasing vitality, and new social influence. One word however recurs impressively — the word "happy." Manchester under William Temple was a happy diocese.

This tribute was contained in a leader of the Bolton Evening News headed "Godspeed to the Bishop:"

> *Every section of the community is in Dr. Temple's debt...Dr. Temple is a man of very rare mental and moral type. He is an intellectual giant — one of the first half-dozen minds in this country; a splendid expositor and interpreter of ideas; a great and sympathetic administrator; a first class philosopher and writer; a cogent and persuasive preacher; a tremendous worker; and finally a most humble and lovable man.*

From Manchester Temple went to York, succeeding Dr. Cosmo Lang as Archbishop, while the latter succeeded Randall Davidson as Primate of all England and the first subject of the King.

Temple was enthroned in York Minster on January 10, 1929. He was 47 years old. For the next 13 years he was to labor and lead as Archbishop of York and Primate of England.

This, we believe, was Temple's greatest period. The Second World War was perhaps his finest hour. Refusing to spare himself, he died in harness as much a war casualty as if he had been killed on a frontline or in aerial combat. But it was as Archbishop of York that his powers reached their full maturity, he produced his greatest books, and his influence was strongest and most far-reaching, in his Diocese and Archdicese, in the whole Church of England, in the national Life, at the Universities, in the Ecumenical Movement, and in all Christendom.

This was the period in which I met William and saw him at work —

At Bishopthorpe, York

in the United States in 1935-36, in England and Scotland the great summer of 1937, and at the World Conference of Christian Youth in Amsterdam in 1939. I had the privilege of visiting the Temples in the Palace, acting as the Archbishop's Chaplain in the Minster, and preaching at the Parish Church in Bishopthorpe to a star-studded congregation, with the Archbishop reading Evensong. This was the Sunday before the Edinburgh Conference.

One of Temple's first decisions was that a good deal of the grandeur of the Palace, its fabulous gardens, and the lavish hospitality indulged in by his predecessor, would have to go. Lang was a bachelor, and a lover of pomp and circumstance. William and Frances would have to live more simply and set an example of moderation.

Temple had a Diocese as before, that of York, and the Northern Province, the Archdiocese of York, as an additional responsibility. York was basically rural, where Manchester had been urban and industrial. But Temple had eight years as a Bishop under his belt and knew exactly where he was and what he had to do. For a longer period than that he had been a national figure; and this of course was what he was to be with accelerating progression for the rest of his life.

The quiet and restful beauty of the Bishopthorpe surroundings meant a great deal to both Temples and were a constant source of refreshment. The routine that William started out with and stayed with as steadfastly as the totality of his life allowed, went this way. Mattins were said in the palace chapel by Temple and his chaplain, the Vicar of Bishopthorpe. Then came family prayers, for the staff and guests: a Scripture reading with a short exposition by the Archbishop followed by prayers that included intercession for the nation, the diocese, and the parishes of the latter in rotation. From the chapel he went to the dining room where he opened his own letters and ordered them while breakfast was being brought in. By 10:00 o'clock, usually after a short walk in the garden, he was with his secretary, ready to dictate which he did flawlessly and as a rule without the necessity of consulting a file or any other document. By 11:00 o'clock he was back in his study or had left Bishopthorpe for engagements in London, the province, or the diocese. Fridays he tried to keep free from outside engagements.

William worked very closely from the start with the Archbishop of Canterbury, Cosmo Lang, who looked upon him as a younger brother, admired him, and leaned on him increasingly. He and Mrs. Temple kept the rooms in the Lollards Tower (at the North end of the court of Lambeth Palace) which Archbishop Davidson had given them on Wiliam's accession to the See of Manchester. There were four comfortable flats in the Tower which were put at the disposal of selected Bishops by the Archbishop of Canterbury. These quarters which the Temple's kept until May 1941 were a London headquarters for William and a great convenience and aid for his multifarious activities.

It is sometimes hard to see the woods for the trees. This useful proverb applies to Temple in his great York period. His labors were so massive and the quantity and amgnitude of his achievements so immense that it is not easy to keep a clear perspective on the human figure

47

in which we are interested.

I propose accordingly to break down the woods in the following way. We shall look first at the Archbishop as preacher and teacher; second as the writer of books; third as an apostle of Christian unity; and fourth as a social thinker and prophet of national righteousness. I shall write of these tremendous themes as simply and compactly as possible. My aim and hope is to see the trees — to be able to visualize this remarkable man as he was in the period from 1929 to 1941, which I believe was his supreme period.

PREACHER AND TEACHER

William Ebor. was both a preacher and a teacher all his adult life. He was a man of words and a minister of *the* Word. This was what he lived for; it was his vocation. And it was the central activity of the Archbishop, engaged in on a scale and with a range given to few men in history. His great position, fantastic facility, and flair for getting across to diverse audiences insured that he would be heard as much as his energy and management of time allowed.

It is necessary to stress that he was both a preacher and a teacher. Both impulses were strong in William and they were related, rather closely related, but at the same time they were distinct.

Most of the time when Temple preached he also taught. This was the cast of his mind and personality. It was not possible for him to be an evangelist in the manner of a Billy Sunday or a Billy Graham. Yet he was an evangelist and a very effective one. As a missioner to the universities, he was outstanding in his nation and generation and this edge of his influence cut most penetratingly during the decade of the 30s.

The secret of his power was the concentration of his being. His aim as he faced young men and women or any other congregation was in the words of Paul the Apostle to be the ambassador of God in Christ. "Now then we are ambassadors for Christ, as though God did beseech you through us." (II Corinthians 5:20) His strength was his sense of the Divine presence, his certainty respecting the character and will of God, the absoluteness of his personal consecration.

These qualities came through when Temple was preaching, they shone as by emanation of light — the light that never was on sea or land. He used words, but it was the Spirit uttering Himself and taking hold of waiting human spirits that was the innermost reality. This preacher had no need of rhetorical pyrotechnics or flamboyant gestures. These would have intruded and in any case they were alien to him.

Stillness and elevation were the notes of William Ebor. as a preacher. The Word became sacramental. Was it St. Francis of Assisi who once called the Word the 8th Sacrament? There were elements of worship, prayer, mystical communion, and sacrifice in a mission service in which he preached or a clergy retreat which he led. No doubt this held of other sermons as well, though there must have been variations as on a scale. Often the teacher would come through more, for this was strong in

Temple. But I remember as yesterday his sermon at Edinburgh in the High Kirk of St. Giles at the opening Service of the World Conference on Faith and Order. Not so much the full sermon perhaps, which was on a text from Ephesians, as the Archbishop's face and voice at the end and his devotional conclusion with a special prayer of his own composition.

What came through and has remained with me was a quality as from another world, what one can only describe as the sense and presence of the Holy. The same quality was even more marked in the Archbishop's sermons at St. Mary's Oxford in the winter of 1931. They were eight of these on successive evenings, Sunday to Sunday, delivered to a packed Church mostly with undergraduates, with many seated on the floor. Increasingly as the week wore on, there were hushed moments of suspense, climax, and preternatural intensity. The teacher was there, to be sure, and the prophet was not absent. But principally it was as if we were in the temple where we "saw the Lord, sitting upon a throne, high and lifted up." We heard the seraphims, as "one cried unto another, and said, Holy, holy, holy, is the Lord of hosts: the whole earth is full of his glory." And before us was one who was like unto the high priest before the altar of sacrifice and surrender, and there was a light that shone on his face, as it were an angel. And as he spoke, quietly out of a great stillness, many of us like Isaiah of old "heard the voice of the Lord saying, Whom shall I send, and who will go for us? Then said I, Here am I: send me."

All, it is safe to say, in those great congregations were touched. Many were reached. Not a few were grasped. I shall never forget the queues of students lined up in the mornings waiting to see His Grace. Often the lines would be a hundred yards long. F.R. Barry, Vicar of St. Mary's, later Bishop of Southwell (a neighbor of Holywell with whom I used to walk home every Saturday morning in term after I had celebrated the Holy Communion at Newman's High Altar), has spread on the record this tribute and estimate:

> It 'stopped the rot' in the Christian life of post-war Oxford. There are large numbers of men and women rendering influential Christian service all over the world today who owe all that is best in them to that week. It was, indeed, a decisive moment in the history of that generation, and the influence still endures and spreads.

This mission was but one of many to the universities. To Cambridge he went also on the same errand — and to London, Leeds, Newcastle, and Trinity College, Dublin. To the United States he came in 1935-36, for lectures at Harvard and the University of Chicago, the College of Preachers, Washington, and the Student Volunteer Movement convention for North American·students at Indianapolis. And of course here and there he did a deal of preaching. Primarily in the lectures we see the teacher, but again the line is by no means hard and fast.

BOOKS

One of the phenomenal things about Wiliam Temple was his literary output. He published in his lifetime not less than 35 books and Heaven knows how many tracts, single sermons or lectures, and articles in learned and popular journals, to say nothing of the leaders and other pieces he wrote for the periodicals he edited.

His first publications were for private circulation, printed in 1904, his last year as an Oxford undergraduate. Significantly these were essays on *Robert Browning,* his first and last poetic love, and *The Province of Science,* on which his father had lectured at Oxford on the Bampton Foundation in 1884.

His first book, *The Faith and Modern Thought,* was published in 1910 and consisted of addresses to the London Intercollegiate Christian Union. Thereafter he averaged one book a year for the rest of his life. Some were volumes of sermons and addresses; others were more ambitious lectures like *The Nature of Personality, Plato and Christianity,* and *Church and Nation* (the Bishop Paddock Lectures at General Theological Seminary, New York in 1915). His first two major books were *Mens Creatrix* (1918) and *Christus Veritas* (1924).

After his enthronement as Archbishop of York in January 1929, there is a lacuna in his publications, but this was but the lull before the mental storm. He was very busy with the Lambeth Conference (his first) of 1930. In 1931 he published *Christian Faith and Life,* his sermons at the Oxford Mission and a book destined to go through 11 printings. From 21 November 1932 to 2 March 1934 he delivered periodically at Glasgow University 20 lectures on the famed Gifford Foundation. These were published in 1934 as *Nature, Man and God.*

This was Temple's *magnum opus.* It is basically a philosophical work, enormous in scope, brilliant in dialectical skill and sustained argument. The title is especially significant, for the three themes of man, nature, and God, either in this order or in the one Temple elected more realistically to follow, were the staples of European philosophy from Descartes on.

In Chapter VII of this book the reader will find a summary of the Archbishop's argument in *Nature, Man and God.* Here it is sufficient to cite Dean W.R. Inge, no mean critic. Writing of *Nature, Man and God,* he said: "It would be a great achievement for a university professor; for a ruler of the Church it is astonishing."

The second notable literary achievement of the York period is the two volume work *Readings in St. John's Gospel* (1939, 1940). This is not an easy work to classify. It is really *sui generis* — in a class by itself. Essentially it is a devotional work in commentary form. The Archbishop in these two volumes gives us the ripe fruit of his meditation on his favorite Gospel and Biblical writing over a period of at least a third of a century.

Temple's biographer, Dean Iremonger, thinks that Readings in St. *John's Gospel* is "the greatest devotional treatise written by an English Churchman since William Law's *A Serious Call to a Devout and Holy Life.*" Professor Reinhold Niebuhr on this side of the Atlantic wrote Temple after perusing the first volume: "I have finished half of the *Readings in St. John's Gospel* and find the book tremendously stimulating, more than anything of the kind I have ever read. I think it represents a new medium in its combination of devotional and scholarly treatment."

One can be sure of this, that this devotional book has been more widely read and will continue to be more influential than anything else that came from William's pen except possibly *Christian Faith and Life* and *Christianity and Social Order*.

We must not overlook a series of small volumes that the Archbishop turned out both in the middle and toward the end of the York period. His American tour in 1935-36 was especially productive, resulting in four published volumes. They were: *The Centrality of Christ* (Published in England as *The Preacher's Theme Today*) containing the College of Preachers lectures; *The Church and Its Teaching Today* containing his Noble lectures at Harvard; *Christianity in Thought and Practice* — the Moody Lectures at the University of Chicago; and *Basic Convictions* — his address at the Student Volunteer Convention, Indianapolis.

It is easy to record the publication in one year of four books, though surprising enough to cause one to raise his eyebrows. But when one realizes that these were all made up from stenographic reports of spoken lectures or addresses; and when one learns that a lecture was normally given from notes and headings on one sheet of ordinary stationery — as the Archbishop showed me at the College of Preachers — the feat becomes really astonishing. One can only exclaim, What a man! What a brain and mind!

Temple's mind was in many ways like a dynamic, well-oiled, tireless machine. The analogy is very imperfect and of course speedily breaks down. But it indicates part of the story and one impressive aspect of the man. Both the thinking of the man and the arrangement and expression of his thoughts were extraordnary in their orderliness. His Grace told me that for the most part he found it unnecessary to revise the stenotype scripts of his lectures with a view to publication. All he needed to do was check or indicate the paragraphing along with the spelling and punctuation.

This was the way four books got written, to my knowledge.

Three more small books that are notable came from his pen and/or mouth after the war began. In 1940 *The Hope of a New World* was published. This is one of the finest, most creative of all Temple's books. The title and first half of the book came from 6 radio broadcast talks made by him in September and October of 1940. The last of the six talks on "A Christian Civilization" has the breath-taking sentence which has influenced my thinking profoundly and is one of the most important statements in the history of religion and theology. This is the Archbishop's dictum:

It is a great mistake to suppose that God is only, or even chiefly, concerned with religion.

This year, 1940, found Temple as Archbishop starting a Lent Book Series. For this series he wrote the second volume himself, entitled *Citizen and Churchman*. (The first was *The Two Moralities* by A.D. Lindsay, Master of Balliol.) That same year 1941, while still Archbishop of York, he penned one of the most widely read and influential of his books, *Christianity and Social Order*. It was not published until after he was enthroned on St. George's Day (April 23) 1942 as Archbishop of Canterbury. Within a short time it had sold well over 150,000 copies.

51

In 1910 a great gathering was held in the city of Edinburgh. It was called the International Missionary Conference. The Chairman of this Conference, commonly credited with having initiated the modern Ecumenical Movement, was Dr. John R. Mott. Present were many young men who were to become prominent in their Churches and in the Reunion movement as the decades came and went.

Among these was a young Oxford don named William Temple. He had been a member of the Preparatory Commission on Missionary Education and attended the Conference as a steward, acting in this capacity for the S.C.M. along with Neville Talbot and Walter Moberly. Other Anglican names involved in the Conference that were or would become famous were Edward Talbot, Walter Frere, Henry Scott Holland, and Charles Gore. The Conference provided for its future by the appointment of a Continuation Committee with a secretariat. The Secretary chosen was Dr. J.H. Oldham.

William Temple was destined to become the leading figure in the Ecumenical Movement prior to Pope John XXIII and Vatican II. The period of his primacy as a leader came in the decade of the 30s when he was Archbishop of York. He was superbly equipped by learning, conviction, and temperament for the stellar role he was to play.

His starting point was the Church in the New Testament and behind that Church the mind of Christ as portrayed especially in what he describes in *Readings in St. John's Gospel* as "perhaps the most sacred passage even in the four Gospels — the record of the Lord's prayer of self-dedication as it lived in the memory and imagination of this most intimate friend." In commenting further on this high-priestly prayer of John 17, he writes: "But the unity of the Church is precious not only for its utility in strengthening the Church as an evangelistic agent. It is itself in principle the consummation to which all history moves...The unity of the Church is something much more than unity of ecclesiastical structure, though it cannot be complete without this. It is the love of God in Christ possessing the hearts of men so as to unite them in itself — as the Father and the Son are united in the love of Each for Each which is the Holy Spirit...His prayer is not only *that they may be one;* it is *that they may be one as we.*"

William goes on, revealing incidentally the source of the loftiness and exaltation that take hold of him at his height as preacher and writer: "Before the loftiness of that hope and calling our little experience of unity and fellowship is humbled to the dust. Our friendships, our reconciliations, our unity of spirit in Church gatherings or in missionary conferences...how poor and petty they appear in the light of the Lord's longing."

In the high-priestly prayer we have the mandate for Reunion. The secretarian divisions of the empirical Church are shocking and scandalous in the light of this prayer. The true follower of Christ is bound to seek for real unity, and, as he seeks, to agonize, realizing the open wounds in the Body of Christ. The basis of full unity can only be a common faith and a common order: life and work are important but vague terms and by themselves are insufficient as a foundation for a Church that is One, Holy, Catholic, and Apostolic.

Bishop Charles Brent, the American Episcopalian, was the prophet and apostle of organic reunion on the basis of faith and order. He was out in front of the cautious Archbishops and English Anglicans for a time, but by the Lausanne Conference in 1927 the National Church Assembly was ready to move and asked the Archbishops to apoint an English Anglican delegation. Temple of Manchester was one of the nominees. At Lausanne he was deputy-chairman of the section that dealt with "The Nature of the Church," impressing most favorably Chairman William Adams Brown of Union Seminary, New York.

Reunion — a reconstituted ecumenical Church — as the goal, is one side of the picture or, as Temple might say, the dialectic. The other side is the unity already existing among Christians and its origin and nature in the work of the Holy Spirit. The truly instructed Christian — instructed that is in the Scriptures and the mysteries of the Kingdom of Heaven — dare not let go of either side.

It has always been seen by the thoughtful, through the Middle Ages and back to the great Augustine, the Colossus of the Christian West, that the Church had an invisible and heavenly as well as a visible and earthly aspect. This insight had stood the Reformers, at the time of the Reformation, in good stead. To some extent, indeed, they embraced the truth of the mystical Body, the heavenly City of Augustine, too unwarily and with too much alacrity. But certainly Luther and Calvin never expected the resort to Biblical authority to have the alarming centrifugal action that in fact ensued, with schism piled on schism for the next three centuries.

The 20th century is characterized by a sharp reversal in the matter of Christian union and unity. It is one of the chief glories of this checkered time, with its world wars and savage, sweeping revolutions, that the entrenched fissiparous trend within Christendom has been arrested and turned around. Our time has witnessed the recovery of the ideal of unity and ecumenicity — that there should be *one worldwide* Church.

This does not mean one uniform Church, organized in a total way. The Church of the first centuries and of Christianity's golden age had a strong ecumenical consciousness but there were differences of administration, and even of doctrinal emphasis.

The Lambeth Conference of 1920 issued *An Appeal to all Christian People* that was both a sign of the times and a forceful positive influence. Basically it was a call for moving toward fellowship grounded in unity among Christians as the divinely appointed antidote to the divisions and enmities of a war-wounded world.

In Great Britian energetic steps were taken in response to this appeal by leaders of the Established Church and of the Free Churches. Meetings and "conversations" began between Anglican representatives appointed by the two Archbishops and Free Church representatives appointed by the Federal Council of Evangelical Free Churches. For six years these deliberations continued. When they ended a report was issued that contained a special memorandum from the Anglican representatives including Archbishops Davidson and Lang. These Churchmen addressed as follows the critical question of the status of the Free Church Ministries:

> *It seems to us to be in accordance with the Lambeth Appeal to say, as we are prepared to say, that the ministries which we have in view in this memorandum, ministries which imply a sincere intention to preach Christ's Word and administer the Sacraments as Christ has ordained, and to which authority so to do has been solemnly given by the Church concerned, are real ministries of Christ's Word and Sacraments in the Universal Church.* "

This was a position to which Temple ever adhered. It represented a milestone in the rising ecumenical consciousness of the Churches generally and helped to make possible the Faith and Order Movement. He believed deeply in this Movement of which he became not only the titular head but the great symbol figure.

The climax of his leadership came in the success of the move to merge provisionally the two hitherto separate bodies or wings of the Ecumenical Movement, namely, "Faith and Order" and "Life and Work." At Utrecht in May 1938 representatives of 70 Churches came together. Under Temple's superb direction in the Chair and as the accepted leader of a world movement, the draft constitution, the doctrinal basis, and the plan of membership of the World Council of Churches were drawn up for submission to the Churches. Temple was named Chairman of the Provisional Committee and W.A. Visser t'Hooft General Secretary, with William Paton (London) and Henry S. Leiper (New York) as Associate Secretaries.

Before the outbreak of World War II, 40 Churches had officially applied for membership in the World Council and within the decade 1939-1948 more than 60 others had joined. In England the going was at first choppy, as a good many Anglo-Catholics were uneasy and stand-pat, and reactionary conservatives like the Bishop of Gloucester (Dr. A.C. Headlam) were unalterably opposed to membership in the World Council by the Church of England. That worthy had, as a matter of fact, very nearly torpedoed at the last minute the unity and harmony of the 1937 World Conference on Faith and Order. Bishop Angus Dun, my old teacher in Divinity School, came to the rescue in a stirring speech and William, very pleased, dubbed him Horatio at the bridge.

Efforts were made to oppose the World Council in the Church Assembly, but the Archbishop was able to head this off and to get through a Resolution welcoming the new development and accepting by the Church of England the invitation to membership. The following February (1939) he was able as Chairman to write the Vatican Secretary of State to inform the Holy See of the establishment of the World Council and to invite exchange of information with appropriate agencies as well consultation unofficially with Roman Catholic theologians and scholars.

To sum up, there was no limit to Temple's openness to all Christians who on the basis of existing unity in Christ desired to deepen that unity and to advance in accordance with His Will to the recovery of organic, ecumenical oneness on the pattern of the ancient undivided Church. It was the strength of his conviction along with his patience, charity, and prudence that made William Ebor. the acknowledged, incomparable leader of the Ecumenical Movement. One cannot but regret that he did not live to know Pope John XXIII, another priest-prophet, and witness his mighty work on behalf of ecumenical recovery and *aggiornamento*.[1] This was not to be but these are the two men who will be forever remembered as Apostles of Unity and Ecumenical Statesmen in the 20th century.

It is fitting to quote here a remarkable personal letter from William. It is one of the longest I ever had from him, running to four full pages. Usually they were two pages. This particular letter was heavily censored, as the War was on. This was because he tells of bombs that had fallen at Lambeth, where of course he had rooms and frequently stayed. I include the first part of the letter which mentions both German planes and a paper I had sent him on the proposed Episcopal-Presbyterian Concordat which is the context of his suggested solution of the problem of straightening out Orders.

Bishopthorpe,
York
September 23, 1940

My very dear Charles,

Your letter or paper on the Concordat arrived just as we got back from a glorious month (August) in Somerset. We had wonderful weather and the days were divine. But we were on the direct route from Cherbourg to Cardiff, so the German planes came over every night. No bombs fell very near us, but several close enough to be unpleasant....

We came back through London just after the attacks there began; the sirens went off and we had to sleep in a strange place, but heard no bangs. (He then describes subsequent bombings of Lambeth, and several words are scissored out by the censor.)

Now about your paper. I will send it on to Alec Vidler and hope he will publish it. At one stage I was consulted about the Concordat when the Form of Commission was something like this. "Take thou authority to exercise the office of a Presbyter in this Church"...I wrote to Bishop Parsons to say that would not do at all. Ordination (as distinct from licensing) is to the ministry in the Church of God.

I understand the present Form to rest on an *avowed* ambiguity...If all this were clearly understood, I could reluctantly accept it, because it would compromise nothing which is not compromised already, and I see no early hope of agreement *on one side* about the reality of Presbyterian Orders.

[1]Updating or modernization

The only satisfactory solutions, I think, are two. (1) Let us and them *both* be conditionally ordained by the Orthodox and put the validity of our Orders beyond question even at Rome. Politically that is good; but as we believe we are ordained it is hardly sincere. (2) — My own solution. Let them come to us for ordination in the historic ministry of the Church; and let the consecrating bishops receive Holy Communion *the previous day* from the presbyters who are to be consecrated bishops and then transmit the historic succession to their own folk. So we should hold apart till the schism was on the eve of being healed, but should on that eve publicly testify our recognition of the *reality* of their ministry and sacraments. What do you think of that?[1]

Yours v. affecty
William Ebor.

SOCIAL THINKER

Temple did his formost work in relation to society and national life during his York Archiepiscopate. We conclude this chapter with a summary of a complex subject, confining ourselves very compactly to the high points and a few observations on some of the difficult issues raised.

William became William Ebor. in early 1929 when he was 47 years old. He was in the prime of life mentally and spiritually. Experience in various directions, including eight years as a Bishop, had seasoned and disciplined him. He knew the responsibility that being in authority and therefore accountable to enduring concerns inculcates. He never lost completely, I believe, the freshness and spontaneity of his youth; a touch of boyishness, which Santayana discerned as belonging to the English character, clung to him always. Still we are dealing with a man who has come to the maturity of his powers, including judgment and sense of limitation.

The most acute analysis of Temple as a Social Thinker is the Rev. W.G. Peck's essay in the slender but telling volume *William Temple: An Estimate and Appreciation* by six friends and associates, published in 1946. Mr. Peck pays this great man a well deserved tribute: "William Temple was the latest of those great prophets of social righteousness whom God has raised up in the English Church. None made a more single impact upon the mind and conscience of the nation; none was more gladly heard by the common people; none gave himself more fully to the support of social justice."

This is the correct starting point. It is the thing that we need to keep

[1]My next letter from the Archbishop was dated July 30, 1940. It closes this way. "I hope the tyranny will soon be overpast. Then it will be essential that we get ahead with World Christian Unity. It is a great relief to me that the Church of England has adhered to the World Council of Churches.

With best love
Yours v. affectly
William Ebor.

in the forefront of our minds as we look at Temple's efforts and consider his ideas as he grappled with the human problems of England. He was never merely or mainly a theorist. He was concerned with persons and personal values. And he always approached them from the standpoint of Jesus, the Incarnate Son of God, and the principles and standards of the Kingdom of God which He enunciated.

Peck's treatment of Temple has the value in addition of anaylzing the sources of his social ideas in the philosophers and philosophies that influenced him. And Peck has studied carefully the development of these ideas.

Development there certainly was. As a young don at Oxford he was convinced that socialism was a corollary of Christianity. In 1908 in *The Economic Review* he wrote that the Gospels "taught nothing less than evolutionary socialism...the alternative stands before us — Socialism or Heresy."

We need not be too shocked or surprised by this. The Zeitgeist or Time-spirit at that time was moving strongly in the direction of a social Christianity. In America this was the era of Walter Rauschenbusch. (1861 - 1918) He felt and thought the same way, and was sure that a new era of reform on the socialist pattern was at hand. In fact, when one reads Rauschenbusch one cannot tell whether he is preaching socialism or communism: the two appear more or less interchangeable with him. The late Bishop Oxnam of the Methodist Church was a disciple of Rauschenbusch and I believe never got over the latter's socialist teaching. There were many others.

Another more personal illustration may be useful. When in 1927 I entered the Episcopal Theological School, Cambridge Mass. (now the Episcopal Divinity School) I experienced two striking novelties. I was in constant contact with the highest standard of living and the most casual acceptance of wealth in my experience. And for the first time I knew and was thrown with men, scholars and theologians, who were Socialists — Christian Socialists. Where I had always thought in terms of Democrats and Republicans, they voted the Socialist ticket — for Norman Thomas.

After Franklin D. Roosevelt came to power and in fighting the Depression began to reach for a mixed economy and a welfare state, these mentors of mine began abandoning Thomas and voting for Roosevelt. A similar or at least a comparable development is discernible in Temple. He certainly ceased to be a socialist even of the "Christian" variety. He became critical of the Labour Party, resigning from it in 1925 (he had joined it in 1918), though I believe the immediate reason was disenchantment with its foreign policy position. In July 1939 on the Boat Train from Amsterdam to the Hook — our last visit and the last time I was to see William — he said to me in the course of a conversation touching on internal affairs in Great Britian: "After all, the best way to get on is for the Conservatives to do the right things."

This offhand remark should be set beside a considered analytic judgment in Lecture III of *Nature, Man and God*. The Archbishop is illustrating his theory of Hegelian dialectic, drawn from his mentor Edward Caird, Master of Balliol, that a dialectical movement of thought nor-

57

mally is suggestive of large periods and movements of history. Also the synthesis is always a reassertion of the thesis with all that has proved valuable in the antithesis worked into it.

Now comes the clincher in one of his proposed illustrations, taken from parliamentary history. The Conservative party of Great Britian, at its best, represents the thesis, standing for the actual situation as it had developed historically. The antithesis — always generated out of the contradictions of the thesis — is the Liberal party, attacking various forms of privilege and restrictions on individual liberty. The Labour party is an extension of the antithesis, influenced and motivated by concern for the wage-earning class. But the synthesis at any given moment is to be found in the continuing Conservative party, combining the thesis and the antithesis of the last generation. "This is recognized in the principle avowed by some detached Radicals that while they are eager for drastic reforms they wish to see these enacted by a Conservative Government, because that will secure that the country is ready for them."[1]

Dean Iremonger speaks of William's "gradual movement to the Right during later years" and in his biography betrays some sense of concern, if not criticism, of the change that had come over his hero. He notes the influences of Lambeth Palace, defined as an atmosphere not a domicile, but believes that a more important factor was the Archbishop's complete absorption in what he was convinced was his mission, "namely holding up and bearing witness to the Divine purpose which "is presented to us in the Bible under the name of the Kingdom (Sovereignty) of God."[2]

W.G. Peck gives a more satisfactory account of the development of Temple's social thought. Noting that it was sometimes suggested that the Archbishop was losing interest in the Christian social witness, Peck says, "This was never for a moment true." What was true was that Temple found himself in perplexity as he sought to apply the *ethico-social idealism* of his Oxford and following periods to the intractable problems visible on every side. "This Idealism, because of its lack of awareness of natural order and of human morphology as related to that order, had nothing to set, upon the natural level, against the false materialistic 'Naturalism' and 'Realism' which, assisted by popular pseudo-science, had spread in the age of Industrialism."

Moreover, the Archbishop had by now begun to be skeptical of hopes placed in the political forces of Socialism. "He perceived in them a preference for 'the good citizen' to 'the good man,' and a lack of any sure conception of 'the good city.' " At this time, also, he was laying more emphasis upon personality in its importance for social thought and action. This emphasis can be seen in his Penguin Special written early in the War (1941), *Christianity and Social Order,* and in 1944 in his William Ainslie Memorial Lecture he carefully clarifies his position: "I do not for a moment believe that our belief in the inherent value of the human person can be maintained except on the basis of

[1]*Nature, Man and God,* p. 59
[2]*William Temple,* p. 512

58

the conviction that he is himself the focus of that principle which gives to history its meaning."[1]

In the light of the biggest and most threatening revolution of our century, Totalitarian Communism based on Marxism-Leninism, this is a prophetic declaration and a momentous one. As is well known, many British Fabian socialists have been less than firm in the face of the allure of the Soviet experiment. Never however even for a moment was William Temple in danger of being taken in by the Marxian brand of Socialism.

He was deeply stimulated by the ideological challenge of Fascism, especially in its Nazi form, and Communism. This can be seen in his six broadcast talks in the early autum of 1940 on "The Hope of a New World." They were almost immediately published under the same title, with several addresses and sermons on related themes added. William wrote me that he was sending me this book and in my copy of it under my bookplate the words "A present from the author" are written.

I have always believed that this is one of the most important of Temple's writings. In my book *Communism and Christ* I have quoted as its concluding words the inspired vision of society based on the sovereignty of a God who is Love, with which the Archbishop closed his great Coronation Sermon in St. Paul's Cathedral. That sermon had been delivered at the Empire Day service in 1937 and was the only piece in *The Hope of a New World* not composed in 1940. Temple chose it, most fittingly, as the concluding chapter of this book.

The broadcast addresses on "The Hope of a New World" are a kind of Christian manifesto, directly answering the ideologies of Fascism and Communism and calling Christians and men and women of good will to consider seriously what was wrong with the old world and what must be thought and done if the world beyond the war is to be truly a new world. In these addresses, which are a kind of climax in Temple's York period, he is truly a prophet-soul and rises, I believe, to great heights.

Also — though Peck does not make the connection — these addresses sum up the mature thought of Temple on social issues, and may be read as a Preface both to the coming Penguin special *Christianity and Social Order* and to the pronouncements and witness of the Canterbury Archiepiscopate on which Peck lays particular stress.

Temple begins with what he labels his jeremiad, and he does not mince words. What is wrong with the old world? The sum and substance of the answer is this: "we have neglected God and His laws."

Historians of the future, declares the Archbishop, "will admire very much about the nineteenth century and its products in the early decades of this century. But they will, I am sure, express a bewildered astonishment at the attitude to God and to faith in God, which increasingly prevailed in that period — I mean the attitude which regards God and faith in God as an optional extra, so to speak, to be added according to taste when the requirements of a decent human life have been met — the attitude often expressed in the astonishingly silly saying that a man's religion is a private affair between him and his Maker."

[1]Quoted by Peck in *William Temple: An Estimate and Appreciation.* p. 65

When it is realized that the view of religion noted by the Archbishop is precisely that of the United States Supreme Court, voiced explicitly by Mr. Justice Black and the premise of its innovative, precedent-shattering decisions in school cases involving prayer and Bible-reading, one is given to think furiously. Of course the real scandal is not so much the actions of the Court, though they were grave, but the acquiescence of the American people in them, led by the supine leaders nearly unanimously of the large, respectable Church denominations, Catholics sad to say as well as Protestants.

But that was just the start of the sword of prophecy, wielded fearlessly by William Ebor.

He goes on to say, "We have forgotten that we are God's creatures equally with the other animals and with the earth itself. Leaving God out of account, we have found ourselves able to utilize all natural resources for our purposes, and have regarded ourselves as lords of creation."

It would be pleasant to record that this Churchman foresaw and anticipated the environmental and ecological crisis and reaction, and I believe that to some extent he did. But he was too intent upon the rediscovery of the natural order of things, God's order, in the economic sphere, and upon pinning down the modern reversal of dominant roles as between consumption and production, to forsee the current dilemma of man. This dilemma comes into sharp focus in the energy crunch in the United States, with the lustful consumer the center of the problem as much as the avaricious producer at least in the West. What is to be said about the OPEC nations, mostly Muslim, is another matter.

In his influential Penguin Paperback, *Christianity and Social Order*, Temple comes down hard on the concept of a Natural Order or Natural Law. He intends something like the traditional Stoic-Catholic Natural Law, though he would doubtless draw its boundaries less rigidly and flatly. He has a flawless definition of Natural Law: in contrast to what the phrase means to a modern scientist, it meant to older Christian thinkers "the proper functions of a human activity as apprehended by a consideration of its own nature." The great value of this concept, he thinks, is that it holds together two aspects of truth, the ideal and the practical.

Temple treats trenchantly the idea and meaning of freedom in *The Hope of a New World*. Again, in the light of where we are today he is astonishingly prophetic. If, as the modern world so widely thinks, freedom is chiefly being allowed to do what I choose, the result inevitably will be a society which is a welter of selfishness. But there is an older view of freedom; its authentic formulation is, "We must obey God rather than men."

At the end of the talk on "God and Freedom," Temple says: "Our present duty is to secure the freedom we defend not only from external attack but from internal decay. If the aim of the last war was to make the world safe for democracy and freedom, our aim in this war must be to make freedom and democracy safe for the world." It is dismaying to read that statement and realize how completely we have ignored this duty, in Church, State, and Society. Apparently prophets in our time are paid no more heed than they were in Bible times.

Finally — and Peck puts a good deal of weight on this — the mature Temple broke away from anything that smacked of statism. The Greeks saw man as a political animal and ethico-idealism always tends to make the political order socially inclusive. Fascism does this in an extreme form and Communism, though theoretically committed to a relative view of the State, is unable in practice to endow the larger community with any transcendence of political coercion. In fact, because of its commitment to total revolution, Communism so far has exceeded Fascism in the degree to which it has established total power in the Total State.

It is one of his distinctions that William as Bishop of Manchester prior to 1928 saw the fallacy of Statism and as Archbishop of York in the following decade of peril and temptation held steadfastly to the prior reality of the natural Community and the limited instrumentality of the State.

We are perhaps ready now to sum up. William started out always as a Christian personalist. The first reality and the one conditioning all else is a personal God who is sovereign but whose sovereignty is that of Love. It follows that man is the child of God, for he is created in the Divine image. This is his dignity and gives us the governing principle of Christian Ethics and Christian Politics — respect for every person because he is a person.

This idealism must not preclude realism, for man has as part of his original equipment an animal on which the Creator has stamped, so to speak, his image. The combination is the glory of man, and it is also his problem. For man's nature is flawed by the self-centeredness with which he is born. This bias to selfishness has infected his "higher nature," his spirit and reason: and this flawed or "fallen" condition inevitably spreads into and through society. Politics in particular reflects this unideal situation; it is largely a contention between groups in which self-interest is uppermost. The statesman has no choice but to recognize this. "The art of government in fact is the art of so ordering life that self-interest prompts what justice demands."[1]

God however has a purpose. It was to embody it and bear witness to it that Jesus came — came proclaiming the Kingdom of God. For the Kingdom, He taught, lived, and died on the Cross. For the Kingdom and because of the Divine purpose, the Son of man and Son of God was raised from the dead, and the Church came into being. The power of Love to transform came into play, altering the whole perspective on Creation. And thus from the primary Christian Social principles of God and Man come three derivative principles. They are Freedom, Fellowship, and Service.

William Ebor. took these things with the utmost seriousness because he believed in God and His Christ. This faith — for him it was utter trust — made all the difference. He held back nothing. Without fear he waded into many questions and various endeavors, such as the Malvern Conference of January 1941. His conclusions in the matter of concrete programs were exploratory and tentative; he was never doctrinaire; and it should be kept in mind that in general he was not ad-

---

[1]One of Temple's choicest epigrams. It is from *Christianity and Social Order*, Chapter 4.

vocating political actions but attempting to sensitize and mobilize Christian citizens. He remained as a social thinker something of an eclectic, for which he was sometimes criticized, but this in his position was a strength, for it kept doors open in various directions and it enabled him to remain primarily a Christian prophet and apostle.

Nor must it be forgotten that this man had the ear of the nation. Clergy and laity respected him, indeed honored him, even when some had reservations. The common people heard him gladly, and among students and intellectuals in and out of the universities there was no figure of comparable appeal.

Former Prime Minister Edward Heath, a Conservative, was willing to write a Foreword to a new edition of the book, *Christianity and Social Order* (1976)[1] "The impact of William Temple on my generation," he wrote, "was immense. His personal influence was not limited to those of his own way of thinking. It extended to those who held no religious belief and to those whose political views did not march with his own. It embraced the whole spectrum of those who were seriously concerned with the social, economic and political problems of the day."

[1]Published by Shepheard-Walwyn, Ltd., London and Seabury, New York — with an excellent critical introduction by Ronald Preston.

CHAPTER FIVE

HIS FINEST HOUR

In the Middle Ages there was a great deal of discussion of the active versus the contemplative life. Like nearly everything, this goes back to the Greeks and received definitive treatment at the hands of Aristotle. His intuition and conviction at this point are reflected in his conception of God. The Aristotelian Diety is not an active Being in any ordinary sense. He has no need to be, for His perfections are so luminous and self-evident that all things are moved by the *Eros* which He, unwilling and unknowing, inspires.

The God of the Bible, based on Yahweh of the Hebrews, a God of war and always and in the end, as Whitehead says, the rationalization of a tribal Deity, is very different from the God of the Stagirite, entirely given over to self-contemplation. The Judeo-Christian God is active. He is active in making the world, so much so that on the seventh day He rests. He is active also in redemption, going out to man, and in abiding with man as a strengthening, guiding, teaching Spiritual Presence.

The active genius of the God of the Bible is dramatically described in the Gospel of John when Jesus says to the Jews who are criticizing Him for healing on the Sabbath, "My Father worketh even until now, and I work."(John 5:17) Immediately, Jesus is refuting the idea that the Sabbath-rest of the Lord after the finished work of Creation means idleness. But He is saying also something very important about His Father and something ultimately and everlastingly true.

God is the living Lord. He is energy, power, purpose, direction, enlightenment. Jesus is active and constant in good works because He is the Son and He is the one whom the Father has sent. If one pauses to think about it, this is a continual theme and thesis in this Gospel. "I must work the works of him that sent me, while it is day." (9:4) "The Son can do nothing of himself, but what he seeth the Father do. For what things soever he doeth, these also the Son in like manner doeth. For the Father loveth the Son, and showeth him all things that he himself doeth; and greater works than these will he show him, that even you may marvel." (5:19, 20 AV and Temple's rendering.)

We are like what we worship. This is why worship — and that which both informs it and issues from it, prayer — are so important. William Temple knew this, and more and more as his life progressed he invested worship and prayer with the highest priority. He knew that in the spiritual order everything depended on contact with God and the constant, ever-present sense of the Divine Reality and Power (Sovereignty).

63

This meant contemplation but never contemplation, never worship, never prayer, divorced from action. "The farmer who cares for his land and neglects his prayers is, as a farmer co-operating with God; and the farmer who says his prayers but neglects his land is failing, as a farmer, to co-operate with God. It is a great mistake to suppose that God is only, or even chiefly, concerned with religion. But of course the truly Christian farmer cares for land and prayers alike."[1]

These words tell us a great deal about the man William Temple, and about the priest-prophet, and about the Archbishop, first of York, and finally, in the midst of the fiery crucible of war, of Canterbury — the Primate of all England.

This was an activist. This was a great man of action. This was a Prelate who believed in the Church Militant — and that "Like a mighty army/Moves the Church of God."

It is doubtful whether since the days of the Apostles there has been any Churchman whose days and nights have been more filled with doing the works of God. He was tireless. He had an almost infinite capacity for taking pains. He was unselfish. He was generous. He took for granted that the vocation of the Christian is *servanthood*.

It is possible that he took on too much, that he was too ready with words, that he despatched assignments and engagements with too sweeping a facility. This was his nature and his special gift. And what a steward he was, of the talents and endowments entrusted to him!

William had, I believe, a secret. But it was not really a secret. It was something the disciple is promised in the Gospel by the Master. It is rest — peace — deliverance from anxiety and all self-concern.

Most of us are restless — at least a good deal of the time. We have a long way to go from the point of view of integration, and therefore of dedication. We are imperfectly at peace. This affects our work and our service. St. Augustine knew the problem. "Our heart is restless, until it finds rest in Thee."

Augustine traveled a rough road before he found this rest. William, on the other hand, from his youth up, was at rest in the Lord. He never knew what serious distraction was. Therefore he had a whole self to give; and he was able to work with a maximum of efficiency and effectiveness, of concentration and endurance.

It is a fantastic story — that of this priest-prophet, bishop, archbishop, who never seemed tired, who was always ready to go another mile, who seemed almost not to have a self to think of. And it was not that he had no physical problems. He suffered from gout all his life — from childhood. It was extremely painful and partly immobilized him, when the attacks came. I experienced this with him, empathetically, at Edinburgh in 1937.

And William had only one good eye. All that reading and remembering — all that mental mastery, rested on 50 percent of a normal visual equipment.

One was apt to forget these things and to think of the Archbishop as a superman physically and mentally. No doubt he was in some ways — in his inherited photographic memory, for example. But there was

[1] *The Hope of a New World*, p. 70

64

more than nature in the character and achievement of this man. There was grace, there was Super-nature. The Spirit was mightily in it all — the Spirit that is like the wind which bloweth where it listeth and we see only fruits and consequences.

Temple had already been a War-Archbishop. But now, from St. George's Day (and Shakespeare's Birthday) April 23, 1942, he was *the* War-Archbishop. London was his base. He was at the heart of the Nation and Empire. He was the King's first subject. There was no assignable limit to his moral and spiritual influence in the time of the testing of a Nation.

What happened is history. Written at first on the tables that are hearts, it was eventually spread on the books. He did not have long to live and labor in the new position. He did not know this, but it would have made no difference if he had. He lived each day fully and victoriously, as if it were the only day left. He had no special concern about the future, and I believe that he had no doubt whatever as to the outcome of the War.

I remember as yesterday a conversation I had on May 31, 1941 in front of the Dean's office in the yard of the Yale Divinity School. I encountered there most unexpectedly a German clergyman and missionary who had served in Japan. He had come to me with an introduction from a mutual friend, had been my house guest, and had lectured to my theology class at the Virginia Seminary on Luther. He was not a Nazi but he was a German and felt that he had to defend his country. We had numerous talks about Luther on the State. My friend at that time argued that Luther would have accepted Hitler; I begged to dissent from this.

The spring of 1941 had been a bad one for Britian. The Nazis had taken Yugoslavia, all Greece, and Crete. Rommel in Africa had become a byword and the British situation under Wavell in North Africa was precarious in the extreme. The Germans were sitting on most of Europe outside the Soviet Union, and it looked to me as if the seizure of Gibralter would not be too difficult. If that were to happen, the British fleet in the Mediterranean could be bottled up. The moral effect of such a happening would be great. And Hitler could then take his time about picking off Great Britain.

No doubt this view was amateurish and over-simplified, but I of course knew nothing at that time of Operation Barbarossa (code name for the invasion of Russia) and it never occurred to me that Hitler was not planning to proceed with adding North Africa and the Middle East to captured Europe. That was the logical and realistic way in which to win the war.

So I described to my German friend what Hitler's strategy then appeared to be and said, "It looks to me as if Hitler's plan is working out well. He may be close to a great success."

"Yes", replied this German pastor, "I think you are right. I think this is Hitler's plan. Things are going very well for us."

Three weeks and one day later, on June 22, Hitler struck at Russia, as Napoleon had done 129 years before. It seems incredible that he would have abandoned what looked like a sure thing for a giant gamble. But he had made many gambles, and they had paid off. And the stakes were very high; they encompassed German hegemony over the world-island (Afro-Eurasia) and an indefinite Nordic future. (Hitler had adopted via Haushofer the Oxonian, Sir Harold Mackinder's Geo-Political theory.)

Thus it was that a great reversal, one of history's most fascinating patterns, came about. No doubt what Tolstoy wrote of Napoleon, was even truer of Hitler: "God was tired of him." But in the ineluctable wisdom and justice of His providence, Hitler was allowed to choose and seal his own doom. "Whom the gods would destroy, they first make mad." That is, they allow them to make themselves mad.

At least as we got into mid-summer and a Navy brother-in-law came up to New Hampshire from Washington full of the notion that Soviet Russia would fall in six weeks, I argued sharply against such dogmatism. I said, "No one can be sure of that. Hitler has taken on much more than he realizes."

All this is set down to illustrate the superb faith and serenity of William Ebor. et Cantuar. I had been very worried by the fall of Greece and Crete and what looked like a debacle in Africa, with Egypt on the brink. I remember writing to him in a pessimistic vein.[1] He was not affected and never seemed the slightest bit discouraged. He had written earlier that Britian was ready now for any invasion and that many hoped the Germans would try it.

As Archbishop of Canterbury William's opportunities were nearly unlimited both for building up the morale of his countrymen and for proclaiming the meaning of the Christian Gospel as they looked beyond the conflict to a new day and a new world. The level of his utterances was uniformly lofty, and it speaks volumes both for this great man and for the English people, the most civilized, I believe, then and now in the world, that he addressed them as he did and that he was heard gladly.

Winston Churchill, granted his genius as a rhetorician, had an easier task than William Temple. Churchill addressed his people as a chieftain, arousing them to pride and passion, energy and endurance. This great chieftain, though a civilian, belonged to the race of fighting men. For him words were goads, and he was a master both at setting them down and uttering them in his stinging, growling voice.

Temple too was a master of assemblies and an artist in words. But his object and technique were alike very different. His aim always was to lift men and women up to the Divine point of view, to bear witness to the mind of Christ, to remind human beings even in the midst of warring madness that they were the children of God.

To this end he appeared on many platforms and under the most varied auspices. He identified fully with all sorts and conditions of

---

[1]Cf. Sir Winston Churchill's summary of this period: "Looking back upon the unceasing tumult of the war, I cannot recall any period when its stresses and the onset of so many problems all at once or in rapid succession bore more directly on me and my colleagues than the first half of 1941. The scale of events grew larger every year; but the decisions required were not more difficult. Greater military disasters fell upon us in 1942, but by then we were no longer alone and our fortunes were mingled with those of the Grand Alliance. No part of our problem in 1941 could be solved without relation to all the rest... Our physical resources were harshly limited. The attitude of a dozen Powers, friendly, opportunist, or potentially hostile, was unknowable."

The Grand Alliance, p. 3

people, and without regard to occasions or dangers of assembly. He spoke on assorted themes, related to the variety of occasions, but with one primary, central, overmastering emphasis. This was — and remember that a fierce War was on — our need for a new integration of life: Religion, Art, Science, Education, Politics, and Economics. Such an integration is possible only if there is a Purpose, ultimate and all-inclusive, capable of imparting unity, power, and direction to civilization.

Such a purpose cannot be merely human; it must be Divine; it must be expressive of the Will of God. There is such a purpose, said Temple, a Biblical prophet always; it is presented to us in the Bible under the name of the Kingdom of God, or sometimes as the summing up of all things in Christ, or as the coming down out of heaven of the holy city, the New Jerusalem.

Temple's last book, published in 1944, the year of his death, is entitled *The Church Looks Forward*. It contains 25 sermons and addresses, mostly the latter and a great many broadcast addresses, delivered over a period of 18 months, after he was enthroned as Archbishop of Canterbury. There is a vast range in audiences and subjects, but the same theme runs through all of these preachments: God's Will, shown forth in Christ, gives us a mandate and program for national and world reconstruction beyond the dislocating ravages of war.

It is clear that the Archbishop felt that this was in a special way his mission. It was to this end that he had come to the Kingdom at such a time.

In his Enthronement Sermon he declared, "My chief desire is to enter on my office as His bondman and His witness; and I ask all of you to hold me to this by your stedfastness and by your prayers."

15 months later, in July 1943 he gave an overseas broadcast address on "The Crisis of Western Civilization." This address he felt, as he looked at the whole volume, struck the keynote of all.

The deepest meaning of the war is that it is a struggle between the adherents of two completely opposed theories of life. "The United Nations" are standing for freedom, justice, and the supremacy of moral law, while "the Axis Powers" stand for the State as the object of supreme allegiance, unamenable to any higher authority or law.

The first outlook was the result of the combined influence of Rome, Greece, and Israel plus the love emphasis of Christianity. The statist concept is older and had been more widely followed than the Western synthesis; it is the creed of barbarism.

The Christian tradition of the West, resulting from the fusion of the three elements of Roman law, Greek philosophy, and Hebrew-Christian theism, rests on three fundamental postulates: the essential unity of the whole created order including man; man's distinctive endowment whereby he chooses the ends he will pursue — the meaning of morality; and the infinite value of man as the child of God and the object of His love, destined for eternal fellowship with Him.

The modern period saw the breakup of the old Christian order and the emergence of the various departments of life, such as politics, commerce, art, and education, clamoring for autonomy. The State was made an end in itself. So was the accumulation of wealth. Such slogans as "Business is business" and "art for art's sake" came in.

Great developments have resulted but they have ended in chaos, as the war proves. "Our task in the coming period is to lay hold on all the cultural and economic wealth which the epoch of departmentalism has developed and integrate it once more in a coherent pattern of life with some intelligent principle." The Christian religion offers such a principle. Our hope is in an advance to "a more faithful Christian discipleship than has yet been seen on any large scale."

Temple in such statements as these, and in his serene optimism respecting the future, set great store by the Ecumenical Movement and the worldwide Christian Church. It was not merely individual Christians but the Church that was called to leaven the lump and make possible the advance of the Kingdom of God. In this connection he played a key role in the formation and inauguration of the British Council of Churches. This was the British arm of the World Council, and there was opposition to this development as there had been to Anglican adherence to the World Council. Temple, patient and prudent as always but firm as a rock, won through and commemorated what he felt was a significant victory when the British Council was inaugurated at a great Service in St. Paul's Cathedral on September 23, 1942. Temple as the newly elected President of the Council preached the sermon. Stressing that there had been no compromise of distinctive principles, he added: "But in days like these, when the basic principles of Christianity are widely challenged and in many quarters expressly repudiated, the primary need is for clear and united testimony to Christianity itself. The difference between Catholic and Protestant is very small as compared with the difference between Christian and non-Christian, between those who do and those who do not believe that in Jesus Christ God 'hath visited and redeemed his people.' "

Another and even more controversial issue was the attitude of the Church of England to the new united Church of South India. It is difficult at this remove to realize the vigor and rancor of the opposition to this scheme of union which had in it elements of compromise or benign neglect from an interim standpoint but promised to end up with a reconstituted and fully valid Apostolic and Catholic ministry. Temple had followed the South India development from its inception in 1919, was deeply interested in it, and was sure that it must go forward. The tide of the Ecumenical Movement was favorable to the Union. He was able to secure from Convocation in both Houses final advice that was constructive and that slammed no doors. However, his last pronouncements on South India to Convocation were so lacking in his customary lucidity that an intimate friend wrote: "They seem to be genuine, but it is a tired William who is writing, and the arrangement is not so clear and logical as usual."

This was true. He was bound to be tired. From the time of his enthronement he had carried an incredible and an ever increasing load of work. It ramified in innumerable directions and under the abnormal conditions of war he was not inclined to draw in or spare himself at any point. In a personal, handwritten letter to me under date of January 14, 1943, the Archbishop wrote: "I get more and more immersed in this

68

job. I have a list of over twenty people asking for early interviews, and all my time is pledged for six weeks ahead." He adds that he is hoping soon to do something to strengthen the staff here (at Lambeth), so as to shovel off a good deal of the less important stuff."

One doubts that he got round to this in any thorough way or that he was able temperamentally to cut down on his activities and husband his strength. Indeed the thing that is impressive about Temple's Canterbury period, which was to constitute the final chapter of his life, is the manner in which he gave himself in multitudinous ways to the concerns of the time.

It was not so much that his activities changed or that much that was positively new came into play. Rather it was a matter of intensified action in areas already well carved out: as a prophet possessed by concern for justice and well-being for all people, as a pastor dealing with the problems of persons under the strains and bereavements of war, and as a spiritual leader in Church, State, and Society.

We have already noted and illustrated his bold and tireless work of prophetic witness. It would be impossible to overstress the depth of his conviction with respect to the social mission of the Church which for him was a part of the evangelization of Britian. For William Temple there was no such thing as the Gospel, to which something called the Social Gospel might or might not be added. No, there was but one Gospel — the Good News of the living God who in His love had sent His Son in our flesh to draw all men unto Himself and to heal and save and renew the world.

"The Church looks forward" was the title and motto of a campaign launched under the special aegis of Temple in the autumn of 1942. A series of meetings was held at which both Archbishops appeared and which had as their purpose proclaiming Christ as the Lord of all life. At such meetings held in large halls in great cities the Primate of all England did not hesitate to declare that the Christian religion has a message for society as well as the individual. "We are concerned to insist that it also has its message for the ordering of society itself, and that the social structure, as well as the lives of individuals within that structure, is subject to criticism in the light of Christian principles."

This was indeed an arresting phenomenon. It is no wonder it caught the imagination of people all over Great Britain. Here was an Archbishop of Canterbury who was not only a scholar-philosopher, recalling Anslem of Bec, the second Norman Archbishop of Canterbury. Here in addition was a man modern to his finger-tips who had the spirit of the Old Testament prophets.

In addition to "The Church Looks Forward" movement, a new form of Evangelism appeared which was interdenominational in character. Meetings were held that were known as "Religion and Life" meetings and Temple did not hesitate to approve and take part in them. Whenever he did, he was enthusiastically received and left a conspicuous mark.

As a pastor and a Father-in-God, the Archbishop came up against the same type of problems and issues that he had met and dealt with as Rector of St. James' in World War I. In addition as Archbishop he had specific responsibilities connected with the Armed Forces and the war effort. Pretty well bombed out himself at Lambeth Palace, he and Mrs. Temple made a point of appearing where there was trouble and loss and ministering by word and example to the victims of war. Next to the King and Winston Churchill, the sturdy figure of the Archbishop in clericals and gaiters became a symbol of strength where the front line was everywhere.

He took special interest in the work of the Chaplains in the Armed Forces and delighted in all opportunities to visit the troops and Home Fleet. In various ways he was consulted by persons with pacifist scruples and parents or others who had lost loved ones in the war. In such situations he was peerless, knowing exactly what to say and how to say it. He was especially well-equipped and helpful where he was dealing with bereavement, for his faith in what he liked to call the larger life beyond the veil was so vibrant and unquestioning that he was bound to communicate strength and reconciliation.

Spiritual Leader is perhaps the most satisfactory summation of William Temple's role as Man and Archbishop in the War and his last years. It has been truly said of him that at the start of the War he set for himself one standard: that he would speak only for the Christian conscience. He not only followed this in what he said. He exemplified it by example as much as by precept. Two illustrations will bring out the power of his example and the greatness of the man.

We have already seen how in the First World War William set himself like flint against hatred of the Germans and everything that was small and vicious. In the second War Temple was in the position of having to deal with frequent requests for special days of public prayer and, on occasion, putting out special Services by authority. A difficulty that he confronted and that confronted him on such occasions was his disbelief in direct prayers for victory.

This led to criticism of Services put out by him and on his authority; and there was the additional factor, deeply distressing to him, that neither his predecessor, Lang, at Canterbury nor his successor at York, Cyril Garbett, agreed with him on this scruple. They had no hesitation about direct and unqualified prayers for victory.

The issue is of so much interest to the thoughtful Christian, and so important from the angle of estimating the man and the Christian, William Temple, that it seems well to quote *in extenso* a 1944 letter from him to his brother Archbishop at York:

> *I am afraid I distress you by the fact that forms of prayer which I draw up do not contain direct prayers for victory. I have always felt that it is wiser to avoid this, and I have publicly stated that it ought to be avoided...*
>
> *I have tried always to draw up prayers which do not range against any of our fellow-Christians in Germany or elsewhere, because it seems to me that the primary concern in prayer — and I mean 'primary' quite seriously — must be the approach to the Father of all men, with recognition that all His other children have the same right of approach, and that if we pray as our Lord taught us, we are never praying against each other, because we are always praying not that what we want shall be done, but that what God wants shall be done, and that we may be used for doing this...*

I am very much encouraged by knowing that on this point I am in agreement with Abraham Lincoln, who seems to me to have led his people in war more Christianly than pretty well anybody in history.

I am very much touched and impressed, as an American, by this tribute to Abraham Lincoln. It is entirely justified. And one can be even happier and more gratified when one realizes that in this Robert E. Lee agreed with Abraham Lincoln.

Both men were deeply Christian, as I emphasized in 1960 at the first Civil War Centennial Assembly in St. Louis, Missouri when I spoke on "The High Water Mark of American Spirituality." I was much gratified, as the grandson of Confederate soldiers, to be asked to speak by General U.S. Grant, 3rd, Chairman by Presidential appointment of the Civil War Centennial Commission.

The second illustration of Temple's quality as a Spiritual Leader in wartime is afforded by his efforts on behalf of the Jews in Europe after the ghastly unloosing by Hitler of what he was pleased to call the final solution. In view of the impact of the Television film *The Holocaust* and the earlier criticism of Pope Pius XII (whether just or not), the clarity and integrity of William Cantuar. in dealing with this horror is topical and noteworthy.

The first point is that from the beginning the Archbishop made the cause of victims of famine, refugees, and the slaughter of the Jews his own. He did not delegate such matters to others, but intervened personally at official levels. With the Jews there was caution for a time, not about intervention but about publicity, lest excuse be given to Hitler for further excoriation of this people as friends of Britain. When by early 1943 it was clear that nothing could make the Nazi treatment of the Jews any more evil than it was, the Archbishop (on March 23) moved in the House of Lords that, in view of "the massacres and starvation of the Jews and others in enemy and enemy-occupied countries, this House desires to assure His Majesty's Government of its fullest support for immediate measures...for providing help and temporary asylum to persons in danger of massacre who are able to leave enemy and enemy-occupied countries."

In supporting this motion Temple made a powerful speech, setting forth suggested actions by the Government and in particular urging that in view of the magnitude of the problem one person of high standing should be appointed to make it his first concern. In closing he protested against procrastination of any kind.

The Jews are being slaughtered at the rate of tens of thousands a day on many days, but there is a proposal for a preliminary exploration to be made with a view to referring the whole matter after that to the Inter-Governmental Committee on Refugees. My Lords, let us at least urge that when that Conference meets it should meet not only for exploration but for decision. We know that what we can do is small compared to the magnitude of the problem, but we cannot rest so long as there is any sense among us that we are not doing all that might be done. We have discussed the matter on the footing that we are not responsible for this great evil, that the burden lies on others, but it is always true that the obligations of decent men are decided for them by contingencies which they did not themselves create and very largely by the action of wicked men. The priest and the Levite in the parable were not in the least responsible for the traveller's wounds as he lay there by the roadside, and no doubt had many other pressing things to attend to, but they stand as the picture of those who are condemned for neglecting the opportunity of showing mercy. We at this moment have upon us a tremendous responsibility. We stand at the bar of history, of humanity, and of God.

Upon the death of William, the World Jewish Congress paid him a tribute which was unusual in its perceptiveness and which may continue to make glad all who loved him for the great soul he was. This is a part of what our Jewish brothers said:

Lamented by the Christian world, the premature death of Dr. Temple will be particularly mourned by the Jewish people whose champion he was. His maintained interest in the welfare of our much persecuted brethren was not rooted, as is the case with many theologians, in an attitude of sanctimonious pity. He approached the overwhelming problem of the destiny of the Jews in a mood more positive more comprehensive, more liberal, and, above all, more human. His interest in Jews was not a by-product of his sacred duties.

The picture of Temple as Archbishop of Canterbury with the War on is by now reasonably clear. It is not easy to get into focus the whole sweep of his activism, but essentially it is what his life had been from his Oxford days on except that the tempo was stepped up and the Archbishop moved with an ease and freedom greater than he had known in any previous period of his life. It would seem that his consciousness both of the vast issues of the War and of the heavy volume of sacrifice it entailed imparted to his daily life a heightened sense of urgency.

There was no anxiety in this; even a clearly discernible declining level of health, with ever increasing bouts of gout as the tell-tale sign, does not seem to have depressed him or caused him to alter the even but swift tenor of his ways. There is a vivid account of a portion of one of his days which the then Bishop of Winchester, Dr. Mervyn Haigh, has left on record. From it we can see as in a perceptive portrait by a great artist what the Primate was like in his last phase — the time is less than six months before his death.

The main occasion is a "Religion and Life" meeting, the day May 5, 1944. On the previous day he had had a busy afternoon and evening at Swansea. He got back to London in time for a meeting in the morning of the 5th, and by the afternoon had reached Bournemouth. Prebendary Boyd, Vicar of Bournemouth, met him and carried him to his Vicarage for tea. "At 6:20, before addressing an immense gathering at the Pavilion on *The Cross,* and on a hot evening, he declined an invitation to be driven in a car and walked by himself (more than a mile). On his arrival at the Pavillion there were 2,500 inside, and fully 1,500 outside who could not get in. I had to meet the Archbishop and ask him to walk some way to S. Peter's Church and speak to as many of the 1,500 as could be got there, for a few minutes. This he readily consented to do. Half an hour later he came back to the immense meeting in the Pavilion and he spoke to them for a full hour, again without a note, on *The Cross* — the finest address that I ever heard him give and I think in many ways the finest I ever heard anyone give. On returning after all this to the Vicarage for supper he appeared both then and after-wards as fresh in mind and body as if he had done nothing at all all day."

That was the way it seemed. He was like a well-oiled machine, pump-ing away with a total lack of effort, so it appeared. But even machines have to be renewed; and William was an organism, programmed for a definite, finite, non-renewable space of time. This organism was run-ning down and he was burning it out. During his last summer he was never entirely free from gout and the pace demanded of him was break-neck speed — no time for rest, no way to avoid mounting pressures and clamorous demands. Everything was complicated by the flying bombs. Canterbury was largely spared but Croyden with its airdromes was a target and suffered widespread damage.

On July 11 Temple with his wife and chaplain met the Suffragan Bishop of Croyden and toured the eleven parishes of this unit of the Diocese of Canterbury. As the party left the first of the parishes, they heard a loud explosion indicating that a bomb had struck about half a mile away on the opposite side of the main road. "Which way do we go now?" the Archbishop asked. "This way," replied the Bishop point-ing to a column of dust in the direction of the explosion. Temple's side-splitting laughter, which no one who ever knew him can forget, rang out as they resumed their tour. Several more hits were registered before they were through, but they were unscathed and of course the people of Croyden and indeed of all Britain were buoyed and braced by the valor and high spirits of their Spiritual Leader.

At Lambeth it was far from restful. There was no direct hit, but the flying bombs were falling all around, with one at the end of the Palace garden and another across Lambeth Road beside Lambeth Bridge House. One man was killed by this bomb. The Temples and the Palace and Office staff were never injured, but life was very disrupted and sleep at night seldom undisturbed.

At length the season arrived for a summer holiday, which the Tem-ples took at their favorite haunt on the top of the Quantock moors on the Bristol Channel, not far from Wales. It went along happily and normally, but did little to repair the physical ravages sustained by William's powerful organism. He suffered more or less constantly from his old enemy, the gout, as he returned to London and a scheduled broadcast on September 2 for a National Day of Prayer. He had to use a stick to get into the pulpit for this broadcast, and from then on it was downhill for the Archbishop.

For a time, as long as it was humanly possible, he refused to give in, carrying on with important scheduled engagements even though he had acute gout in both knees and had to be carried into his Cathedral in a chair to deliver a Charge to the clergy at a Synod on September 18.

On the next day it was clear that he was seriously ill, though from September 21 to 23 he saw his ordination candidates individually in his bedroom and at the end gave his Charge to them gathered around his bed. This was his last ministerial act. His last celebration of the Holy Communion had been at the altar of Luton Parish Church on Sunday, September 3 — the Day of National Prayer.

On October 2 Temple, acting on his doctor's advice, went to West-gate by the sea. He was kept as quiet as possible and his engagements were canceled through November. The Vicar of St. Saviour's, Westgate twice celebrated the Holy Communion in his room. On October 22 he received two American Bishops, Oldham of Albany and Hobson of Southern, Ohio who bore a letter of greeting and commendation to him from President Roosevelt.

He still wrote letters, a message to his Diocese on the 23rd and a letter to Cosmo Lang, in which he spoke of a specialist's opinion that he had an independent infection that was the keeping the gout alive. The next day he wrote in the same vein to the King's Private Secretary. (This was characteristic. In one of my first letters from him in early 1936 he mentions sending a letter to King George V's Private Secretary and conveying to his Majesty a story about the King I had told him.)

On Thursday the 26th he had breakfast and read *The Times* as usual. The Sister who was his nurse came in to make up his bed, when sudden-ly he said: "I feel very faint." His wife dashed out to get help and brought back a heart specialist who did what he could, but in vain. He asked the Archbishop whether he was in great pain, and His Grace replied, "No, but I can't breathe." A few minutes later he breathed his last, and without pain, entirely peacefully, William's great soul departed from his body.

The shock of his death was very great. It was truly a traumatic blow. Nearly everyone remembers where he was and what he was doing when President Kennedy was assassinated. I remember also how I got the news of my great Friend's passing. Canon Charles Smith of Washington Cathedral in some way had heard and called me at All Saints', Chevy Chase because he knew how close I had been to Temple. I of course could hardly take in the news. With the intellect I grasped the event, but not with the heart for some time. I was too numb. It was a heavy blow, and it seemed for long that a bright light had gone out.

The Provost of the Queen's College, Oxford, R.H. Hodgkin, Tem-ple's onetime colleague and long-time friend, wrote of his sudden death, that it "seemed to shake the western world as if one of its pillars had been removed." That describes exactly my personal state: it seemed as though one of the pillars of my universe had been pulled out.

Such a reaction was wrong — and temporary. There was about the Archbishop's life and career a splendid completeness. He had known and done everything. There were no more heights really to scale. He went out with his gaiters on, accoutered for action in the name of Christ. He was spared, as he had wished and hoped, the ordeal of a painful and lingering illness. He was spared also the misery of having to face and struggle with the psychology of frustration and let-down in a disillusioned postwar world.

One thinks of the bitter personal blow which the victorious fighting Chieftain Winston Churchill had to take and live with. The war was not over in the Pacific when he was turned out of office, repudiated at the polls by a majority of his fellow-countrymen, so that he had no part in the peace negotiations and decisions. In the *Preface* of the first volume of his great six volume classic, *The Gathering Storm*, published in 1948, he writes bitterly: "The human tragedy reaches its climax in the fact that after all the exertions and sacrifices of hundreds of millions of people and of the victories of the Righteous Couse, we have still not found Peace or Security, and that we lie in the grip of even worse perils than those we have surmounted."

Churchill, who received the Nobel Prize not for Peace but for Literature, delivered one of his greatest speeches before Parliament on June 18, 1940. It was the morrow of the ignominious capitulation of France. The French did not believe the British could or would continue the war alone. Churchill in this speech had addressed himself to "our inflexible resolve to continue the war." There are few passages in literature that rise to a nobler height than the peroration of this Address.

> *What General Weygand called the Battle of France is over. I expect that the Battle of Britain is about to begin. Upon this battle depends the survival of Christian civilisation. Upon it depends our British life, and the long continuity of our institutions and our Empire. The whole fury and might of the enemy must very soon be turned on us. Hitler knows that he will have to break us in this island or lose the war. If we can stand up to him, all Europe may be free and the life of the world may move forward into broad, sunlit uplands. But if we fail, then the whole world, including the United States, including all that we have known and cared for, will sink into the abyss of a new Dark Age, made more sinister, and perhaps more protracted, by the lights of perverted science. Let us therefore brace ourselves to our duties, and so bear ourselves that, if the British Empire and its Commonwealth last for a thousand years, men will say, 'This was their finest hour.'*

It is this passage and its concluding phrase that suggested the title of the present chapter. Temple had of course as Archbishop of York up to 1942 thrown himself into the War and all its issues with characteristic energy and selfless dedication. But he was the junior Archbishop both in years and in position. When unexpectedly (from his viewpoint) he was translated to the See of Canterbury in the very thick of the struggle, but in the wake of the acquisition as allies of the Soviet Union and the United States, he embraced eagerly the call and challenge of spiritual leadership.

As we have seen, he interpreted this opportunity of service broadly. He saw as his field not only the War and the war effort but Britain and the world after the War; he saw as the Divinely appointed instrument not only the Church of England but all the Churches of Britain and the worldwide Ecumenical Movement of which he had become the representative Leader.

With fidelity to the Gospel and the mind of Christ, he saw the Kingdom of God as at hand in a new way and proclaimed in season and out the Sovereignty of God over all life, and that this Rule is the Sovereignty of Love. With a total dedication, seldom matched in the history of the Church, he gave himself to this high-priestly and prophetic mission. In the end it was for this, spending himself with astounding selflessness, that he gave his life.

Those last years, lived in the shoes of his father Frederick Cantuar., had in them a glow and an intensity. They showed the man William, always marked by unity and continuity, a figure whose symbol like that of his Master was the seamless robe, lifted up in the Spirit to the highest level of his superb faculties and qualities.

It has seemed to me as I have brooded over the life and character and sanctity of this incomparable Man that the Canterbury years were his finest hour. William had borne throughout his life more of a cross than most people including his friends realized. In the last period he literally burned himself out. To the long years of discipline, denial of self, presenting his body a living sacrifice (Romans 12:1), there was added as a culmination the gift of his very life.

Looking at the world and the Church more than three decades after that sacrificial Life and Death, we may perhaps wonder whether it was worthwhile. Were he present today, he would be disappointed and surprised. But he would not be dismayed. He was never a Utopian. His view of human nature was realistic, his concept of Original Sin definite and strong. He would, I think, find special comfort in the Gospel of John. He might well quote in his own translation the words of the Prologue which are optimistic but only in a qualified sense: "And the light shineth in the darkness, and the darkness did not absorb it."

Light and darkness remain, as no doubt they will continue to abide, strangely intermingled, so long as time endures. But we must never forget that history is dynamic and progressive. This corresponds alike to the nature in its fullness of man and to the nature and purpose of God. He is the living Lord. If at times He seems to be a God "that hideth himself," at other moments in history he manifests Himself in power and great glory.

They will sing of the ways of the Lord,
that great is the glory of the Lord.
(Psalm 138: 6. B.C.P. 1979)

Recently in the American Theological Society there was a Presidential Address by Professor Frederick Ferre entitled *Toward Transformational Theology.* Professor Ferre's thesis, which drew heavily on a systematic study of the theological thinking of his father, the late Nels F. S. Ferre, was that theology, unlike philosophy which is tied to evidence from the actual, is "free to choose a norm on the experiential pole that takes account of the forward vector of history."

The norm that it is bound to choose is the Christ event, God's *agape* in his Son. This criterion partakes both of the selective actual and of expectant futurity. It constitutes the leading edge of history as well as being its center: we may describe it as simultaneously center and frontier.

On this view the function of theology is not merely or even mainly to understand the world; it is to transform the world. This need not and should not mean that theology ceases to be a conceptual activity. The function of the theologian is to think it in such a way as to open it to change toward the highest ideals implicit in the Biblical vision.

Thus it is the ultimate power of transformation that is the focus of the theologian's trade.

As I reflect on the life and work of William Temple, I keep thinking of Professor Ferre's pregnant concept. William Ebor. et Cantuar. was, it seems to me, not merely a prophet of coming social justice. He was implicitly the prophet of a transformational theology. We cannot tell

76

what will be, but our faith is in the living God. "Source, Guide, and Goal of all that is — to him be glory for ever! Amen." (Romans 11:36. NEB)

In God's good time — in the *Kairos* He chooses and in which men and women faithfully and fittingly respond — we shall see the kind of Forward Movement in Church and State and Society that William saw in vision and imagination, and for which he gave, not in vain, his life.

CHAPTER SIX

A MODERN SAINT

Any discussion of Saints or sanctity must begin with the New Testament. Specifically, it will start with the Epistles of Paul, the earliest Christian writings that have come down to us.

Paul is writing in his Letters to local Churches. All over the Roman Empire there are assemblies or congregations of persons who have heard of one Jesus called Christ or Messiah and Son of God and of His Life, Teaching, Death, and Resurrection. They have not only heard but have seen and believed that God has spoken in His Son a revealing and saving Word.

It is these assemblies or churches that Paul addresses. Typically he will start a Letter in this way: "From Paul and Timothy to the church of God at Corinth and to all the saints in the whole of Achaia." (II Corinthians 1:1)

In general the word *hagioi* or holy ones means the persons dedicated or sanctified through Baptism and the Holy Spirit who make up the Church. The word is used and understood democratically rather than aristocratically. It refers more to the calling of God than to moral and spiritual achievement.

In time this was to change drastically. In both East and West the Saints came to be thought of as an elite spiritual class. They were the men and women who by their holiness in life and their fidelity unto death had set a lofty example and had won official recognition and canonization by the Church.

Sometimes this process takes a long time; in other cases it happens quickly. Thus it was four centuries before Sir Thomas More was canonized. For Thomas Aquinas it came about in less than 50 years following his death. (He died in 1274 and was named a Saint by Pope John XXII in 1323.)

Francis of Assisi was canonized two years after his death on October 3, 1226.

There is truth and reality in both sides of the equation with respect to Saints. In general the Churches of the Reformation tried to return to the New Testament outlook. The Roman Catholic Church continued to hold the aristocratic view, that great holiness is rare and should be especially noted and celebrated. Anglicanism as usual attempted to come in between with a *via media*, but its first solution of confining the Calendar of Saints to the Biblically elect was arbitrary and not very inspiring.

Probably we can say that today over much of Christendom a consensus has emerged, and that this result is a good example of what Archbishop Temple considered the dialectical character of truth.

To say that all baptized members of the universal Church are Saints is manifestly misleading and in fact stupid. On the other hand, the extreme aristocratic view with its combination of authoritarianism and promotion from below (a sort of regulated democracy) is too restrictive and may be stultifying. The ordinary congregation in all churches needs to feel the beauty of holiness as manifest in the lives of all Saints, living and departed, remote and near. Individual Christians need to feel that the qualities of the Saints are for them, too and are in fact what the Church and Christianity are all about.

I believe that increasingly this working synthesis has taken hold of the modern Church regardless of denominational lines. The Feast of All Saints seems to be a Sacramental, embodying and communicating this. It beautifully reenforces the great article of Faith, confessed whenever Christianity's primal Creed is said: "I believe in the Communion of Saints."

Then there is the superb hymn written by William Walsham How and first published in 1864. Vaughan Williams' noble Tune, *Sine Nomine,* was composed to accompany *For all the Saints* in the English Hymnal of 1906.

> *For all the saints, who from their labors rest,*
> *Who thee by faith before the world confessed,*
> *Thy name, O Jesus, be for ever blest.*
>
> *O blest communion, fellowship divine!*
> *We feebly struggle, they in glory shine;*
> *Yet all are one in thee, for all are thine.*
>
> *From earth's wide bounds, from ocean's farthest coast,*
> *Through gates of pearl streams in the countless host,*
> *Singing to Father, Son, and Holy Ghost,*
> *Alleluia, Alleluia!*

Finally, there is the modern hymn, *I sing a song of the saints of God,* originally written by an English lady, Lesbia Scott, for her children and first published in the United States by the Morehouse Publishing Company in 1929 from sheets issued by the Society of SS. Peter and Paul in London. It was included in the Episcopal *Hymnal of 1940.*

The text of this hymn is something to conjure with. It truly fires the imagination. At All Saints' Church, Chevy Chase, Maryland during my 10-year Rectorship from 1943 to 1953, we were blest with, and wrestled with, the largest Sunday School in the Diocese of Washington, and one of the two or three largest in the Episcopal Church. We used this Hymn extensively, especially in the inclusive Family Service we eventually developed and featured. No other hymn was more effective or inspiriting. The children loved it, and the parents and other adults were surely not far behind.

Our point here, in citing this hymm, is to get before us what I am suggesting is an implicit and widespread modern synthesis in the understanding of saint and saints. This is perhaps a good example of the ancient intuition, *Lex orandi lex credendi* — the law of praying is the law of believing. Here are the words of this joyous and delightful hymn.

I sing a song of the saints of God,
Patient and brave and true,
Who toiled and fought and lived and died
For the Lord they loved and knew.

And one was a doctor, and one was a queen,
And one was a sheperdess on the green:
They were all of them saints of God — and I mean
God helping, to be one too.

They loved their Lord so dear, so dear,
And his love made them strong;
And they followed the right, for Jesus' sake,
The whole of their good lives long.

And one was a soldier, and one was a priest,
And one was slain by a fierce wild beast:
And there's not any reason — no not the least —
Why I shouldn't be one too.

They lived not only in ages past,
There are hundreds of thousands still;
The world is bright with the joyous saints
Who love to do Jesus' will.

You can meet them in school, or in lanes, or at sea,
In church, or in trains, or in shops, or at tea,
For the saints of God are just folk like me —
And I mean to be one too.

These lines are moving even when simply read. When sung to the tune of *Grand Isle* by John Henry Hopkins (1940) by a sizeable, variegated congreagation, they are stirring and enkindling to an incredible degree. One feels that he knows what Saints are and that they are all about us now in modern life. They lived not only in ages past. They are marked by love and devotion to the Lord Jesus, shown in daily life and in Christian qualities. Saints are joyous too, and the world is made bright by them.

There have been many attempts to identify Saints and define saintliness. We have all heard the answer the small girl gave to the question, "What is a Saint?" She replied, "It is some one who lets the light shine through."

Dean W.R. Inge, writing in 1899, said: "Men of preeminent saintliness agree very closely in what they tell us. They tell us that they have arrived at an unshakeable conviction, not based on inference but on immediate experience, that God is a spirit with whom the human spirit can hold intercourse; that in him meet all that they can imagine of goodness, truth, and beauty; that they can see his footprints everywhere in nature, and feel his presence within them as the very life of their life, so that in proportion as they come to themselves they come to him. They tell us what separates us from him and from happiness is, first, self-seeking in all its forms; and, secondly, sensuality in all its forms;

that these are the ways of darkness and death and hide from us the face of God."[1]

Saint-Beuve remarks somewhere on the fact that the phenomenon of grace appears extraordinary, eminent, and rare even from the purely human point of view. "Penetrate a little beneath the diversity of circumstances, and it becomes evident that in Christians of different epochs it is always one and the same modification by which they are affected: there is veritably a single fundamental and identical spirit of piety and charity, common to those who have received grace; an inner state which before all things is one of love and humility, of infinite confidence in God, and of severity for one's self, accompanied with tenderness for others."

This is a useful description of what might be called the essence of saintliness. Saints are persons who have been grasped, and are deeply conscious that they have been grasped, by the grace of God, with the result that they feel the power of the new being in Christ and show forth the fruits of love, humility, utter trust in God, a deepened sense of sin in themselves, and benevolence toward others, especially the poor, the helpless and the disadvantaged.

Another way of saying it is that saintliness is holiness and is in some measure the reflection of the holiness of God. Holiness is not easy to define. It is almost the same thing as saying Divinity. But we can possibly say that holiness as an attribute of God represents the transcendent union of *otherness* and *goodness.*

In the Book of Leviticus in the Old Testament we read: "For I am the Lord your God; you shall make yourselves holy and keep yourselves holy, because I am holy." (11:44. NEB) The context here is ceremonial rather than ethical, though the latter may well be and I think is implied in the commandment. In the Epistle to the Colossians there is a superb complementary passage in which St. Paul distills the full meaning of holiness as the mark of God's people. "Then put on the garments that suit God's chosen people, his own, his beloved: compassion, kindness, humility, gentleness, patience. Be forbearing with one another, and forgiving, where any of you has cause for complaint: you must forgive as the Lord forgave you. To crown all, there must be love to bind all together and complete the whole." (3:12-14. NEB)

Here we have a description of the Saint that is universal: it applies at all times and places. But there is a new condition that characterizes the modern world and that bears on, or may bear on, the estimate of sanctity in the case of a given individual. It is particularly relevant in the instance of the subject of this book, Archbishop William Temple.

In the 19th century as a result of the Industrial Revolution a whole set of new problems and human concerns arose. There was a novel focus on social order and the structure of society, because of the rise of very large numbers of industrial workers wholly dependent on daily wages.

In the agrarian or pre-industrial order, which means in effect all previous history, comparative or essential stability was built into the system of economic life. Man lived on and from the soil. The masses could not be thrown out of work, at least completely. Barring some

[1]*Christian Mysticism*, p. 326

spectacular catastrophe, there was always land to till and the opportunity to grow food. There was nothing between man and nature.

With the industrial revolution, and still more today with the advent of more and more complex technology, the masses of men are removed from nature and are dependent on an immensely intricate system known as the economy. The economy is in fact a second nature, and is the structure of reality to which the vast majority of people in the developed Western world are related.

Writing in 1912 a remarkable lay-theologian Baron Friedrich von Hugel noted that "This world, and these difficulties and helps, are, in their special intensity, range, and complication, a genuinely new experience in the history of mankind. It is the world of the West-European and North-American workmen, with their special requirements, passions, and mentality, as these have developed within the last sixty years."[1]

The general phenomenon of which the Baron speaks and which we have emphasized has had in the ensuing years prodigious consequences. Compounded and assisted by the destructive legacy of the First World War, doctrinaire Socialism was able actually to precipitate the sweeping revolutions of which it had dreamed and which its more radical prophets had predicted. (Mussolini was an ex-Communist and Hitler's Nazi party was the German National Socialist Workers Party.)

Von Hugel does not use the term Communism but he has Marx and like-minded socialists in mind when he perceptively describes what they offer us as "a distinct, indeed a highly militant and dogmatic Creed, of an apocalyptic, millennial character...It is a sort of Kingdom of God, but without a King and without a God."[2]

Twenty years later, in 1933, addressing the York Diocesan Conference, Temple describes Communism as "undoubtedly the most serious menace which has threatened the Christian faith in the civilised world for some hundreds of years." It is, he added an economic system, a philosophy, and a religion.

This was at the height of the influence of Communism on intellectuals in the Western world. Middleton Murray had just written a book entitled *The Necessity of Communism*. The October Club was going strong in Oxford University. I was a witness to its rise and dynamic appeal.[3] I do not know whether Cambridge had a similar open organization, but it certainly outdid its older sister in producing Communists who were able to infiltrate the British diplomatic service. (Reference is made to Philby, Burgess and MacLean.)

The important point however is that Temple was not just against Communism. He was among the prophets and apostles of the modern Church who were keenly aware of the spiritual as well as the physical problems of workers in the industrial era and who strove mightily and consistently to do something about it. In his student days he was drawn temporarily to some form of Socialism on Christian grounds, but increasingly and decisively he came to doubt that this was the answer.

[1] *Eternal Life*, p. 303
[2] Ibid. pp 310, 311.
[3] See my *Communism and Christ*, p 144 (Ch V).

But he did believe, and he stuck to the belief, that the Church must speak out on issues of principle in the structure of social order. Specifically, he held that the priority of God and His purpose and the inherent value of man as a person created in the image of God were the two primary Christian social principles. From these he advanced to three derivative principles essential to an order that could in any sense be called Christian, namely, freedom, fellowship, and service.

Temple's great burden and basic conviction are summed up in this sentence: "The aim of a Christian social order is the fullest possible development of individual personality in the widest and deepest possible fellowship." He was explicit also in urging that the Church through her members has a central responsibility and that Evangelism and the missionary movement are indispensable and must be given the highest priority if true social progress is to be made.

Near the end of his Penguin Special, *Christianity and Social Order,* published in 1942, Temple wrote: "I should give a false impression of my own convictions if I did not add here that there is no hope of establishing a more Christian social order except through the labour and sacrifice of those in whom the Spirit of Christ is active, and that the first necessity for progress is more and better Christians taking full responsibility as citizens for the political, social and economic system under which they and their fellows live."

William Temple's concern for his fellow men and his understanding of the role of environment in the development of persons and personal values do not make him a Saint. They do indicate the modernity both of his grasp of the realities of a world based on industry and his understanding of the Good News of God and His loving purpose for the whole life of man. If we should find that William in character and spirituality fulfills the universal criteria of sanctity in the Christian Church, his unique apostolate toward society and the common good will complement this towering personal and religious stature. And it will insure our recognizing that we have in this remarkable man the very prototype of a *modern* Saint.

In fact, if we hold before us steadily the image of William Ebor. et Cantuar., and the Bishop, the priest-prophet, the Don, the Oxford undergraduate, and the schoolboy, before the Archbishop, as portrayed in the preceding chapters of this book, and as writ even larger and more stunningly unique in life, we can hardly escape drawing two conclusions.

The first conclusion is that by every test recognized throughout the Christian centuries, and impressively supplemented by the evidence of the peculiarly modern challenge to Christianity, William stands before us as indubitably of the stuff of sainthood. The very phrase is suspect, ringing not quite true, from the point of view of one mood, imposed inevitably by the spirit of modernity heavily influenced by the bias of the secular. On the other hand — how dialectical we naturally are! — when we actually bring before us real saints, Peter and Paul and Stephen and John, Augustine, Thomas Aquinas, and Francis of Assisi together with many men and women less well known, possibly almost unknown, but of the same stuff as these illustrious worthies, we are embarrassed by our hesitation and timidity in the face of the terms saint and saintliness, even sanctity and sanctification.

The second conclusion, which really is secondary but is nonetheless of intense interest, is that in William we have a classical case of the once-born type raised to the level of the authentic saint.

It remains to deal in summary form with these two points.

Anatomy of a Saint

Dean Iremonger has a description of Temple the man in his long chapter "The New Primate of All England." It follows summaries under the heads: The Man of Letters, The Churchman, The Father-in-God, — and is followed by The Prophet and The Philosopher, the last being a separate chapter by a distinguished student of philosophy and an authority on Whitehead, Miss Dorothy Emmet.

This is the Dean's conclusion. "Such was the House of Life as Temple saw it, and into every part of it his abundant personality penetrated, spilling over, as it were, from one room to another, till there was no corner where he would not claim for the Gospel the right of entry and assent the indisputable priority of God. Here, too, was the Master of the House, *speciosus et amabilis* — to welcome, to consecrate, and to control — whose guiding hand his hold never relaxed...And here he lived that spiritual life which was his whole life."

The finest and best-rounded account of Temple the man that has so far appeared is the sketch by his colleague and friend A.E. Baker, Canon and Prebendary of York Minster, in the slender volume already alluded to in these pages more than once — *William Temple: An Estimate and Appreciation.* Baker's portrait of this great and simple man is a charming one, but it is not the less penetrating and profound on that account. What emerges as dominant in the personality of the Archbishop is the love of God and the love of fellow human beings. And this was not two loves but one indivisible passion and affection that flooded his human being and commanded him in all his relationships.

But Let Canon Baker speak for himself:
> *But the deepest interpretation of William Temple's kindness and tenderness, of the patience and friendliness which would not be angry, is not natural but supernatural. They were an integral part of his faith, which was the soil and root of his life. He filled his mind with the thought of the perfection of God as Jesus revealed Him, a perfection which takes shape in an unwavering kindness, endless forgiveness, complete freedom from any approach to indignation; and it meant for him that the immediate goal for a Christian is a universal and imperturbable kindness of heart. It was trust in the Father of our Lord Jesus Christ which could not be roused to violence of speech or action.*

Almost the primary expression of the Archbishop's Christianity, Baker goes on,
> *was a humble, modest, intensely practical and never-failing recognition of the value of other people. He was the most generously and effectively tolerant person I have ever known...*
> *He cherished the image of Christ which is stamped on every human soul, and cared keenly for the feelings and needs of people whose*

lives had been entirely different from his own. He had a sense of fellowship with all God's children — with people of every race, of every nation, of every class, and of every denomination...

And now he is dead. He believed quite simply that we should pray for our departed friends, and ask them to pray for us...But if indeed it is possible for our prayers to help him and for his prayers to help us, what, he being the man he was, will be their object? Surely it will be that men should discover that love of God and love of their fellows are two sides of one fact which is to be the source and crown of their lives'; that Christians should make actual their fellowship, and give their lives to extend and intensify it, with those of other Christian societies, of other social and economic classes, of other nations and races — without limit; that it should make us ashamed, as being a denial of the fundamental moral law, that we and ours should be content to enjoy any privilege when we are not striving to secure it for others; that we should practise what he taught, that fellowship is the sacrament of the Kingdom of Heaven.

These two testimonies by men who knew Temple well and who had meditated too, seriously, on his life, are sufficiently conclusive. They say in effect about all there is to say of the most fundamental elements of saintliness, though I believe neither writer actually uses the word or broaches the thesis that this Archbishop belongs among the Saints of the Church.

I believe that he deserves to be and will be numbered among the holy and humble men of heart whom the living Church designates as Saints, either by canonization or by consensus. I see him as at once of the ages and of an age, as both universal in notable spiritual qualities and in a peculiar way a modern man — a prophet and apostle of the post-industrial era. Accordingly it is fitting for me to state the case in my own way, simply and at the same time summarily, utilizing the device of numbering my points.

1. William's life and being from childhood to mature manhood to the fullness of age, though not old age, was God-centered. There were no breaks, no discontinuities in this central consciousness. God was ever present for him, as much so as the air he breathed, the sun which warmed the earth, the love of father and mother which surrounded him from his earliest consciousness.

There was for William nothing vague or indefinite or loosely mystical about his God. It bore no relation to the state of a New England Unitarian I came to know after I entered Harvard University. A Unitarian, quipped my friend, himself one, is a person who has a lively, sustaining faith in he knows not what. Young Temple was taught by his father that God was a God of character — the highest and holiest conceivable — and he was warned of the danger of lowering one's conception of God.

The lesson stuck. He never lowered his view of God or lost the certainty of the Divine being. His God was the living God of the Bible, a God who had a Will and a Word, a God who unveiled his heart of Love in the life and teaching and death and resurrection of His Son Jesus. "And the Word became flesh...and we beheld his glory, glory as of the only-begotten from the Father, full of grace and truth."

These words were for William the alpha and the omega of his thinking, willing, being. More than anything else, they were for him determinative. They were destiny. His whole life rested on them.

2. William led a life bounded by Church and Bible. It was thus that he was nourished spiritually and by lifelong immersion and habit in worship and prayer. Integral to this, its supreme expression, was the Holy Communion. He said at one time and another many wonderful and helpful things about worship, prayer, and Communion. These sayings, of which we can give only a taste, show infallibly the depth and maturity of his spiritual life.

Of worship Temple wrote:

> Throughout our growth as Christians worship is a duty; as we advance it becomes a delight; and at all times a true act of worship is the fulfillment — for a moment — of the true destiny of our being... But God, if we once understand Him, we can all love...All can love Him, because for each He is the Life of Life; by Him I live; by Him I came to be; by Him I aspire, so far as I aspire at all, to better things. If I realize Him, I must love Him. So I may fitly be commanded to love Him; and from this I shall go on to love my neighbor, for God's sake if not yet for his own. But as I become more perfectly united to God, I begin to love my neighbor as God loves Him, that is for himself, or for the good thing that he at least can be and can bring into being. In the perpetual return of our hearts and minds to God in worship we both enjoy a foretaste of our perfect happiness, and find the renewal of spiritual strength by which we do the work which fits us for it. [1]

As to prayer, there is no doubt that William was always and increasingly a man of prayer. As he grew older, he came to feel that it was the most important thing. On one occasion he said that "what we need more than all else is to teach the clergy to be teachers of prayer." And to persons invited to conduct retreats for his ordinands, he was wont to say, "I am entirely convinced that prayer is the principal thing."

When it came to his teaching about prayer, there was no one whose ideas were purer or more exalted; yet he was practical and persuasive. And very Scriptural. Here are some samples:

> This means that the essential act of prayer is not the bending of God's will to ours — of course not — but the bending of our will to His. The proper outline of a Christian prayer is not, 'Please do for me what I want,' but 'Please do in me, with me and through me what You want.'

> When we come into our Father's presence, our Lord seems to say, we should be so filled with the thought of Him that we forget all about ourselves, our hopes, our needs, even our sins; what we want most of all and therefore utter first is that all men may know how glorious God is and reverence Him accordingly — 'Hallowed be thy name.' (How often do we pray that? We say it every day, but do we pray it?)

> The two sons of Zebedee once approached the Lord with a prayer which perfectly illustrates the wrong way to pray: 'Master, we would that Thou shouldst do for us whatsoever we shall ask of Thee...' To such a prayer for selfish advantage can be one answer: Can you share My sacrifice? (St. Mark 10: 35-38)

[1]*Christ the Truth*, pp. 230, 231.

The essence of prayer is to seek how we may share that sacrifice.
It finds its fullest expression in the Eucharist where we offer ourselves
to Christ that He may unite us to Himself in His perfect self-offering
to the Father — that self-offering to which He dedicated Himself in
the great prayer which St. John now calls us to hear with adoring
wonder...what is, perhaps, the most sacred passage in the four
Gospels. — (St. John 17)[1]

3. The third thing that is most striking about William Temple the
man is the degree to which his being was emptied of self. This is a great
and severe test, for as he taught with such clarity the deepest human
problem is man's native or original self-centeredness. This is always the
state and fate of the animal, but man stamped with the image of God
has within him the gifts of reason, self-consciousness, and self-transcendence. He can choose up to a point the objects he will attend to, the
ends he will serve, and the center around which his life and being will
revolve. Temple believed devoutly and as a fact of experience that God's
grace shown in the overwhelming love of Christ could reduce the hold
and thrust of self and even supplant it as motive and center. Here is
this specific, self-revealing analysis:

Our question, therefore, is this: How can the self find it good to
submit willingly to removal from its self-centeredness and welcome
reconstitution about God as its centre? There is, in fact, one power
known to men, and only one, which can effect this, not only for one
or another function of self (as beauty and truth can do), but for the
self as a whole in its entirety and integrity. When a man acts to please
one whom he loves, doing or bearing what apart from that love he
would not choose to do or bear, his action is wholly determined by the
other's pleasure, yet in no action is he so utterly free — that is, so
utterly determined by his apparent good...The one hope, then, of
bringing human selves into right relationship to God is that God
should declare His love in an act or acts of sheer self-sacrifice, there-
by winning the freely offered love of the finite selves which he has
created.[2]

In another related passage the Archbishop speaks very characteristically of "that objectivity of direction which is called humility, and
which consists not in thinking little of self but in not thinking of the self
at all."[3]

That is quite an extraordinary statement, but for its author it was
a matter of daily experience and the mark, not of his spiritual achievement, but of what God's grace had achieved in him. There were many
who marveled at the mass of work he was able to accomplish and at
the constancy of his untroubled serenity. The secret was self-transcendence and self-emptying. His business was the Kingdom of God, and its
goals galvanized all his energies. He was able to utilize half-hour periods
or less, which most of us trifle away, to compose his books or write
letters.

Canon Baker quotes Reinhold Niebuhr (a tough-minded rather than
tender-minded thinker) on the key to Temple's personality: "It is safe to
say that not only in public characters but also in private individuals

[1]*Readings in St. John's Gospel,* Vol. II, pp. 305-307.

[2]*Nature, Man and God,* pp. 399-400. [3]Ibid., p 423

few of us have known any person whose life and personality were so completely and successfully integrated around love for Christ as their focus and source and crown."[3]

4. We have stressed William's serenity of soul and his impressive freedom from restlessness. With this, not surprisingly, he was a very happy person, given to high spirits and robust, hearty, even explosive laughter. As is well known, he was famous for his laughter, which was frequently side-splitting and was evoked often by his own jokes. He enjoyed them hugely. And there was so much that this wonderful man enjoyed. He gave God much, indeed from long habit of self-surrender he offered Him all; and God gave him back the gifts of happiness and joy.

Canon Baker again is unerring in his close observation: "It is true to say that he looked at the world and his work with the eyes of a child, and enjoyed them like a child. It was one of the marks of his genius that he retained, as knowledge increased, the freshness of vision by which a child appreciates the plain facts more vividly than most grown people. But it is saying the same thing to say that he tried to see the world and to act in it as though with the eyes and the will of God."

5. Throughout this book we have noted and laid weight on Temple's concern for society and his social thought. He was very steadfast and consistent in this burden and advocacy. Some of this came out of his training in philosophy and the trends that were to the fore in his Oxford days.

Plato was an early hero to William, and the attachment continued. No one who is thoroughly exposed to this most divine of the Greeks, can ever be the same again. The sub-title of *The Republic* is *Concerning Justice* and this remained Plato's most absorbing concern, as it had been that of his master, Socrates. I can never forget, or ever get over, my discovery that for Plato the deepest evil of injustice is not what it does to the victim, but the injury it inflicts on the soul of the perpetrator of the unjust act.

William undoubtedly was affected by his Platonic studies, and there was in addition the heavy emphasis upon politics and society in the thinking of idealists in philosophy: Edward Caird, T.H. Green, and of course their master Hegel. For all his personalism, the young philosopher and theologian could never contract into individualism. His view of man and his destiny was dialectical as between the individual person and society.

But, above all, there was the feeling of the young aristocrat, the child born to the purple, for the underdog. He never forgot that privilege was not something conferred on the basis of merit. His heart burned for the worker deprived of educational opportunity, for the poor and the oppressed, and for the unemployed — particularly the unemployed! And as he studied and preached the Gospel of the Kingdom of God, he was grasped by the unshakeable conviction that Christianity was called to Christianize society just as surely as it was to preach repentance to sinners.

William was a Churchman from his childhood up. We have empha-

[3]Op. cit., p. 110

sized this. Possibly we have not said enough about his love of the English Church and his Churchmanship. Never a Party man, he was what was called when I first lived in England in the 1930s a Central Churchman. He was at once an Evangelical and a Catholic and saw this too as a dialectical truth and reality. But in accepting and loving and serving the Church, he did not forget that Christ proclaimed a Kingdom and that as the Body of Christ the Church was called to the same service of that Kingdom. And the Kingdom for Temple was ever Sovereignty — the Sovereignty of Love.

All this is very important, not as an interesting side issue, but as central in the conviction and the confession of William Temple. This is the Churchman whose voice was the mightiest in the Christian world in the period of the World Wars for claiming the kingdoms and republics of this world as the Kingdom of our God and His Christ. It is this aspect of Temple — his witness and contribution as prophet and social thinker in the industrial and technical age — that marks him as a modern Saint.

Recently, dipping into selections from classical Christian mystics, I came across two passages which arrested — I might almost say, froze — my attention.

The first is from the unknown English mystic of the 14th century who wrote *The Cloud of Unknowing*.

> *Lift up thine heart unto God with a meek stirring of love; and mean Himself, and none of His goods. And thereto, look thee loath to think on aught but Himself...And...forget all the creatures that God ever made and the works of them...let them be, and take no heed to them. This is the work of the soul that most pleaseth God.*

The second selection, which might almost have come from a Buddhist scripture, is from St. John of the Cross.

> *When you stop at one thing, you cease to open yourself to the All.*
> *For to come to the All you must give up the All.*
> *And if you should attain to owning the All, you must own it desiring Nothing.*
> *In this spoliation, the soul finds its tranquility and rest. Proudly established in the centre of its own nothingness, it can be assailed by naught that comes from below; and since it no longer desires anything, what comes from above cannot depress it; for its desires alone are the cause of its woes.*

Temple no doubt would have seen truth in the tenor of these passages. In the concentration of the mystics of God, he would have seen valuable witness to the first priority of the Christian. "God is." "In the beginning God." "That God may be all in all."

But to pull down a curtain, shutting the soul from converse with all the creatures of God; and to root out all desire, parting company with joy, happiness, sympathy, love — this surely would be a kind of blasphemy and the contradiction of Christ and Christianity.

St. Francis in his love of all God's creatures, even the ministering agents of nature, is truer to the spirit of Christianity and is the prototype of the deepest Christian sanctity. William Temple is in the Franciscan succession, and he would be at home in the Dominican!

6. William Ebor. et Cantuar. as a Saint! How would it have struck his contemporaries? Let two witnesses be heard.

The first is the late Sir Walter Moberly, a life-long friend. He wrote.

*I have had what was, I presume, the experience of all Temple's older friends. More and more was added to the old affection and admiration something for which 'reverence seems the only possible term. No one could make less claim for himself or take it more wholly for granted that he met you on equal terms. But his ever growing stature became such that, to look at him at all, one must look **up** at steeper and steeper angles.* [1]

That is indeed a fitting and telling tribute, worded with a delicate finesse.

The second witness is really a corporate one and involves an interesting story. The crisis period of the latter 30s was marked by an increasing polarization of theological thought among the theologians of the English Church. The younger men turned conservative on dogma and the Bible. Orthodoxy of an intelligent kind appealed to them. The older generation was tainted to too great an extent by optimism and liberalism.

The Archbishop, ever open to the mind and heart of the young, and by training and temperament an apostle of comprehension, was the ideal sponsor of efforts at communication and understanding as between the two broad schools of thought.

Three informal conferences were held, convoked by Temple. The first two were in 1940: in January and April. A third and enlarged session came four years later at Canterbury after William had become the Primate of All England. In fact, it was in the last year of his life. In the background was the proposed scheme for the union of churches in the Church of South India. There were some strong feelings about this, especially among the more authoritarian younger men. So there was some tension in the air and sharp criticism and discussion. Temple was known to favor the Union in South India, and some young theologians were afraid they could not utter their views.

This, of course, was wrong. He wanted complete freedom and candor of discussion, and was ready to listen to all views. Because of his humility and courtesy and rare quality of spirit, divisions were broken down and all benefitted. A member of the younger group spoke for all when he wrote that they knew "that we had been meeting with a man of prayer and a saint. That realization overshadowed everything else. It was not his great intellect, or his astonishing gift of understanding, or the wideness of the theological rift, that made the deepest impression, but the fact of his holiness."

"A man of prayer and a Saint!" This was William at the height of his unique career, in many ways unparalleled, and as he was cut down in floodtide, a casualty and a martyr of the War. This is the way he was remembered and will be remembered in the history of the Christian Church.

A Once-born Man

The above seems to be the only heading for the concluding portion of the present chapter. I considered such variants as "A Once-born

[1] Quoted by Iremonger, p. 515

Spirit" and "A Once-born Saint," but either of these wordings would be misleading.

We are born human beings, not disembodied spirits. We must develop, one way or another, as flesh and spirit, as soul and body, as psycho-physical organisms. And we are certainly not born Saints. A Saint is made, not born.

William Temple, as is now clear, was a particular sort of man. We have stressed the constancy and continuity which one finds in his character, his career, his whole life. It was, to a most unusual extent, of one piece.

This suggests a master key to an understanding of William. He is a classical example of the *once-born* spiritual type; a concept and popularized by William James in his *Varieties of Religious Experience*.

Most of James' *varieties*, as a matter of fact, seem to be twice-born types. I forget whether it was Temple's friend, Oliver Quick, or F.R. Barry at Oxford who remarked that the singular thing about William James' celebrated book *The Varieties of Religious Experience* was the lack of variety in it.

This is true. But the great religious figures do tend to be men who found their way through intense struggle, crisis, even convulsion, to reconciliation and peace with God.

St. Paul is the classical example. St. Augustine and Martin Luther are equally instructive, parallel examples of the twice-born man. Less extreme examples are St. Francis of Assisi and John Wesley. But both men went through a severe spiritual crisis before finding peace and unity of soul in loving and serving God.

Outside of Christianity, Isaiah and Jeremiah, Gautama the Buddha and Muhammad the camel-driver, seem clearly to fall within the twice-born category, though in a less spectacular manner than, say, an Augustine.

In Christian history there are saints who fall in the once-born class or approach it. Two notable instances are Origen of ancient Alexandria, who flourished around A.D. 230, and St. Thomas Aquinas (A.D.c. 1224-1274). Both were very great theologians, and less men of affairs than William Ebor. et Cantuar. But they afford parallels of considerable interest.

Origen presents the first picture in Christian history of a Christian boy. (We except here St. Luke's account of the boy Jesus at 12.) He was the son of a martyr and was a Christian from his birth. He was educated by his father Leonides, and the thorough training the boy received included daily memory work in the Holy Scriptures. Origen was eager, precocious, reverent, and athirst for knowledge, human and divine. In time he attended the catechetical school, where he was a pupil of Clement. When his father was thrown into prison in the Severan persecution, the boy was only restrained from following Leonides by the tears and entreaties of his mother. He wrote his father not to let any concern for his family, consisting of a wife and seven sons, affect his resolve to be faithful unto death. Leonides kept the faith, was beheaded, and had all his property confiscated. Origen became a teacher in his teens, first of "grammar," then at 18 as head of the Catechetical

School following Clement, who was a marked man and felt it wise to retire.

The point is that Origen's life, in contrast to such saints as Cyprian, Jerome, and Augustine, was from start to finish of one piece. It was like a seamless robe, and there are many parallels between Origen and William Temple.

I have always felt that there was a striking personal parallel between Temple and St. Thomas Aquinas. In a major article *William Temple Archbishop of Canterbury*, which I was asked to do by the editors of the American *Christendom* at the time of his enthronement, I developed this comparison. Both were large men, of genial, happy temperament, yet self-directed from childhood toward a perfect dedication to God and toward serving him with the mind. Both were men of prodigious industry. Their powerful minds were applied to enlisting philosophy, in the largest sense, as the handmaid of Christ's religion and His reign in all life. They were in agreement in giving absolute priority to prayer and the Blessed Sacrament of Christ's Body and Blood.

We think of Aquinas as being Italian, but in reality he was a German. He was closely related to the reigning house of the Kingdom of Sicily: his father, Count Landulf of Aquino, was a nephew of Frederick Barbarossa and a prominent figure at "the Apulian court of the impious Frederick II." His mother, a countess in her own right, was of Norman stock and could trace her descent back to the Anglo-Saxon kings. Pope Honorius III was Thomas' godfather.

As a man he was large in body, cherubic in countenance, "of the color of new wheat" in complexion. His mind likewise was great, spacious and sunny within. His whole life was of a piece. As a boy he turned from the world and worldly ambitions, dedicating himself to God's service. All the power and ingenuity and wickedness of his proud family were not sufficient to turn Thomas from his chosen way. And the child was "father of the man;" never for the slightest moment did the man turn aside. No more "whole" personality has made a conspicuous mark on the Christian church.

William, it seems to me, resembled Thomas as a person to an unusual degree, There was a parallel in their childhood and boyhood, as well as in their physique. William was massive in stature; he was ruddy and fair of face. He was to a remarkable extent whole in nature. In temperament he was sunny, placid, unfailingly cheerful.

Temple, one felt, hardly had nerves. He had few if any complexes, was little given to introversion, functioned habitually with something of the smooth power of a flawless machine. Such qualities stood him in good stead as a presiding officer at assemblies, conferences, and committees. In 1937 at the World Conference on Faith and Order at Edinburgh I had the opportunity to observe William as its President at very close range and for a period of two and a half weeks.

His mind was the counterpart of his body. It was massive and spacious, comprehensive and well rounded. It appeared to have no rough edges, no gaping fissures, no sharp edges. In bent it was constructive rather than inquisitive, tending to impose upon the vast range of material made readily accessible by a phenomenal memory the order and harmony of his personality. He was singularly free from the sense of contradiction in things, just as he seemes to have known in his own experience little of failure or of crisis. Was there ever a man who so little wearied in well-doing?

There is a verse in the Sermon on the Mount, the last one in chapter 5 of St. Matthew, which has troubled many Christians and many theologians (it is not intended to place the two in antithesis). The Authorized Version translates the verse: "Be ye therefore perfect, even as your Father, which is in heaven, is perfect." The Revised Version alters this to read: "Ye therefore shall be perfect, as your heavenly Father is perfect." Subsequent translators have tended to agree with the instinct of the Revisers, and in the New English Bible we find this rendering: "You must therefore be all goodness, just as your heavenly Father is all good."

Is such affirmation meaningful and appropriate, given human nature as Christian theology has understood and evaluated it? We know the answer of a Luther, even with redeemed and justified man in the picture. "The old Adam has in us ten thousand deaths to die." John Wesley, on the other hand, following the doctrine of the mentor of his Oxford days, William Law, was convinced of the essential validity and existence of Christian perfection. In his famous sermon on *Christian Perfection* he asserts that "a Christian is so far perfect as not to commit sin." In his Journal he records a debate with Count Zinzendorf. The latter says, "I acknowledge no inherent perfection in this life. This is the error of errors." To which Wesley replies, "But I believe that the spirit of Christ works this perfection in true Christians." Elsewhere he interprets the perfection open to the Christian as fulfilling essentially the two great commandments of the law, the love of God with one's whole being and the love of neighbor as oneself.

William Temple, it seems to me, is a good illustration of the Wesleyan idea of Christian perfection, though the phrase is not one he would have used and he would have been uncomfortable with any application of it to himself. Moreover, there is one heresy which Temple particularly feared. He said repeatedly that there was only one heresy which was truly damnable, and that was Pelagianism. Pelagius was a British monk, and some would say that his heresy is one to which the British have always tended. Perhaps this is one reason for Temple's insight and concern.

This however is a different issue from sanctity and Christlikeness. What Pelagianism does is to affirm the moral and spiritual competency of man. It calls in question man's utter need of Divine grace and his absolute dependence on God. Temple was sure, as Wesley was, that "our sufficiency is of God" and that salvation is from the start to finish the work of the Triune God, Father, Son and Holy Spirit. But it is also a work in which we freely cooperate.

It is worth noting that Temple's ideas on freedom were very definite and more in line with the long Christian tradition than with much modern talk of freedom and confused assertion of it as the supreme value. In his Gifford Lectures he dismisses both freedom conceived as moral or psychological indeterminism and "stark determinism." He defines freedom as essentially determination by the good. "Freedom is not absence of determination; it is spiritual determination, as distinct from mechanical or even organic, determination. It is determination by what seems good as contrasted with determination by irresistible compulsion."

Such an outlook enables us to see how Temple can be very anti-Pelagian and at the same time see human life and character as steadily and increasingly under the sway of God. This is what Temple was — a God-centered man from his childhood up, concerned in the most concrete way to reflect the spirit of Christ and to do the will of God.

In reading (and re-reading as I have done again and again at different periods) his great Lecture IX on Freedom and Determinism it is impossible not to see the author drawing aside the curtain and revealing his own inmost selfhood. If he writes with the insight of a Paul and an Augustine — and if he keeps in view as a good philosopher the universal condition of man — this does not mean that he speaks out of the depths of the experience of these souls and countless others like them. When he invokes as an hypothesis a self-disclosure of the Spirit of the Whole and, while not claiming that such ever can be proved, refers to the mind finding that it is confronted with "something akin, yet transcendent, and discovers a new power of self-forgetfulness increasingly to pervade both thought and conduct," one is sure that the scholar-archbishop is unconsciously portraying his deepest and ever-formative experience from childhood on. Here is the secret of his extraordinary integration of self, with will but its cutting edge of action, and the shining radiance of his habitual self-forgetfulness.

If we ask what was the route traveled by this unusual person and character to get where he infallibly arrived, and that not late in his life, the first answer is, by Christian nurture. Horace Bushnell, in the nineteenth century, wrote one of the seminal books of the time on that subject, "Christian Nurture." He had in mind essentially what William James generalized in the concept of the once-born type spiritually. But he was describing the social and psychological conditions of this type of Christian personality and was doing so in reaction to the long Puritan and Evangelical insistence upon conversion or a conscious second-birth. If a child was reared in a Christian home and trained in a school under Christian influence and allowed to grow up in the atmosphere of a Christian church, then Christianity would be second nature to him as a matter of course. There would be no occasion for any radical crisis of faith or moral experience. Faith in God as Father and in Jesus as Lord would come as naturally as breathing — and as the love of mother and father did.

We do have information, as we saw in chapters I and II, on William as a child and as a youth which throws much light on the man. His father, Frederick, was his idol and the image was never altered. He of course had been Archbishop of Canterbury from 1897 to 1902, and William said of him at his own enthronement: "He was and is among men the chief inspiration of my life."

His mother, also, Beatrice Lascelles, the niece of three Dukes, and her family and family connections played a stellar role in the moulding of his outlook and basic psychology. A self-made man rarely gets over his background and harsh compulsions.

William had none of this to contend with. He was a true aristocrat in the conspicuous lack of self-consciousness that seems always to have characterized him.

American churchmen and churchwomen will be interested in a personal item involving the late Henry St. George Tucker, Bishop of Virginia and Presiding Bishop of the Episcopal Church. He was Chairman of the Board of Trustees of the Virginia Theological Seminary at the time I was elected by them to the Chair of Theology at the age of 28. I got to know Bishop Tucker quite well and admired him greatly. I always regarded him as the epitome of the aristocrat — a man as plain in some ways as an old shoe and entirely lacking in side. He seemed, more than anyone else I have known, to have no self-consciousness at all. Nothing fazed him or troubled him.

William Temple reminded me of St. George Tucker, after I had come to know him; and in a letter to the New York Times following the death of Tucker I instituted a comparison of the two prelates along the line indicated above. This was much appreciated by the Tucker family. I might add that St. George was the oldest of thirteen children and that his Mother was a Washington and the last girl to be married from Mt. Vernon. At Seminary faculty meetings I have heard Tom Nelson, another Virginia aristocrat, say: "St. George is a Washington; the Washingtons have no nerves."

But we have done. In taking leave of Temple the man and the Saint, I wish to adopt and make my own one of the finest of all the tributes ever paid him. It is from a short memoir written by the late Dr. George Bell, Bishop of Chichester, and himself one of the notable ecumenical Christians of the period of World War II. He wrote:

Temple had...vision, imagination and courage. He was a man of extraordinary intellectual and spiritual power, as well as of extraordinary industry. He never spared himself, though he never gave the impression of haste. And in the midst of his activity he kept the serenity and simplicity of a child. 'Ministers of good things,' said Richard Hooker, 'are like torches, a light to others, a waste and destruction to themselves.' William Temple had all the vividness and swiftness of a flame. It was like a flame that he sped through our whole firmament, filling every corner of it with a new splendour. It was like a flame that he communicated warmth and light to all who saw or heard him. We cannot expect to look upon his like again in our lifetime. [1]

---

[1] *William Temple and His Message*, Ed. A.E. Baker, p. 47

CHAPTER SEVEN

BASIC IDEAS

William Temple was a highly trained scholar. At Rugby and Oxford, as we have seen, he received a superb classical education. In addition, he was steeped in English poetry and in both ancient and modern philosophy. Upon taking his B.A. degree with a double-first in "Greats" or Literae Humaniores, he was elected a Fellow and Lecturer in Philosophy of The Queens College. Here his job was to teach philosophy.

It was inevitable that a churchman with this background should be a man of ideas. It was as a young don that he was ordained and began a preaching career that ended only with his death. Always he was in fantastic demand and he was never at any time a man to spare himself. Like the Japanese, the word "No" was, at least in this respect, not in his vocabulary.

It would be interesting but difficult to compute the number of sermons Temple preached in the 36 years of his ministry. No doubt the addresses and lectures he gave would double the total. His biographer, Dean Iremonger, wrote of him: "Temple was a born teacher. He was one of the few among his Chrstian contemporaries who was never known to preach without teaching."

This teacher-preacher lived with ideas from his youth up. It was his mission to propound ideas, discuss them, develop them, and propagate them. This did not mean dry-as-dust concepts. Quite the contrary. His aim was to explain, clarify, and drive home. Thus he was essentially a popularizer. But he dealt with the coin of ideas rather than images and illustrations.

With his remarkable facility, he was ready to speak on almost any subject or occasion. Many of his sermons, addresses, lectures, and charges got into books or were published separately as pamphlets. He published in his lifetime no fewer than 35 volumes. Other published items probably number as many or more.

From 1910 on (the year he became Headmaster of Repton) Temple was a busy, active man, involved in a central way with affairs and institutions. In view of this, his literary achievement is fantastic. Of his magnum opus, *Nature, Man and God*, delivered first as Gifford Lectures, Dean Inge wrote that for a professor such an achievement would have been remarkable, for a busy prince of the church it was astonishing. Nevertheless, Temple's basic ideas were few and they never changed very much. His genius lay in reiteration and in versatility of expression and application.

The first source of these ideas was Christianity — the Gospel of Christ and its meaning for all life. It must never be forgotten that William Temple was brought up as a Christian boy. His environment for longer than he could remember was of worship, prayer, Bible-reading, and Church. He could not remember when he had not expected to become a priest and preacher.

The second thing that was bound to be influential in this man's thought and life in their interaction was his thorough classical education — in school and at Oxford. He came especially under the influence of Plato — the second of the three dominant forces in his mental life, he always said. The other two were St. John and Robert Browning.

In addition, at Balliol in Oxford the Master was Edward Caird, a Scottish philosopher-theologian who had succeeded the great Benjamin Jowett. The latter's immense reputation rested supremely on his translation of Plato and commentaries on that master's thought. Jowett as a young academic had been caught up in the German orbit and had been a zealous student of Kant and Hegel. In his prime he backed away from systematic metaphysics and in the spirit of Plato put his stress on philosophy as wisdom of life. Caird, on the other hand, was and remained a Scottish Hegelian. This means that he was a monist in philosophy — an apostle of unity and a resolver of conflicts, intellectual and otherwise; and that he was an able and fearless dialectician. Dialectic is a scholastic name for logic, but it implies truth-finding by the method of overcoming opposition and contradiction and thus attaining synthesis.

Temple came inevitably under the powerful influence of Caird. This influence was an abiding one. Temple acknowledged it handsomely on many occasions. He believed that he owed to Caird his basic method in thought and his deep immersion in the essential principles of Dialectic.

If we look not only at *Nature, Man and God* (published in 1934), but also at his two earlier major works, *Mens Creatrix* (1917) and *Christus Veritas* (1924), we become aware of the deeply dialectical character of Temple's basic thought. The first of these writings, *Mens Creatrix*, was intended as an Essay in philosophy. It was planned in 1908 when the author was a junior don at Queen's College, Oxford engaged in lecturing on philosophy. This was just prior to his ordination as Deacon on December 20, 1908. The writing was done in snatches over eight years. Characteristically, one may feel, Temple finished what he then supposed was his one fling at philosophy on the eve of his marriage to Frances Anson, when he wrote till late into the night. In a chapter entitled "The Method of Intellect and the Province of Truth," he states that the essential quality and method of the intellect may be summed up in this way:

> *Contradiction is at once its enemy and its stimulus. It finds incoherence in its apprehension at any given time and reorganizes its content to remove that incoherence. Contradiction is what it cannot think; and yet contradiction is what makes it think.*

Temple speaks here of Logic as "the theory of Theory" and of its close relation to politics. We do more than scent: we cannot fail to see the influence of Hegel and also of Bradley. Moving in another connec-

97

tion from theory to fact, Temple is optimistic respecting the British Empire and its meaning for the future. "In this fact of the British Empire, then, we have 'the noblest project of freedom that the world has seen.' " He is impressed with the example of South Africa, failing in rebellion and then supporting the British Crown; and with the action of the Crown in New Zealand, moving to protect the Maoris from its own subjects. "Here already we see in the Imperial Government the germ of a World Government deriving its authority from a moral need. This Empire does not stand in the line of succession with Assyria, Babylon, Macedon and Rome; it is a new kind of fact."

Optimism of this kind was implicit in idealist philosophy and the young Temple was evidently under this influence to a considerable extent. I am unable however to find any trace of explicit idealism or mentalism in *Mens Creatrix*, and this conclusion is borne out by an earlier book, *The Nature of Personality*, published in 1911 and consisting of Oxford lectures delivered in Lent Term 1910.[1] In this work Temple reveals the impact of a strong current in all serious ultimate thinking of that period, namely, the primacy of personality as a moral and metaphysical category. In all his writings we find that he is a strong personalist. It is over the role and import of personality in philosophy that Temple the Archbishop breaks with Whitehead the metaphysician in *Nature, Man and God*. The latter in his cosmology stops short with the category of organism and presents God and the world as completely correlated to each other. Temple sees in the world qualities such as self-determination by reference to apprehended good which carry a philosopher beyond Organism to Personality. The principle that accounts for the world-process must account for the fact of self-transcendence and Organism cannot do this unless it is expanded so as to be properly named Personality. *"Personality is always transcendent in relation to Process."*

This emphasis on personality is nothing new in Temple. He explored it systematically as a young don at Oxford. It was in the air he breathed intellectually before that — at Rugby and no doubt in the teaching and speaking of his father, Frederick Temple. For it is Christianity which increasingly over the centuries, and climactically in the nineteenth and early twentieth centuries, focused on as supreme the concept of personality. In all William's writings we shall find him holding to and holding up the category of the Person as ultimate. The reason is that at the heart of the Christian Gospel and of the religious system to which it gave rise is a concrete Person, Jesus the Christ, the Incarnate Word of God. This is the master-idea of William Temple from first to last. It explains why of the three master-influences on his thought two are St. John and Robert Browning.

Mens Creatrix is a rather curious book. It bears on it clear traces

---

[1] I find that in 1942, following Temple's enthronement as Archbishop of Canterbury I wrote as follows: "Temple the Archbishop reflects the commotions that have shaken the world of philosophy. He has now definitely broken with traditional idealism. Whether this break is as sharp as Professor Horton (Walter M.), following apparently the view of Professor Widgery, indicates, may be a question. In *Mens Creatrix* (1917) Temple is specific in declining to commit himself absolutely to Realism or Idealism and minimizes the controversy between them." *Christendom: An Ecumenical Review*, Winter 1943, p. 37

of a precocious but youthful mind. It was planned as something massive and definitive, as a kind of *Summa*. It was intended to exemplify a systematic dialectic, moving from the four converging lines of the four philosophical sciences of Knowledge, Art, Morality, and Religion "which do not in fact meet" to see whether theology can answer "Man's search for an all-inclusive system of Truth." Thus Book II, "God's Act," is the attempt to supply the convergence, unity, and system. The attempt is only that. For some reason, perhaps because he was tired and wanted to get the long effort behind him, perhaps because he wanted to finish before he got married, Book II is a sawed-off presentation which does not stand up well beside Book I, "Man's Search." This Book contains 292 pages, Book II only 72.

Christus Veritas (in the American version *Christ the Truth*) is seen by the author as a theological rather than a philosophical Essay, a companion to the older work. In the new book the Christian revelation is in full view from the ouset. It is nevertheless a highly dialectical writing, alike in conception and in execution. The author sets out from the "Outer Circle," with three chapters: The Structure of Reality, The Apprehension of Value, and Religious Experience, to the "Inner Circle," which likewise has three chapters: The Nature of Man, History and Eternity, and The Nature of God. Then we have as Part III "The Core of the Argument" with three chapters: The Godhead of Jesus Christ, The Person of Christ, and The Holy Spirit and the Church. Now the procedure and the argument are dialectically reversed. Part IV "Inner Circle" has three chapters: God in the Light of the Incarnation, Eternity and History, and Man in the Light of the Incarnation. Finally there is the return trip to the "Outer Circle," Part V, also with three chapters: Worship and Sacraments, The Atonement, and Love Divine: The Blessed Trinity.

It is a beautifully architectonic volume and there is a deal of philosophy in it as well as large stretches of theology. As a whole, it is much more mature and far more ably executed than *Mens Creatrix*. It does illustrate the judgment of Archbishop Michael Ramsey and others that Temple was essentially a philosopher rather than a theologian.

His magnum opus, *Nature, Man and God,* confirms this point. It is notable as a systematic treatise, attempting to look synoptically at all reality. The hand of the theologian is visible. There is no doubt, even with the limitations imposed by the the Gifford Lectures, supposedly as in some manner limited to Natural Theology, that the Archbishop-author is above all a man of faith, seeing God in Christ as the central and controlling reality of the universe. Nevertheless, with a magnificent sweep, he sets out from the picture of the world offered by science, identifying here with the neo-realist Whitehead rather than his original idealist mentors. Another influence undoubtedly was the dialectical materialism of Marx and Communism. He had been a student of Bergson's *Creative Evolution*, as we know from *Mens Creatrix*. But it would be incorrect to suppose that, even in *Nature, Man and God*, he had simply thrown idealism overboard.

The Archbishop sets out from matter, evolution, and slowly emerging mind. He asserts emphatically that in the real world as grasped by science apprehension takes place within the world, not the world within apprehension. However, once mind appears associated with human reason and self-consciousness, it becomes evident that there is a close and surprising correlation of mind and the order of the world which it apprehends. Science itself is a supreme example of this; other instances are aesthetic experience, moral values, and religion. The full consideration of this activity of mind leads from a doctrine of Immanence to one of Transcendence of process. This is Temple's *second* dialectical transition. The first was the reconsideration of the evolutionary, material world-picture, impelled by the realization of Mind as a factor in that picture.

Once Transcendent Mind is reached, it is relevant to examine its actuality and self-expression in the creation. What is its relation to the order of nature? Is it self-revealing and self-communicating and in what mode? This leads on to religious experience and the nature of spiritual authority. It also brings the mind up short at the point of confrontation by Evil, the serious problem it raises for Theism, and its implications for the relation between finite minds and Transcendent Mind. This is Temple's *third* dialectical transition. Now he must deal with such large questions as value, history, eternal life, and the universe as sacramental in the light of the Living and Transcendent God.

The Nineteenth Lecture on "The Sacramental Universe" is one of the ripest and richest of all Temple's pronouncements. Incidentally it clinches his "realist" outlook and starting-point. Here occurs one of the Archbishop's strongest and most oft-quoted assertions. "It may safely be said that one ground for the hope of Christianity that it may make good its claim to be the true faith lies in the fact that it is the most avowedly materialist of all the great religions." He adds, after noting the most central saying of the Christian religion that "the Word was made flesh," that by the very nature of this central doctrine "Christianity is committed to a belief in the ultimate significance of the historic process, and in the reality of matter and its place in the divine scheme."

In a sense Temple has in this invocation of the doctrine of the Incarnation gone beyond what his argument at this point entitles him to. His final transition is going to be a shift to theology grounded in the self-revelation of God in Christ. Natural theology, as he understands and employs this term and discipline, cannot produce the light that will satisfy reason and point to the resolution of all contradictions, especially those thrown up by a candid consideration of the phenomenon of Evil in all its range.

Incidentally there is a gripping sentence in Whitehead's small volume, *Religion in the Making*, which bears on Temple at this point in his argument. "Every simplification of religious dogma," wrote Professor Whitehead, "comes to shipwreck upon the rock of the problem of evil." Before we look however at Temple's measure of the final need and task of thought, it will be of interest to see where he sees himself after contemplating and expounding the Universe as sacramental. This is his summary paragraph:

> Thus the view of the universe which I have called sacramental asserts the supremacy and absolute freedom of God; the reality of the physical world and its process as His creation; the vital significance of the material and temporal world to the eternal Spirit; and the

100

spiritual issue of the process in a fellowship of the finite and time-enduring spirits in the infinite and eternal Spirit. Matter exists in full reality but at a secondary level. It is created by spirit — the Divine Spirit — to be the vehicle of spirit and the sphere of spirit's self-realization in and through the activity of controlling it.

In this comprehensive statement we have a summation not only of the implications of the universe seen as essentially sacramental but also of the results of Temple's argument following the route of reason applied to experience in its fulness, but without appeal to the authority of any specific revelation. He has gone as far as one can go along this route.

In his final review chapter (or lecture), *The Hunger of Natural Religion,* Temple clears the ground for a final dialectical transition which is to a full-blown theology grounded on a specific self-revelation of the Divine. The Christian theologian — he is clear — has as his task the viewing of the world, all life, and the immanent-transcendent God in the light of Jesus Christ seen as Incarnate God, as representing at once an unveiling of the Eternal Father and an act of the living God with a view to bringing good out of all things, even evil itself, and doing for man that which by himself, self-centered as he is, he is unable to do.

Such a conclusion strongly suggests, as is the case, that in Temple we have to do with a thinker who is much more than a moral, a metaphysical, and even a religious philosopher rolled into one. We have to do with a thinker who is first of all a religious person, a converted Christian. This being so, Christianity seems to him necessary for the completion of thought as well as of life. It is only in the light of the knowledge of the glory of God in the face of Jesus Christ that the intellectual hypothesis of an eternal purpose grounded in an eternal will eternally fulfilled can become a sure and certain conviction. Thus Temple stands also squarely in the great tradition of Anglican theology, which views Christianity as above all the religion of the Incarnation and seeks to see all things in the light of the fact that in Jesus Christ the very Word of God became flesh. For him truth is a dialogue between reason and faith, philosophy and religion, but in the end it is religion, the religion of the Incarnation, that enables the mind as well as the heart to be satisfied.

Temple in *Nature, Man and God* remains Temple the philosopher with a compulsion to see a rational whole freed from contradictions and therefore able to satisfy the mind. The Gifford Lectures which were brought together in this book were delivered in Glasgow in 1932-33 and 1933-34. This was almost the moment of the rise to power of Adolph Hitler. From then on to the plunge into a Second World War, the world was dominated by the specter of totalitarianism.

There was not only Hitler to be considered, but Mussolini in Italy and Stalin in the Soviet Union. It became increasingly difficult to see the world as the beautiful harmony that the idealists in philosophy were bound to discern, and in fact felt they could discern. This growing discontent surfaced in the Oxford Conference on Life and Work in 1937. The influence of Barth and Brunner, of Reinhold Niebuhr and Paul Tillich, was strongly felt.

Temple, who was a power in the ecumenical movement precisely because of his sensitivity and openness to all the winds of the Spirit, was keenly aware of this problem of philosophical impedimenta. He deals with this issue and indicates a shift of emphasis in his own philosophical outlook in an important article in the periodical *Theology* of November, 1939. In a Letter to Miss Dorothy Emmet under date of 16 July 1942 he describes with characteristic clarity the change of which he is conscious in his perception of the whole.

> *What we must completely get away from is the notion that the world as it now exists is a rational whole; we must think of its unity not by the analogy of a picture, of which all the parts exist at once, but by the analogy of a drama where, if it is good enough, the full meaning of the first scene only becomes apparent with the final curtain; and we are in the middle of this. Consequently the world as we see it is strictly unintelligible...*
>
> *Theologically, this is a greater emphasis on eschatology. Another way to put it is that the* **Logos** *is not to be conceived as a static principle of unity, but as an active force of moral judgement which calls upon us to be fellow workers and agents.*

In this letter and in a magisterial exposition of St. John 1:5 ("The light shineth in the darkness, and the darkness did not absorb it.") in his *Readings in St. John's Gospel*, the Archbishop goes far toward reaching out a hand to what has come to be called "process theology" and to what Professor Frederick Ferré has called "transformational theology." The importance of this is evident if we keep in mind the social thought of Temple the priest-prophet and his strong consistent motivation to preach constantly in its relevance here and now the Kingdom of God. Against this background the realism of the Archbishop as he expounds the provisional dualism of St. John is especially striking:

> *As we look forwards, we peer into darkness, and none can say with certainty what course the true progress of the future should follow. But as we look back, the truth is marked by beacon-lights, which are the lives of saints and pioneers; and these in their turn are not originators of light, but rather reflectors which give light to us, because they themselves are turned to the source of light...To (St. John's) deep spiritual insight it is apparent that the redemption of man is part, even if the crowning part, of a greater thing, the redemption, or conquest, of the universe. Till that be accomplished the darkness abides, pierced but unilluminated by the beam of divine light. And the one great question for everyone is whether he will 'walk in darkness' or 'walk in light.'*

So far we have dealt with the foundations, so to speak, of the thought of William Temple. We have laid out in outline the pattern of the deeper levels of his philosophical theology. It is time now to turn to another aspect of the mind and thought of this priest-statesman who was always an educator.

There is a sense in which Temple was a popularizer. Dr. W.R. Matthews writes somewhere that "of all the men I have known he (Temple) was the most able 'to speak pamphlets.' " This was strikingly illustrated in the Archbishop's American lecture tour in 1935-36 when in the course of a month he delivered four sets of lectures and produced from the stenographic transcriptions of his spoken words four books.

He had done the same sort of thing earlier, in some cases using sermons as the filler for printed volumes. Later on, especially in the war

period during the last years of his life, he was able to gather up addresses and sermons and fit them into books. And of course throughout his
career as Bishop and Archbishop many charges, sermons and addresses
were separately printed.

When one goes through this category of Temple's writings, one naturally finds considerable repetition. It was in fact his ability to take certain
basic ideas and expound them clearly and simply in varying contexts
that made him the leader he became. He was always to a degree the
intellectual but he was also the spiritual advocate and persuader — the
preacher with a word from God and about God. It will be helpful to
lay out and look at the principal concepts in the pamphlets which this
tireless leader "spoke" over more than three decades.

If one may utilize an interesting distinction made by the medieval
theologians, it may serve to bring out the two levels of Temple's contribution as a philosophical theologian. Thomas Aquinas held that
theology was a theoretical science. Its aim was knowledge. Duns Scotus
differed with the Angelical Doctor on this point, holding that theology
was a practical science since its informing end was salvation.

Temple as a Don and to some extent always was a theoretical man.
A philosopher must always be objectively concerned with what is and
the accurate knowledge of being. It is different with the religious person, which is what the theologian is initially and consistently, though he
is obliged to think through the implications of faith for all life and for
total knowledge or world-view. At least this is the task of systematic
theology. Dogmatic theology conceivably might let up on the systematic
aspect, being primarily concerned to lay out the meaning and implications of the great dogmas of the Faith.

Temple was fully aware of the difference between man the philosopher and man the worshipper. In the second of his Gifford Lectures on
"The Tension between Philosophy and Religion," the Archbishop de-
lineated the sharp contrast in mental habit and outlook between the
respective exponents of these salient enterprises. The objects of attention are the same, but that is all. The difference is that "the primary
assurances of Religion are the ultimate questions of Philosophy. Religion finds its fullest expression in absolute surrender to the Object of
its worship. But the very existence of that Object is a main theme of
philosophical disputation."

The Archbishop then proceeds to exemplify the reality of this contrast and tension by examining what he calls the three central convictions of Religion in its higher forms. These are worth listing as a reflection of the mind of Temple and for their inherent instructiveness. "First
is the conviction that Spirit is a true source of initiation of processes —
a real *apxn*, a *vera causa*.

"Second is the conviction that all existence finds its source (*apxn,
vera causa*) in a Supreme Reality of which the nature is Spirit.

"Third is the conviction that between that Spirit and ourselves there
can be, and to some extent already is, true fellowship, at least such
as is involved in our conscious dependence on that Spirit."

This very interesting analysis suggests clearly the first of the basic
ideas which Temple as a preacher and "speaker of Pamphlets" is constantly dwelling on and pounding home. It is the idea of God. He is

103

here entirely Biblical. The most notable single feature of the Bible is that God, not man, is the chief character and primary agent.

Temple, first as a person, and second as a thinker, is steeped in the consciousness of God. Like Spinoza he is a God-intoxicated man. But there is this important difference, that whereas Spinoza is a Pantheist finding no real difference between God and Nature, Temple is faithful to the essential truth of Biblical Theism, that God is the living Lord. He is a personal Being. He is Spirit. No analogy we have is adequate, but personality is the least inadequate. No doubt the German Lotze's idea that "Perfect Personality is in God only" while our own personalities are but pale copies thereof, is in essence the concept of Temple.

In all that this man of God said whether in Church or in a hall or over the wireless or in print, God, if not in the foreground, was in the background. He lived daily, indeed hourly, in the presence of God. His steady will, so formed by the nature and habit of a lifetime that it needed no special direction or reminder, was to bear witness to the Father and to do His will.

This Divine will was a will of Love. Here Temple is Johannine to the core: and again there is no question of a cliche or of a great thought occasionally interposing itself. No, Temple lived in this consciousness. The love of God revealed in Christ is the Truth. It is what is. It is the meaning of Christianity and life. It is what we are called to realize, in our personal lives, in all our relationships, and in the organization of society.

I have said that Temple's will was steadfastly formed and required no special direction or stimulation. This is true, but there is nothing accidental about this. The secret of the man and his will was in worship. To this he gave the highest priority and he exemplified it continually by precept and example.

In *Christus Veritas* published when he was 43 and a Bishop, he wrote that

> *There is no possibility of increasing our self-dedication until it becomes perfect, unless we deliberately and repeatedly turn our minds toward that love of God, that God of love, to whom we should be dedicated. This is the place of worship in Christian discipline... Throughout our growth as Christians worship is a duty; as we advance it becomes a delight; and at all times a true act of worship is the fulfilment — for a moment — of the true destiny of our being.*

In his thinking of God, Temple is constantly and consistently Christocentric. The Incarnation is for him no abstraction. It is the heart of faith, the key to truth.

Jesus the Christ is the visible image of the invisible God. In Him we see the Father. "I and my Father are One." (John 10:30)

It would be impossible to exaggerate the reality of the Incarnation and its absolute centrality for Temple. This is the way he put it as he addressed Oxford students on the second night of his great mission at St. Mary's University Church in 1931. (It was my privilege to be there that night and each night of the eight nights when the Archbishop spoke.)

> *The doctrine of the Incarnation is not first and foremost of importance because of what it says about Somebody who lived in Palestine;*

it is of fundamental importance because of what it tells us about the eternal and unchanging God, who is and always will be Himself; and if He, in His self-expression, has given perfect expression of his character in terms of human life, then as we look at that life we see the Eternal God. And if the world we know, or any finite world, is to be God's world, it must be because somehow He gives Himself to it.

Above all, it is in Christ and because of Christ that we know God as a Father whose nature is Love. In a little volume entitled *Basic Convictions*, which contains four addresses to students at Indianapolis in 1935, Temple makes this point in a clear and forthright way.

For the Old Testament prophets, God is righteous indeed, but first as King and Judge and not so prominently as Father. In our Lord the righteousness of God is finally interpreted as Love, and the conception of God as Father takes priority over the conception of Him as Sovereign and Judge. These are not eliminated. He is still the King of the world.

His law still prevails over all things that happen. Not one sparrow falls to the ground apart from Him. And if this law is broken it will vindicate itself in the judgment that ensues. God is King and Judge, but these are not the first thoughts of Him. If we make them the first thoughts, we shall misunderstand the whole of man's relationship to Him. First and foremost He is Our Father and we His Children.

At the end of this very powerful address, he says to the students before him something quite memorable and very characteristic of the man.

Therefore, I want to say a very simple thing: never in your prayers begin to ask for anything nor in any way address God Himself until you have remembered Jesus Christ...There you see God. In your prayers, act on His words: 'He that hath seen Me, hath seen the Father.' Only pray to God as you have come to understand Him in Christ. It is worth saying this, I think, because I find many people who are regular in their prayers and earnest in their discipleship who yet habitually address God primarily as a Soverign; and those whose imaginations easily form pictures, clear or otherwise, form one, perhaps modeled upon Daniel's vision of the Ancient Days, of a King enthroned and full of sovereign dignity. It is true as far as it goes but does not go all the way. The throne of God for this world is, after all, the Cross, and it must be to Jesus that our minds are turned when we want to speak to God,

In this connection it is remarkable that Temple, philosopher and Archbishop, broke with Greek Philosophy and Orthodox Theology on the issue of Patripassionism or Suffering in God. He did this as young man and never changed his mind or moderated his deviation from Tradition. For him the controlling thing was love of God in Christ.

Here is a characteristic passage taken from one of Temple's lectures at the College of Preachers in Washington, D.C. (It was here that we first met.) These lectures were published under the title, *The Centrality of Christ* (in Great Britain as *The Preacher's Theme Today*). Said the Archbishop:

Or, then, consider what is the most distinctive feature of the Gospel: 'God so loved the world that He gave...' The divine passion. For unless we are obsessed with the purely Hellenistic notion of the divine 'apathy,' we cannot suppose that the giving of Christ by the

Father cost Him nothing. The divine passion is that which is entirely absent (I believe this to be perfectly true) from every other religious system in the world except so far as that system has learned from Christianity. It is the point which awakens most indignation in Moslems; it is the point where even the tenderness of Buddhism completely fails.

With his deep sense of God and certitude regarding the Incarnation, the living God making Himself known through a flesh-and-blood Person, sharing fully our humanity, it was inevitable that for Temple Revelation was a critical doctrine. To this idea we turn now.

Indeed the notion of revelation is central for any Christian theologian. In addition to the factor of the Incarnation, the Bible as a whole is the Book of the Word, and the Word is a revealing Word. It symbolizes a God who is the Living One and whose nature it is to communicate.

God speaks, and His Word goes forth. At first in the Bible this image is very anthropomorphic. It is the image and likeness of a magnified man — a King who commands by voice and his word is obeyed. Even the priest-theologian who composed the first chapter of Genesis, one of the great pioneer abstractions in the history of human thought, had scarcely got beyond this anthropomorphic image.

Nevertheless, the progress of Biblical thought is ever toward a substantial Word, a going forth of God Himself in a specific mode of being as He speaks, implanting order and reason and communicating with the crown of His creation, the human being, man and woman. The climax of this Biblical development, assisted no doubt by the influence of Philo Judaeus, the remarkable Jew of Alexandria who was a contemporary of Jesus, is John 1:1. By a sure inspiration, he starts his climactic Gospel with the identical first phrase of Genesis: "In the beginning."

> In the beginning was the Word
> The Word was with God.
> The Word was God.
> He was with God in the beginning.
> Through the Word all things came to be,
> And apart from Him not one thing had its being.

St. John then introduces one of his most telling categories, that of light. It is, of course, of the very nature of light to reveal.

> What came to be in the Word was Life:
> and the Life was the Light of men.
> The light moreover shines in the dark,
> and the darkness has never been able to overpower it.
> . . . .
> That one, John, was not the Light,
> but was only a witness to speak for the Light.
> There was the Light, the true Light
> that enlightens all men.
> coming into the world.

Then in a moment comes the climax, the thrilling, unexpected, overwhelming crescendo, which yet as St. John puts it, is so simply and quietly matter of fact.

The Word was made flesh;
He lived among us,
and we saw His glory,
the glory that is His as the only Son of the Father,
full of grace and truth.[1]

Here we confront the ultimate revelation — God's revealing Word taking the form of human personality.

It has always been implicit in Holy Scriptures that there was a progressive element, something increasingly normative and definitive. The New Testament and Covenant has its context in the Old, but the man Christ Jesus is sharply commanding. He represents something that is boldly new and at the same time the fulfillment of the old. He is that which the Old Testament and Covenant cry out for. He is God's man, far more than a prophet; He is the one long expected and awaited, the Messiah.

But He is so much more than the Messiah, for now the self-revealing God has sent His eternal Word in person, to show the ultimate glory which is Love and to reveal the very heart of God.

If this tremendous thing is true, then clearly Revelation is more than any form of written words or indeed than the sum of all the words of Holy Writ. What is involved in Revelation — in communication, manifestation, self-disclosure on the part of the God who is both Ultimate Being and the Creator of the Universe?

It is one of the distinctions of Archbishop Temple that he saw the importance of this issue both practically and philosophically. The modern study of the Bible as a literary and historical document, fully a human production and therefore calling for analysis and criticism in the manner of any literature, had made the questions of inspiration and revelation very urgent.

The Archbishop, as he once told me, had never been trained in critical Biblical scholarship. The questions that arose for many of his contemporaries respecting the authorship and character of the Fourth Gospel he had never found troublesome. This was a help probably when he came to write his second greatest work, the two-volume *Readings in St. John's Gospel.*

All the same Temple was a modern man. He knew that "the letter killeth, the Spirit giveth life." Literalism and Fundamentalism were not an option for him, and he knew they were not tenable for educated men and women generally. So he was led to give a good deal of thought to the reality and problem of Revelation.

What the precise influences on him were, is unclear. Miss Dorothy Emmet, writing on "The Philosopher" in the official biography by Iremonger, thought that Temple was possibly indebted to Father Herbert Kelly, S.S.M. in relation to his criticism of "revelation in propositions." Father Kelly however disclaimed the credit, giving it rather "to the greater portion of Christian history."

Miss Emmet does say that Temple "has put the view of 'revelation

[1]These fine lines are from the translation of the Jerusalem Bible. The translation of the earlier passages is eclectic and individual, but is influenced by Temple's rendering in his *Readings in St. John's Gospel.*

in events' with a clarity which has caused it to make its mark in contemporary theology." And it is in *Nature, Man and God* that he developed, apparently for the first time, this theory and emphasis. Thereafter in occasional lectures and in various small volumes he reiterates the view that the *locus* of Revelation is in acts or events, not in the words of Scripture or in propositions of any sort.

Temple recognized that in this view he was going against the traditional doctrine of Christendom, Roman Catholic as well as Protestant. This doctrine has been "that the Book itself is the revelation rather than that it contains the record of it."

Temple breaks decisively with this outlook.

> *What we find in the Old Testament Scriptures is not mainly, if at all, authoritative declarations of theological doctrine, but living apprehension of a living process wherein those whose minds are enlightened by divine communion can discern in part the purposive activity of God.*
>
> *Its essence (i.e. of revelation) is intercourse of mind and event, not the communication of doctrine distilled from that intercourse. The contrary opinion, which has so long held the field, is due to the false estimate of conceptual thinking held by Greek and Scholastic and Cartesian philosophers.* [1]

The crown, of course, of this view, and its principal confirmation, is the Incarnation — the coming of God into the world in the person of Jesus the Christ. In this climactic Event we have the fullness of revelation. "He that hath seen Me, hath seen the Father."

Here as always, Temple is strong and very convincing. His position as far as I know, has drawn little criticism. It seems to me, however, that there are two aspects to the Archbishop's construction that raise questions.

The first aspect concerns the Bible and the role of words in relation to the Word. I dealt with this in the small book that Temple invited me to write as soon as he was enthroned as Archbishop of Canterbury. He himself selected the title *The Trinity and Christian Devotion* and projected the work as the Archbishop of Canterbury's Lent Book for 1946. It was produced and published as Archbishop Temple's Lent Book. The Presiding Bishop of the American Episcopal Church, Dr. Henry St. George Tucker, picked the work up as his "Lenten Book" for the same year — the only time in history there has been such a joint selection. But unfortunately the Archbishop did not live to see the book he had so kindly and expectantly sponsored.

In *The Trinity and Christian Devotion* I develop a position on Revelation in relation to the Bible that comes in between Temple's construction and the older, literalist view common to both Catholic and Protestant orthodoxy. There have of course been various efforts to find middle ground of this sort, quite apart from Temple.

Luther was a bold, perhaps a brash pioneer, with his denigration of the Epistle of James and his attractive characterization of the Bible as the cradle in which the Christ is suspended for our knowledge and salvation. Coleridge put forward the mediating view that the Bible

---

[1] *Nature, Man and God*, pp. 312, 316

is inspired because there is more in it that finds me than in any other book. Karl Barth in his earlier phase or phases espoused a middle view of revelation, though it is one that it is not easy to pin down. Somehow one knew that the Word was addressing him in Scripture or through preaching. This was the work of the Spirit: and indeed Barth grounded, or tried to ground, the doctrine of the Trinity exclusively on the reality and fulness of Divine revelation.

The obscurity and difficulty of this approach may account for the fact that Barth as a systematic theologian moved progressively toward a more specific and inclusive Biblicism, emphasizing the unique, organic relation between the Word and the words of Holy Scripture.

In my wrestling with this important issue in the Temple Lent Book, *The Trinity and Christian Devotion,* I took the position that between the deeds of God and the acceptance of the revelation given as true by enlightened minds (this is Temple's version of revelation) there is an intermediate moment or phase of revelation — the written moment which is a moment of recording and at the same time interpreting.

Thus in properly analysing revelation we find three distinct yet interrelated moments: (a) specific revelatory acts of God in history; (b) a definite though not mechanical or magical calling and inspiring of the Biblical writers to record and interpret the Divine activity in the events of history; and (c) an illumination of our hearts and minds so that this revelation lays hold on us and compels our Yea of faith.

The following diagram brings out clearly the anatomy of revelation:

As Perceived by Man	As Given by God
A. Event	Activity
B. Record	Inspiration
C. Apprehension	Illumination

William, to my deep regret, did not live to see my Trinity book in print. I believe that he would have been pleased with it and I think he would have seen and approved my emendation of his definition and location of revelation.

The second question which the Archbishop's confident construct in *Nature, Man and God* raises is that of the universality of revelation. God, he thinks and asserts dogmatically, must be revealed in all existence and all occurrences; or he is revealed nowhere.. Only if He is revealed in the rising of the sun in the sky can he be revealed in the rising of a Son of Man from the dead. Only if He chooses all men for His own can He choose any at all.

The premise here is the rational coherence of the world. We are under the shadow of Edward Caird. Temple's position is at the antipodes of Calvin and the Reformation; it would seem also of St. Paul.

I speak with hesitancy and I may be wrong. I find however that this view of things merges revelation and reason too flatly. It takes in too much territory and assumes much too much knowledge on the part of frail, finite man.

The Bible theologian, I believe, must step in here and correct the monistic philosopher.

109

There are a number of other important ideas that Temple either stresses or that are implicit in his thought and writings. We shall do well to list and note some of these but leave the matter at that point. He was a man of ideas and to canvas them at all thoroughly and systematically would take a volume in itself and a large one at that. I do believe that the round-up of this chapter affords a useful introduction to the ideas of Temple. It should also supplement helpfully the monograph of Miss Dorothy Emmet on *The Philosopher* which Dean Iremonger called on her to contribute to his official Life of the Archbishop.

A very basic idea of Temple that is implicit rather than explicit but should be brought out, is his conception of salvation. For him the Gospel means not a transaction but a transformation; it is the power of God unto life, in the individual and in society.

Another idea that the Archbishop came to see as central and to stress a great deal is the nature and profundity of sin. He saw sins as correlated with Sin, a basic principle. Here he is very orthodox, but he illuminates ancient orthodoxy by a modern insight that appears highly original.

Sin is essentially self-centeredness; and this lies at the heart of experience and individual existence. It is original precisely in the manner of original sin in the classical Christian scheme.

Each of us as a baby from the first moment of sight makes himself the center of the world as regards bodily vision. I am the center of the world I see, and this is always the case.

The same thing is true of our mental and spiritual vision, at first. We are governed entirely by pleasure and pain; each of us is the center of his own world. But this is to have things out of joint: I am not the center of the world or the standard of value. God is. "In other words, from the beginning I put myself in God's place. This is my original sin."

This sinful state does not carry with it guilt. But the state I am born in will bring disaster on me and those around me unless I can escape from it.

Education may help, especially if it leads me into devotion to truth and beauty. But complete deliverance can come only if something wins my heart's devotion, my will's total allegiance. This only the love of God revealed by Christ in His Life and Death can accomplish.

In *Nature, Man and God* the Archbishop gets into the tricky problem of the Fall of man and this too he handles in an original way.

The animal is self-centered, too, but not self-assertive. Man however, when his consciousness advances to full self-conciousness, adds self-assertion to self-centeredness. His inevitable bias is toward what is good for self. Selfishness is built in as man's native condition, with severe and appalling consequences since we are members one of another in point of influence.

Actual human society is to a large extent, though never completely, a network of competing selfishnesses, all kept in check by each one's fear of the others, which Glaucon describes in Plato's **Republic** *and which Hobbes made the basis of his political philosophy in the* **Leviathan.**

Was this necessary? Ought we to say that God made man selfish, predestined him to sin?

Temple says, No; it was not absolutely necessary that this fallen condition should have come to pass. But, he adds, it was "too probable not to happen." God so created the world that man was likely to sin; he was more likely to fall than to ascend with the advent of moral self-consciousness.

Temple gave a good deal of thought to a problem that is actually closely related to sin and the Fall, though this is seldom recognized in our age of over-emphasis on freedom. He valued freedom very highly, as every Christian must. But he thought it necessary to define it carefully, in this following the examples of the Greeks, St. Paul, and the St. Augustine.

For Temple any identification of freedom with indeterminism must be dismissed at once. Indeterminism means without bounds and would be the destruction of morality.

> Freedom is not absence of determination; it is spiritual determination, as distinct from mechanical or even organic, determination. It is determination by what seems good as contrasted with determination by irresistible compulsion.

This is thoroughly scriptural; its affinity with Paul's "freedom wherewith Christ has made us free" is evident. Christianity until recent liberal times has been more concerned with final freedom than with initial freedom.

What then of initial freedom? Temple is fully aware of the problem and has an acute solution. He shies away from fixing on acts of choice as the *locus* of freedom. This merely throws one into indeterminism as the meaning of freedom, which leads to hopeless confusion.

The key to clarity respecting the problem and to a solution is in transference from freedom of choice to freedom of thought, or from action to attention. The mind has the capacity to form free ideas, apart from any corresponding external objects. It is by these ideas that connections in experience are traced and values discovered with the power to unify and to compel attention. Through such attention the personality becomes integrated.

It is the personality with its capacity for the constant direction of attention that is the *locus* of freedom rather than moments of choice and action. This means that self-determination in the act of moral choice is as a rule greatest when reflection is possible, least when immediate action has to be taken.

> In most cases the main decision is not made then; it is made by the discipline or non-discipline of the life of thought or imagination, which determines the general quality of character and consequently also the actions which will be done in the various combinations that arise.

Against the background of this analysis, Temple rightly observes that St. Paul's counsel is shown in its profound significance: "Whatsoever things are true, whatsoever things are noble, whatsoever things are righteous, whatsoever things are pure, whatsoever things are lovely, whatsoever things are of good report, if there be any virtue, and if there be any praise, occupy your mind with these things."

CHAPTER EIGHT

THE FRIEND

I have saved to the end what I regard as one of the most important aspects of William Temple and this book, which is a biography but is also intended as a study of his mind, soul, and personality.

William Ebor. et Cantuar. was by common consent a very great man, one of the Titans of his age. He was certainly the greatest English Churchman of this century and he was generally considered to be the leading Christian and Christian statesman of the period of the World Wars. It is no disparagement of Bishop Charles Brent, a shining light of the American Episcopal House of Bishops, who was the first President of the World Conference on Faith and Order, to say that Archbishop Temple was the dominating figure of the nascent Ecumenical Movement. A new and unexpected but thrilling phase of this movement came into being with the rise to prominence and power of another prophet-soul, Pope John XXIII.

In the providence of God it was not given that those two, William, the English Primate, and John, the Roman Pontiff, were to meet. Nonetheless, they were kindred spirits. William would have been especially pleased by Archbishop Roncalli's choice of John to be his new and Papal name.

There have been a fair number of books written about Temple, including several doctoral dissertations on his thought and a volume of his "Canterbury Letters." In all of them, however, there is nothing, so far as I am aware, that is very satisfactory about the Friend. Nor have I seen anything at all penetrating or significant about the emotional side of William, at least as an adult and a mature man.

Dean Iremonger, soon after he began his arduous labor on the official *Life*, wrote me to request any material I had on the Archbishop, including letters. He remarked that he had a vast mine of material on Temple the intellectual but little on the emotional and psychological side of the person.

This remark, if I remember correctly, was in a second letter after I had replied by outlining the material I had. Anyway I complied with the Dean's request, sending him copies of all my letters from Temple, the relevant portions of the Diary I kept in 1935 and 1937, and a basic article on the man and the Archbishop I had done at the request of the American periodical *Christendom* at the time of his Canterbury enthronement.

Lambeth Palace, S.E.
Dec: 17. 1943

My very dear Charles,
I am immensely interested to know of your
change from academic to parochial life.
It must have cost you rather a wrench;
but on balance I am very glad of it.
One gets the impression that there is in
the American Church too little of this
interchange between the two; and
incidentally, as no Professor is ever
elected to a See, the American episcopate
is rather lacking in theological learning.
We are running very low here in that
respect, and I must try to secure
that some early appointments are
of theologians. Headlam is old and
Kirk is pernickety — so we need a
vigourous and level-headed scholar
very badly.
For yourself I am sure it will be good.

You are too human to remain academic all your life, and you are too much interested in theology to let other concerns completely stop your intellectual work. On the whole it will gain in quality from the fuller human contacts. May you have every blessing in it.

This is near the season when we first met eight years ago and I remember the sight of you inside the cage of the lift that led to n from my room in the College of Preachers. It is not often that a friendship has so marked a birth day as ours has. And happily your visit to England two years later and our meeting in Amsterdam two years after that have spaced out the time so that it has never seemed intolerably long since we last talked together. But I heartily look forward to the next opportunity.

With my best love, and with hearty greetings to you all

Yours v. affectly
William Cantuar

As I had gone to quite a bit of trouble, and knew also that my material was unique and designed by its nature to be of special value to a thorough biographer, I was keenly disappointed to find when the big book came out that nothing from me had been used. Also I could not feel that Dean Iremonger had come to grips with the emotive and affectional side of his heroic subject who in life set so much store by friendship and had so many friends, not a few of whom — Charles Gore for instance — must have been on an intimate footing with him.

Iremonger has one page in which he deals sparingly and somewhat primly with this subject, and incidentally falls into what I knew was error. This is the relevant passage:

> To write of his personal friendships is more difficult. By no conscious effort, but because it was natural for him to do so, he showed to each and all of those with whom he had relations the same tenderness, charity, and understanding, and so gathered a host of friends. Yet to many he remained oddly remote. While some would claim an intimacy with him he himself might have hesitated to admit, to others he seemed either a man without close friends or one whom it was not easy to know. If an attempt be made to account for his apparent remoteness, two suggestions may be hazarded: one (which could be reenforced by the complaint sometimes made of the lack of emotion in his preaching) that the emotional side of his nature did not develop *pari passu* with his intellect — and here perhaps is the one slight complication in his personality — the other that his friends' views of human relationships were more restricted than his own. The almost intellectual affection he bestowed on all alike was so obviously sincere as to enlarge the hearts of any who came under his influence, but it did not satisfy the desire of those — and they are not a few — who wish to possess their friends. He held back from nobody what he could offer of himself, and all that each could gain from contact with him, each was entitled to have and to keep. But he himself remained inappropriable. The world of men was too wide, and the claims on his active sympathy too diverse, for any such embarrassing occupation of his whole personality as would have satisfied the more exacting of his friends. [1]

The temptation is strong to comment on this extraordinary passage, which is more imaginative than realistic. The Dean apparently knew William well, in his own mind, but the man he describes — rather airily and hypothetically it must be admitted — bears little resemblance to the man whom I knew and whom many others must have known.

Never mind — let the passage stand intact; and then let the reader come back to it when he has finished the present chapter and render to himself his own verdict respecting it.

I purpose in this final chapter to tell a story — the true story of my friendship with an illustrious but very human and lovable person — William Ebor. et Cantuar. Yes, this Prince of the Church (though he would never have used or even thought such a phrase), this giant intellect, this servant of God and his fellow human beings who I believe had in rich measure the attributes of the Saint — this man was my special and intimate Friend.

There can be no question of my merely claiming something or pre-

[1] pp. 499-500

suming upon and enlarging out of desire and imagination an ordinary friendly relationship. The words and actions that will count in this narrative will be those of the Archbishop himself, either directly or as corroborating and underwriting a personal account taken from a Diary kept in some detail in 1935 and 1937. Basic to what I fully realize is a story extraordinary is the 30 letters I have from His Grace, written over the last 9 years of his life. All but four are handwritten. Reference has already been made in this book to two or three of these letters, and others will appear in due course in the tale about to unfold.

At the outset it is important for one point to be crystal-clear. The initiative in this friendship at the beginning was the Archbishop's. It was an initiative as pronounced as that of the Divine Will in prevenient Grace, though of course a cooperative element on my part was never lacking. I came in time to love this magnificent human being very much and to cherish with my whole heart a relationship so privileged. But it was not an event I could or would even have dreamed of, on my own initiative.

For me the experience was a tremendous one, absurdly improbable but thrillingly true. At the time, as I went home at the end of the four-day Conference in 1935 at the College of Preachers, Washington, I felt like a character in a most implausible romance. I cannot of course even comment on his feelings or thoughts, but the beautiful part was and is that he remained faithful and apparently unaltered in feeling for 9 years, right up to his death. This was a big surprise to some prelates with whom I was friendly and who expected that the great Man would presently drop me.

The story begins really at Oxford. I was up for 7 terms and in England steadily for two and a half years, except for some of the vacations. I met and talked with an unusual assortment of English theologians, for I was doing my doctoral dissertation on the doctrine of the Trinity and I was eager to collect as many opinions as I could.

I first encountered the Archbishop at Oxford but as an attendant all 8 nights at his mission in St. Mary's University Church. I did one morning set out to interview him, as he was open each morning for personal conferences. When I found a queue of undergraduates half a block long waiting their turns, I abandoned this idea, feeling it was not fair to them. One afternoon however as I was walking in the Parks, I encountered him walking and conversing with an undergraduate.

It was in December, 1935 that Temple visited for the second time the United States. His lecture tour began with a so-called all-star conference of younger theologians and rectors arranged for him. Future leadership was more or less the idea. I was lucky enough to be a member of this Conference.

It began Monday evening the 9th. Temple lectured for an hour on Church and State, without a note. The lecture was preceded, as was customary at the College of Preachers, by a formal signing of the College Register. We filed up one by one to do this, with Temple seated near by.

After the lecture there was an opportunity to speak to His Grace. I did so, saying that we had never met but that I felt as if I knew him, having heard him 8 times at St. Mary's and having passed him walking in the Parks, with our sleeves practically brushing. He was very cordial and said, "As soon as I saw you I was sure that I had seen you somewhere before."

On Tuesday he lectured in the morning and there was a discussion session before luncheon. The afternoon was free but Evensong came at 6:00. After dinner and coffee and informal talk, there was Compline. Following this Service, several men gathered around the Archbishop talking with him for a brief time. I stood with this group for a moment, not saying anything. As he drew away, to go toward the elevator and his suite in the central Tower, he spoke to me particularly and putting his arm through mine, asked me to come up to his room with him for awhile.

I of course went with him and we talked for perhaps 25 minutes. There was nothing very remarkable about the conversation, but the time passed quickly. He bade me goodnight cordially, even affectionately, saying "My dear" a couple of times. I was not sure that he had remembered my name."

(So far I have followed my Diary meticulously. Now I must condense a bit.)

On Wednesday afternoon the Archbishop decided that he would be glad to take a drive on the Virginia side. I took him out by the Lincoln Memorial and Arlington Cemetery, drove through Alexandria and along the River Boulevard to Mt. Vernon, though we did not have time to go in. Then we came back by the Seminary for a cup of tea and a very brief visit with my wife and two-year old daughter, Harriet, whom he always referred to in letters as Henrietta.

On Thursday the Archbishop was extremely busy. He doubled up on his lectures in order to go to Princeton early Friday morning to receive an Honorary Degree. He was out for all meals. I feared I should have no further chance to see him. But after Evensong he asked me when I was leaving and invited me to drop up to the Tower Room at 10:15. (After the Evening Lecture and discussion, he said, he had to go over to Bishop Freeman's to see Mrs. Temple.)

At 10:15 I went up to his suite, expressing doubt that I should stay, knowing how tired he must be after so fiendish a day. He insisted that I remain and again we talked for 20 or 25 minutes. In the course of our conversation (I again quote from my Diary), I expressed my sense of privilege and my gratitude for the favor he had shown me. He expressed in turn his pleasure and sense of close friendship: the other evening I had not been in the room 10 minutes, he said, when he felt that he had known me for years. So it ended, and on parting he embraced me most affectionately.

My Diary then reads: "To me, who had never embraced or been embraced by a male not a kinsman and who had experience of very intimate friendship with men only to a very limited extent, it is not strange that all this seemed more like a novel than life and that I had to pinch myself riding home to make sure I was not dreaming."

This material went to Dean Iremonger and he was evidently disturbed by it, for after he had finished his *Life* he wrote me again. He had noticed, he said, that I spoke of Temple embracing me. He imagined, he went on, that perhaps we used the word differently over here and

115

that I meant he had put his hand on my shoulder or something of that sort.

Unfortunately, as I now see it, I allowed myself to be provoked. I was already hurt that the Dean had used none of my material and had not even mentioned me in the *Life* of the great man. So instead of writing back mildly and getting into a dialogue and learning something, as I would certainly do now, I wrote back snappishly and informed him that there was no difference in our American use of the word "embrace" and that it meant in my Diary entries exactly what it said. That of course ended the correspondence.

The simple truth was that William was a very loving and affectionate person. He once said, according to Canon A.E. Baker, that he envied a dog the privilege he enjoys of showing his affection without anyone thinking he is making a fool out of himself. He knew himself thoroughly and as in all things moved effortlessly, spontaneously (unless deliberation was indicated), and self-confidently. What he did that Thursday night as we said Farewell was to throw his arms around me and kiss me on the mouth. It was natural to him and I am certain entirely a pure action. In 1937 when I visited him it became natural to me.

When we get there and to Edinburgh, I shall quote the one letter he wrote me in which the matter is mentioned. I believe that I did not send this letter to Iremonger, being afraid that in some way it might reflect upon my great Friend.

The first letter I received from the Archbishop (he was an inveterate letter-writer, as any reader of Iremonger will realize) came just before Christmas. It is dated Dec: 20 1935 and was written from the home of Willard L. Sperry, Dean of the Harvard Divinity School and one of the first American Rhodes Scholars. This letter is fundamental, for it is the first objective indication of his side, it illustrates the extent of his initiative, and it set the tone of the corrrespondence that was to follow over the years. The whole letter follows.

> 11 Francis Avenue
> Cambridge,
> Massachusetts

Dec:20. 1935

My dear Charles, (seu Charlie libentius audis),
(I hope you will forgive this familiarity)

I want to send you a line of greeting for Christmas, and take advantage of a lucid interval for the purpose. This place is less exacting in its demands than Washington, or than New York where I preached three sermons on Sunday and delivered five addresses on Monday. But it has been pretty strenuous all the same.

I don't suppose I shall enjoy any part of my programme so much as the days at the College of Preachers; and of that time the best was the opportunity of making friends with you. We must some how keep in touch with each other — which means among other things that you must visit us in England.

If you are ever coming over or will be arriving by about

116

Easter, let me know in good time in case I could fix up an arrangement for you to talk to my "School for Clergy" which is held at Scarborough each year for all four days soon after Easter. That would be great fun.

Please give my most cordial greetings to your wife, whose parents I was delighted to meet here after my first Noble Lecture: — and my best love to your absurd self!

We go on Monday to Bishop Perry at Providence.

May all blessings be with you at Christmas and through the new year.

Yours most affectly
William Ebor:

My next communication was from Presiding Bishop James DeWolf Perry's home in Providence, Rhode Island. It was a handsome, inscribed Photograph of the Archbishop and a Christmas greeting written on notepaper headed Bishop's House, Providence.

From Indianapolis (where he gave 4 addresses to students assembled for the Twelfth Quadrennial Student Volunteer Convention[1]) I received a postcard postmarked December 30. It told me that my new Friend was sailing on the Europa at midnight on January 10, after having dined that evening with the New York Pilgrims.

William's next letter was from Bishopthorpe under date of January 26, 1936. It contains a couple of reactions to famous Americans and a significant account of the "waste" done to his huge body by the Marathon schedule of his American tour. It is no wonder he went home in a *collapsible* condition and was quite ill. This letter also reveals Temple's feeling for King Geoge V. It follows in full.

Bishopthorpe,
York

January 26, 1936

My dear Charles,

I read those articles, which you sent, with immense interest; your own on J.D. (Jefferson Davis) was all new to me, for I really knew nothing about him. I did not know he was anything like so talented as you describe him. The other certainly gave me a new and higher, conception of Jefferson. From the facts cited, it is clear that this conception is right. But it departs a good deal from the legend, doesn't it?

About two days before starting for home I caught, at Chicago, the father and mother of all colds. I had for two days to force a voice through a nearly solid throat, which of course made it worse. So I was rather collapsible on the voyage. Then the wretched thing got into the antrum (a cavity in one's cheek-bone) from which it is apparently most important that it should be expelled — which has not quite happened yet. So I have had to lie low. But I had left the days free for overtaking arrears, so there is little harm done.

---

[1]The writer attended what must have been the 9th of these Conventions at Indianapolis in 1923. Here he met and talked with the famous war Padre, "Woodbine Willie" G.S. Studdert Kennedy.

117

We are overwhelmed with sorrow at the death of the King — who ideally filled the place our system gives to the monarch — simple, personally quite modest, utterly straight and reliable, with sound judgement that sprang from a sympathy with the people amounting to a unity of mind with them. I go to Windsor tomorrow to take part in the funeral service on Tuesday. You may be interested to know that I sent to Lord Wigram (his Secretary) your story about the man who had said of his broadcast that it couldn't be the King; and on getting home found a message from him that the King was delighted with the story.

My warmest remembrances to your wife — and to Henrietta,

Yours v. affectly
William Ebor:

My next Letter, #4, was a typed letter under the date of 20 March, 1936 brought to me by the Rev. Brian Green, well known Anglican Evangelist and Missioner, and introducing and commending him cordially. I got to know Bryan (I believe the correct spelling) quite well, engaged him for a short mission at All Saints', Chevy Chase several years later, and mention him in my book *Communism and Christ,* along with Billy Graham and Oral Roberts in a section headed "Religious Revival." This letter was in a black-bordered envelope.

Letter #5 did not come until 8 months later, but it was a fat one, was filled with affection, and contains several comments on world affairs. In this letter he addresses me for the first time as "My very dear Charles." Its full text deserves to be spread on the record.

Bishopthorpe,
York.

November 27, 1936

My very dear Charles,

Though quite delighted to hear from you, I was annoyed when your letter came, because it was so much in my mind to write to you and I hoped my letter would reach you before you wrote again. But don't ever delay a letter for fear of causing a similar annoyance.

That tercentenary at Harvard must have been a splendid gathering. All accounts I have heard of it make a fine impression of a really worthy commemoration. I am so glad you met some Oxford friends there.

I don't see the J.T.S. (Journal of Theological Studies). Of course one ought to watch it, but time is limited. I try to follow *Mind* a little, and have not time for more specialist periodicals. So do send me a print of your article on Origen if you have one to spare.

Your election must have been a great thrill. I had a letter from a friend staying in New Hampshire, written the day before the vote, in which he said that the only point of agreement among the people whom he met was that it would be a very near thing! I wonder how far that view was general.

We go on, over here, in a rather ineffectual drift in face of a series of critical events in Europe. It is impossible to ascertain the truth — e.g. about attacks on religion (as distinct from clericalism) in Spain, or an Italian occupation of Majorca, or the real contents of the German-Japanese pact, or the meaning of the new Russian constitution. All that is certain is that the hope of a moral regulation of international affairs has suffered a great set back during the past year. A great many of our best folk have swung over to absolute pacifism, which is, I am convinced, a blunder, if presented as a general Christian doctrine, though it may well be an individual vocation.

I am very thankful to think that even if a conflagration breaks out in Europe, your country will not be too badly scorched, and even though we have an eclipse of civilisation, as we may, you will still have the light with which to kindle it again. For you are not as yet exposed to aerial bombardment! I don't think the horror is coming here; but a small turn of events might bring it.

I become more and more impressed by Reinhold Niebuhr as a man who is really thinking about realities.

Well, well. When this reaches you, it will be just about a year since we met at Washington. I dreadfully want to see you again. Yet I hope your coming here will not be in 1937, for the two World Conferences ("Church State and Community" and "Faith and Order") will consume all my time, and I shall have no leisure for friends. Anyhow, when you are coming, let us try at least to fix well in advance a time for you to pay a little visit here, when I will try to be relatively free from engagements.

My warmest rememberances to your wife and to Henrietta — and best love to yourself.

Bless you, my dear.

Yours affectly

William Ebor:

Letter #6 is especially interesting because it is written on stationery headed Chatsworth, Bakewell. It is dated Jan: 8. 1937. (This was William's dating style.) Chatsworth is the famed principal seat of the Dukes of Devonshire, to whom he was related through his Mother. He makes no reference to them or to Chatsworth, though the letter is a long one — more than 3 pages. He talks mostly about the Abdication of Edward VIII, the reactions in England, something Baldwin said in Privy Council about London versus the rest of the country politically, the reactions to Archbishop Lang's broadcast and his own remarks (which drew about 50 letters, one containing a thank-offering of 100 guineas), and Press exaggerations both in Britain and America. Of Edward he says: "The real anxiety is — what will become of the Duke of Windsor? The prospect of steady deterioration is sadly probable: and he had really fine qualities."

This letter starts out with a reference to Edinburgh and the prospect of my being there; so I shall quote the opening paragraph of this missive.

> *It is thrilling to think that you may be coming over to Edinburgh; we can surely get some good times for talks there if you come. But you must come to Bishopthorpe some time too. I shall have some Edinburgh folk for the Sunday just before it starts, and if you can't fix a time sooner you must come then.*

The next letter, #7 is dated April 19. 1937. It is short and is principally about fixing a date (July 31 - August 2) for me to come to Bishopthorpe. He then says: "I hope you won't think me an interfering busybody for having asked that you should be allotted to the Hostel in Edinburgh where I expect to be, and several of the officers and Committees of the Conference. I added that I thought you would be ready to 'fag' for us in a variety of ways."

Letter #8 (June 29, 1937) is just a note to catch me before I left and to reiterate that he is expecting me for the week-end July 31 to August 2. And he repeats an invitation to my wife if she is coming, too.

I am in London now, staying at the Authors Club on Whitehall Place as the guest of Retired Bishop Julius W. Atwood. William had seen "Uncle Bish," as this Friend was known, and had learned that I was going to Oxford on July 24 (his letter "As from Bishopthorpe" was dated July 23).

This Letter, #9, he writes to tell me has to leave Oxford to go home the next morning but will be back in London the 28 and 29th. He hopes we shall meet but in any case can I come to Bishopthorpe on Friday instead of Saturday. "We should get some talk before the nobs arrive next day, though I should have to leave you a good deal alone as there is a lot to finish off. But you would not be in the least in the way!"

He then adds: "By the way I have told the Minster folk that you will act as my chaplain and carry my cross that day (Sunday) — I hope you don't mind! It is splendid to think of seeing you."

We must now suspend letters and try to tell the exciting story of my stay at Bishopthorpe with the Archbishop and Mrs. Temple, followed by the trip to Edinburgh with him and the 16 days of the World Conference on Faith and Order. My source will be a copious Diary I kept at this time. I shall set down only what is documented in this written record plus the first letter His Grace wrote me after the Conference, the importance of which will be clear when it is read.

On Wednesday, July 28 I attended the Archbishop of Canterbury's Reception in the Lambeth Garden for Oxford and Edinburgh Delegates. It was a large affair and there were long lines of people waiting to be received by the Archbishop. In the line some 20 feet from me I spied William Ebor. and Mrs. Temple. I advanced and greeted him, and he me; then I met Mrs. Temple. Later he and I brought tea to Mrs. Temple, Mrs. Harper Sibley (prominent Churchwoman from Rochester, N.Y.) whom I reintroduced to him, and a Mrs. Stebbins, he taking my arm and saying, Come along Charles, we'll get the tea.

As I was leaving, well toward the end of the affair, and was paying my farewell respects to the Archbishop of Canterbury, William advanced and said, "Your Grace, I hope you'll not only meet this man, but get to know him." This resulted in a minute's more conversation with Cosmo Cantuar. When we got around to Oxford and my dissertation on the Trinity, he put on a long face, shook his head disbelievingly, and said, "Dear me!"

On Friday, July 30 I got out of London on the 11:16 non-stop train to York. Temple's chauffeur met me and took me immediately to Bishopthorpe and the Palace. His Grace came down very soon and showed me about within and without the Palace for perhaps an hour. "He was most cordial and friendly." (Diary) Then came tea, with Dean and Mrs. Brillioth (she very blond and the daughter of the great Archbishop Soderblum of Sweden). They had stopped off en route to Edinburgh. Later an Archdeacon Denyer of Ceylon came in, and I walked and talked with him for awhile, before His Grace took him away, having first been taken away himself by Mrs. Temple.

At dinner Mrs. Temple was not present, but a Miss Sinker, one of the Secretaries was. After dinner the Archbishop and I went over the Message of the Oxford Conference, which he had largely written before he had to leave. I had the final text, so we were able to note the changes made in his draft, which were not many. Mrs. Temple came in for a short time with Jock their 8-year old Scottie, with whom I made friends readily.

Then William and I went into the semi-private study or library and talked awhile longer, after he had stopped to dash off a letter to The Church Times. "It was exactly as before: he was very affectionate and embraced me warmly as we parted for the night. Quite an experience." (Verbatim from Diary)

Saturday the 31st passed uneventfully. I was alone most of the morning and read in great gulps volume I of Bishop Bell's *Life* of Randall Davidson. Lang's portrait I noted was not in the Dining Hall. I was fascinated by the portraits in that large Room, with its magnificent ancient Table, of all the Archbishops of York from Cardinal Wolsey through the 19th century. I studied them at length and found that one could readily place them in their respective centuries from observing their garb and faces.

I walked about the Village and visited the site of the Old Parish Church. The Archbishop told me that he had given the Vicar a Sunday evening off as he was sure I should be glad to preach at Evensong. Of course I did not have to have my arm twisted very much. We went over his innumerable hoods and finally chose the Princeton D. Litt. for the Mattins portion of the Minster Service the next day. Altogether a delightful visit on a more or less chatty level.

In the afternoon the "bigwig" notables arrived: Pastor Bergneur, head of the French Protestants, and his wife; Presiding Bishop Perry and his wife and Bishop Parsons of California and his daughter, Harriet; and Dr. Richard Roberts, head of the United Church of Canada, and his wife. There was a fine dinner and much conversation. "But again before bed I had a time alone with His Grace, and he embraced me before we parted." (Diary)

Sunday, August 1 was a memorable day in my life. Probably never before or since have I scaled such heights of glory. I was up at 8:00 for Holy Communion in the Parish Church, with His Grace the celebrant.

121

At 10:30 Mattins in the Minster, with Presiding Bishop James De Wolf Perry the preacher. I acted as Chaplain to His Grace, bearing before him the Cross of York. Then we went to vest for the Choral Eucharist at 11:30 and a second ceremonial Procession. I was fixed up with a handsome Cope of blue and ivory, while the Archbishop was splendor itself in the Cloth of Gold vestments given the Archbishop of York by Lord Halifax.

After luncheon I slept, and at tea there were extra guests. Then came at 6:30 Evensong with the Lord Archbishop of York officiating and Professor Lowry, as he and Mrs. Temple would have it, the Preacher. In the congregation were the notables already chronicled, and according to my Diary "I was in good shape, hardly nervous at all, and had my sufficient reward as His Grace and I walked out after the Service, still in vestments and he said, Thank you very much, my dear!"

After dinner the ladies retired early with some of the male guests. Bishop Perry, Dr. Roberts, the Archbishop and I sat up talking till 11:00, principally about ghosts and psychic phenomena.

They all believe in a good deal along this line, and have had many unusual experiences. Again, after the other two had departed for bed, His Grace and I had a short time together. He was most tender and affectionate and we embraced repeatedly.

The next day, Monday, 8 of the Bishopthorpe party, including the Archbishop and myself, entrained at 10:40 a.m. for Edinburgh, traveling in a saloon. Arriving at Edinburgh and proceeding to Cowan House, we two had tea together, when in honor of the occasion, he said, he broke over and had some cake with his tea. This was the eve of the great World Conference.

I must now compress my story of a friendship. I have already written of the Archbishop's sermon at the opening Service in St. Giles Cathedral and of his tremendous ministry of leadership and friendship reaching out to all members of the Conference, especially those living at Cowan House, during the 16 days of the Conference. I was fortunate enough to be made secretary of a sub-section of Section I on *Grace*. This gave me extra work and responsibility. Then there was a great deal going on, with hundreds of fascinating people from all continents. I struck up a warm friendship with Bishop and Mrs. Whitehead (he was the older brother of the renowned philosopher under whom I had studied, (Alfred North Whitehead); and they took me to see New Battle Abbey and to tea with the Alec Fraziers.

The Marquis of Lothian, soon to be Ambassador to the United States, had just inherited the title and five places. One was New Battle Abbey near Dalkeith where we went. He had walked out of it, leaving it to Scotland. This house dated from 1140, was situated on the river Esk, had a mighty and unique beech tree 430 years old, a lovely formal garden, a fantastic library, 96 rooms, and over 500 paintings by great masters. One, the original Van Dyke of Charles I, was insured for L60,000 and a Botticelli in the private Chapel was insured for L10,000. I saw Chinese wall paper 240 years old, Robert Bruce's saddle, and the font in which Mary Queen of Scots was baptized.

To return to William Ebor. and our relationship, I realized of course that things had to settle down and we could not stay on the level of recent days. I think, as I read my Diary anew and reflect back on that time, that he may well have had some sober second thoughts and realized the need of care and prudence. For a period I was depressed and felt that he was, what some people have claimed about him, cool and remote.

But this was temporary. As the Conference rolled on, and the life of Cowan House where we had our meals with it, I found that my great and good Friend was very much aware that I was around and went out of his way to check on my welfare and to let me know I was on his mind. On Saturday the 7th I noticed that he came into the Dining Room for breakfast limping. His gout had flared up. In consequence I carried out an already formed intention of sending him a basket of nice fruit, since he ate nothing else for breakfast. Also I had the chance on the bus of showing him a copy of my Oxford thesis which had just arrived from Charles Raven, the Master of Christ's College, Cambridge. It was the third copy of this massive document and had reposed in Charles' study for nearly 5 years.

As the days passed, His Grace would take a seat by me at breakfast, if it happened to be vacant, or inquire about my doings if I had missed a meal. According to my Diary on the 15th I had breakfast with him for the third day in a row. And on this evening after I had got into bed (I had caught a mean cold several days before and had not entirely thrown it off) he came by and visited with me for several minutes.

On Tuesday the 17th I record driving home with His Grace and Mrs. Temple in their car, accompanied by Dr. Garvie. I note that the Arch-Bishop in spite of great weariness (he had not got to bed till 2:00 a.m. and had had another fiendish day) was "most lovable and more demonstratively friendly to me than at some times earlier" and that Mrs. Temple also was most friendly. I had had a lengthy chat with her that morning, at the end of a long and difficult session, about her husband.

On Wednesday, August 18 — the last day of the Conference — I wrote: "Then I have said goodbye to His Grace, an hour ago, very formally, and to Mrs. Temple. But that was simply the end of a most satisfactory and happy and moving day for me personally. At breakfast I again ate by His Grace, or rather he took his seat beside me. Then I rode up with him and Mrs. Temple after breakfast. This afternoon, coming back to Cowan House after the final Service at St. Giles, I had tea with His Grace and both before and after had some time alone with him. Clearly we are exactly where we have been; no change at all except increase of the duration of friendship and in the naturalness of our expression of affection for each other. To be sure, I don't think he knows my mind any better, but I have watched him and thought much of him these past days and have grown, I know, in the deepest affection, love, and admiration for him — His dear Grace!"

That sums up pretty well the situation. I wrote him, I imagine in early September after I had got home, or on shipboard en route, expressing my feelings about the summer and its meaning to me in terms of our close relationship. I have no record of what I wrote and I assume that all my letters were destroyed after his death, if indeed he had kept them. I do remember making some reference to Plato and Shakespeare and I think I was trying to voice my sense of the strong bond of love that had arisen between us. At any rate, whatever I wrote, it evoked the following letter, written from Cambridge and a document of singular importance both for understanding Temple and for certifying my good faith in any private accounts, as in my Diaries, of what had happened between us.

This Letter, #10, is in my judgment a masterpiece. It makes clear the Archbishop's self-command and at the same time throws a bright light on his view of affection and its place in a loving relationship. I greatly treasure this letter.

As from
Bishopthorpe,
York.

Sept: 28. 1937

My dear Charles,

It was very delightful to get your letter. I suppose it must be some time now before we can meet again; but it was splendid to see so much of you this summer.

I suppose people differ very much with regard to any demonstrations of affection in friendship. It is obvious that they can be very dangerous. And there is a sort of wisdom in keeping them down. But it is a rather stingy wisdom, I think. And if the dangers are not actually threatening, they may have their place in strengthening as well as expressing what is supremely good. But I won't say more on paper. I would ask you to avoid the subject in letters. It is always possible that unauthorised eyes will see them and put any sort of construction on them.

Here I am in the midst of our Doctrinal Commission at Pembroke College, Cambridge. We hope it is going to be our last session, and it is high time, for I think we are very stale. It is like a small Edinburgh, but all Anglican. J.H. Oldham is coming down tomorrow to talk about the follow-up of Oxford and Edinburgh in this country.

I hope we shall before long see your book on the Trinity. I believe you are doing a great bit of work there. As regards the "social Trinity" of which we spoke — I think "social" does overemphasise the liberality. But I think those theologians must be right — even if the tradition started in a heretical camp — who have held that self-giving must be an eternal activity within the divine Being — not (of course) as a substitute for self-giving to what is other than God, but as the fount of it.

Well, well. Bless you, my dear: my best love —

Yours v. affectly
William Ebor:

Temple's next letter, #11, written some 3 months later, is one of the most theological in the collection. It also expresses his views on two Presiding Bishops. The new one was Henry St. George Tucker of Virginia. It seems worthwhile to publish this entire letter.

124

Bishopthorpe,
York.

December 16. 1937

My dear Charles,

Your letter, written at the anniversary of our days at the College of Preachers has just reached me, and I was much stirred by your having written just then.

I am immensely interested by all that I heard of the Convention. It must have been a very moving occasion. And I am excited by all that I hear of the new Presiding Bishop. I am personally very fond of Bishop Perry, but I have feared the influence which he allowed to Gavin, for whose intellect I have much respect though not for his judgment, and to Dunphy, for whose intellect and judgment alike I have very little respect!

I am sure you are right about Church and State. Both are of God; therefore a total separation between them must be false in principle. The Orders of Creation and of Redemption (to use the German jargon) cannot be merely disparate, if the Creator and Redeemer are One God. But whatever the true relation according to their ideal natures, in this sinful world there must always be tension, and perpetual re-adjustment; between Church and State. Erastianism (subordination of the Church to a State admittedly not perfectly Christian) and total separation, are alike poisonous.

Our own (English) relationship has merits, but is as it stands not permanently tolerable. One sees that the State should (for its own sake) acknowledge not only God but the Church, yet without controlling its spiritual life: and that the Church should inspire the State, without becoming sponsor for particular policies. But this really pre-supposes *one* Church, national and international.

Best love, and all possible good wishes for Christmas and New Year: my salaams to your wife and to "Henrietta".

Yours v. affectly
William Ebor:

Six months elapsed before another letter came from William Ebor. This Letter, #12 describes the way he viewed his book on St. John and contains some thoughts on foreign policy.

Bishopthorpe,
York

June 6. 1938

My dear Charles,

The letter which you wrote on Easter Day (bless you!) was kept waiting for me while I visited Athens (for the centenary of the English Church there). Alexandria (for the centenary of the English Chaplaincy there) Cairo (for the consecration of the new Cathedral there) and Utrecht (for the conference on the proposed World Council of Churches). So here it was with about 200 others when I got home. That is the reason for my delayed answer — together with the fact that I am deep in my book on St. John, and return to it at all possible moments to tackle a few more verses. It is a grotesque sort of book — not a commentary, nor a meditation, nor an exposition, but a setting out of what I find my mind excogitating on the occasion of reading that Gospel.

Athens and Cairo were fascinatingly interesting, though they so filled my time at Athens that we were only once on the Acropolis — for about an hour.

I think I agree with your reading of our foreign policy. The root disaster was John Simon's action and inaction over Manchuria. The failure to stop the Suez Canal to Italy in 1935 was the next.

The great blunder in 1932 (as I think) is that they concentrated on Disarmament instead of Agreement about Armaments. The latter is the vital matter, and would soon lead to the former.

Now we have to build again from the foundations, but your Secretary of State is a great encouragement.

Lots of love —

Yours v. affectly
William Ebor:

Again, six months passed before I received another letter. He is still plunging at his work on St. John and there are comments on Munich and Chamberlain. This is Letter #13.

Bishopthorpe,
York

Dec: 13. 1938

My very dear Charles,

Quite apart from the approach of Christmas, this time of yearprompts me to write to you because of our talks at the College of Preachers when we first made friends.

Since I wrote last (I think) I have fairly plunged at my book on St. John and the first instalment will be published in February. I shudder to think what the scholar-blokes will think of it. But anyhow it disowns any attempt to add to scholarship. Whether it is any use, I can't tell; but what is in it has been of use to me. In other words it has done *me* good to get it ready.

The world is in a horrible state. The cruelty of it is quite horrifying. And both Russia and Germany profess a creed which justifies this, so there is nothing to which to appeal. Personally I despair of our present Government. They seem quite horribly to lack back-bone. Chamberlain brought off a great *coup* by flying to see Hitler, but it was a last-moment escape from a hole we ought never to have been in, purchased at a fearful cost to other people. He seems to me to have clear vision between *very* narrow blinkers. That is better than a universal blur, but it is horribly dangerous.

More and more I feel that Anglo-American friendship is the one real hope.

I trust you flourish. When does the great book appear? And when do you yourself appear again on this side of the Atlantic?

Best love, Charles.

Yours v. affectly

William Ebor.

Letter #14 is a short one. It is under date of April 9. 1939. It is primarily a message of congratulations and good wishes on the arrival in March of my second son, Atherton. It contains this important observation regarding the fix the world was in:

> *What a world we live in! And of course our countries are partly to blame. A real union of all to keep the peace has been the only right or sane policy since 1918 — with readiness to stop aggression by force if necessary. But we have all thought first of our own interests if not of our own skin; so here we are.*

He goes on to say he hopes Macmillan has sent me a copy of his book on the first half of St. John. "If we don't blow up first, the second series will appear next winter." The letter concludes: "I do hope you flourish: Come over again as soon as you can."

Letter #15 was evoked by the news that I was coming to the World Conference of Christian Youth at Amsterdam. There is a salient comment, too, about St. John.

As from

Bishopthorpe,

York

April 27. 1939

My very dear Charles,

How splendid to know you will be at Amsterdam — if the world has not blown up first. When you know your plans, do let me know, in case you could come to us for a day or two first. There is a meeting of the Administrative Committee of the proposed World Council first, and I must go to that. Then I hope to be at the Leaders' Conference; I shall tell them that you will be my chaplain, and must have a room near mine! Then we will get some scraps of talk: otherwise they will keep you so busy that I shall never see you.

I suppose we couldn't cross together — ?

I must go by the night boat from Harwich on July 20 reaching Holland early on July 21. I must leave Amsterdam on July 25, whether morning or evening I don't yet know.

I am so glad you have come out of your "tunnel" into fair weather.

As regards St. John — I had to indicate my position about authorship, etc. but I don't attach any importance to my view, as I am not a real student of that problem. But, as you say, this hardly affects the rest of my book. I am so weary of dissertations on the authorship that I thought it time for someone to say: "Well, someone wrote it anyhow; let's see what he said."

Yours most affectly
William Ebor:

x On looking again at your letter, I see that it is too early for you.

In between the above Letter and the next one, the Amsterdam World Conference of Christian Youth had taken place and William and I had met for the last time. Actually I saw him three times.

I arrived on Saturday, July 22 at 9:30 a.m., as I learn from my Diary. Meetings began at 11:15 and at 4:30 I saw the Archbishop "with whom I had a delightful visit for a short time — after tea in his room." He spoke on Monday at the opening Service on Worship, a subject on which "he was as ever superb." I was presented by him, as I learn again from my Diary, to Dr. Visser t'Hooft. "He came back on the stairs at the Concertgebouw to get me, with characteristic thoughtfulness. He said: 'I want you to meet Professor Lowry. He is teaching America theology.' To my surprise t'Hooft said, Haven't we met before? and I recalled to him our Oxford Conference meeting. Later I sat beside him at lunch, got a number of names of people in Germany, and had a friendly visit."

On Tuesday evening I absented myself from the Archimandrite's address in order "to have a brief farewell visit with his Grace and to accompany him to his Boat Train. I stayed until it pulled out, waving goodbye to the dear man. We had one of the most satisfactory talks, to me, we have ever had. A good deal of politics." We moved from *Mein Kampf* to Plato to Aristotle. "His replies on Plato and, in answer to my queries, on Aristotle revealed an amazingly accurate knowledge. He always remembers the Greek. Two points stick in my mind: (a) Speaking to my point regarding democracy on the toboggan because of man, he said: That's what original sin means, that man left to himself will go the wrong way; and (b) 'The best way is for the conservatives to do the right things.' " (Diary verbatim)

There is no record of it in my Diary, But I believe that we spoke, as always, of meeting again. The outlook was somber but he was not unduly pessimistic. I was excited over my prospective trip into Germany, following the Conference, to travel about and talk and see what it was like under Hitler. William would, shortly, be off on his August holiday.

Letter #16 was not written until just before Christmas. The war has begun and it is short but filled with affection.

Bishopthorpe,
York

Dec: 19. 1939

My very dear Charles,

This is too late to bring you Christmas wishes, but it brings my heartiest good wishes for the New Year.

Your letter was enormously interesting. I wish I had been

in Germany as recently as you. Your impressions were most intriguing. Of course, in comparing 1939 with 1931 you were going back to the nadir of the great depression.

I will see what I can do about the White Paper. The reason for such strictness about the taking of printed matter out of the country is that it can so easily be marked in such a way as to carry messages in cypher.

I share your anxieties about the future, but I have no doubt about the immediate necessity of stopping Hitler.

The pressure of work involved in all the re-adjustments is enormous, and I have to keep my letters short: so best love and God bless you

Your always affectionate
William Ebor:

Letters #17 and #18 have already been cited and quoted. The reader is referred to Chapter IV.

Letter #19, written in January 1941, is about London and its people and the war damage; also about York. It follows in full:

From the
Archbishop of York
Bishopthorpe,
York.

Jan: 20. 1941

My very dear Charles,

I was, as I always am, immensely glad to hear from you. I have sent a note to Lord Halifax to tell him you exist! If you meet him, you will find him personally most charming.

I am at the moment in London, in our rooms at the Lollards Tower, which with the rest of the old part of Lambeth Palace, is still undamaged. It is 10:45 p.m. and no air-raid warning has gone as yet, so we are hoping for some quite sleep.

The London people are glorious — perfectly unflustered, and talking about bombs and araters with that *meosis* which is so great a steadier of nerves. Of course the material damage is now immense, especially since the great fire-raid. But one gets a scale of values which puts these things very low.

York has so far suffered very little. One lone raider dropped six bombs at 5:00 a.m. last Thursday morning — damaged one Church slightly, and smashed about three small houses. That is our worst so far. The Minster is quite untouched.

I have asked the publishers to send you my "Hope of a New World."

My best love.

Yours affectly
William Ebor:

Nearly a year passed before the next Letter, #20, arrived. It tells of a trip to America that did not materialize.

Bishopthorpe,
York.

December 5. 1941

My very dear Charles,

It was delightful to get your letter — of Nov: 15, written just after you had been again in the Tower Room at the College.

Life in England has been free from horrors since the end of May. In the middle of May there were two nights of "blitz" on Hull — the largest city in my diocese, and the area of destruction there is said to be the greatest of any in the country. The King and Queen, who have visited every badly bombed place, endorsed that estimate when I spent a week-end at Windsor lately.

When Van Dusen was here he pressed very hard that I should cross the Atlantic. I have always said that I cannot leave my job and my folk unless I am openly *sent*. At the moment it seemed as if this might happen, but the Abp. of C., after saying he thought it could be right for me to go, went on to speak of something which may mature here at about the time when alone I could have gone, and for which he would want me to be at hand. So "sending" became impossible.

I hope this may reach you round about Christmas; any how, all good wishes for Christmas and the New Year, and much love.

Yours affectly
William Ebor:

My first Letter from Lambeth Palace, #21, was written on May 12, 1942. He speaks of the wonderful service of his enthronement, of the bleak condition of the Palace, and a letter of his, thanking us for a food parcel which we had sent. His letter had never been received. His concluding sentence is, "I am very proud to think my Giffords are being distilled into, or over, your students!" This referred to my using *Nature, Man and God* as a text book in Apologetics.

Letter #22, dated Jan: 14. 1943, has been cited above in Chapter V . He states, "I can only write personal letters by sitting up after bedtime; so they get short. This is short. But it brings much love."

Letter #23, written in June 1943, is both interesting and important. It must be quoted in full.

June 9. 1943
Lambeth Palace, S.E.

My very dear Charles,

I am ashamed of not writing sooner to thank you for

130

sending the *Christendom* in which you wrote about me. I was in a bad patch of health when it came; I had to cancel some engagements and put off all letters that I could. I completely recovered a good while back, but have not yet worked off the accumulation. I am sorry yours was one of the more badly delayed.

And now you tell me of your father's death. He must have been a very impressive man for those who knew him well — and a source of great inspiration. You are older that I was when my father died; I was 21, and in my second year at Oxford. It gave me a curious "shelterless: feeling, and I think that would have been the same however old or mature I had been at the time. I expect you feel something like that a good deal, over and above the actual pain of separation and the empty space in life. I was very much moved by what you wrote about him.

One is a bad judge of what is said about one's self; but, for what it is worth, I thought your article about me, (barring its eulogies!) was very discerning.

Reinhold Niebuhr is over here just now and I am seeing something of him, but not as much as I should like. He is a great fellow.   It will be great when normal travel becomes possible again and you and I can meet. Can't you get sent over here on some delegation? I find it quite impossible, myself, to leave England while the war lasts.

With all my best greetings to your wife and to Harriet — and very much love to you.

Yours affectly
William Cantuar.

Letter #24, dated 22nd June 1943, is "comparatively speaking an official letter" and is typewritten. It conveys at some length an invitation to me to write The Archbishop of Canterbury's Lent Book for 1946. He suggests as a subject The Doctrine of the Trinity and the Life of Devotion. This book was written and published as *The Trinity and Christian Devotion,* but of course there was a new Primate at Lambeth and Canterbury. Temple's Lent series thus began in 1940 with the Master of Balliol's *The Two Moralities* and ended with my volume.

Letter #25, written near the end of 1943, deals with my announcement of a change from academic life to the Rectorship of All Saints', Chevy Chase. William's reaction was in contrast to that of most American prelates with whom I had talked, and the whole Letter is beautiful. It moves me deeply to reread it.

Lambeth Palace, S.E.
Dec: 17. 1943

My very dear Charles,

I am immensely interested to know of your change from academic to parochial life. It must have cost you rather a wrench; but on balance I am very glad of it. One get the impression that there is in the American Church too little of this interchange between the two; and incidentally, as no Professor is ever elected to a See, the American episcopate is rather lacking in theological learning. We are running very low here in that respect, and I must try to secure that some early appointments are of theologians. Headlam is old and Kirk is pernickety — so we need a vigourous and level headed scholar very badly.

For yourself I am sure it will be good. You are too human to remain academic all your life, and you are too much interested in theology to let other concerns completely stop your intellectual work. On the whole it will gain in quality from the fuller human contacts. May you have every blessing in it.

This is near the season when we first met eight years ago and I remember the sight of you inside the cage of the lift that led to or from my room in the College of Preachers. It is not often that a friendship has so marked a birthday as ours has. And happily your visit to England two years later and our meeting in Amsterdam two years after that have spaced out the time so that it has never seemed intolerably long since we last talked together. But I keenly look forward to the next opportunity.

With my best love, and with hearty greetings to you all

Yours v. affectly

William Cantuar:

Less than a month elapsed between the Letter just quoted and a short Missive, Letter #26, written on Jan: 10. 1944 at the Old Palace, Canterbury. He thanks me for stationery and coffee we had sent over but writes especially to call my attention to Leonard Hodgson's book *The Doctrine of the Trinity*. He praises the first three lectures but is disturbed by the criticism of his Giffords which he thinks is founded on a misunderstanding of what he said there.

Letter #27, dated March 16. 1944, expresses delight at Angus Dun's election as Bishop of Washington and the wish that we would make Washington a Primatial See. He wonders whether my move will affect writing his book and brings up Hodgson again, repeating the burden of the previous Letter. This Letter was censored but nothing was cut out.

Letter #28 is a dictated Letter concerned with being sure I am going to be able to write the Lent book. It is dated July 18, 1944 and is typewritten.

A few days later a parishioner Victor Bates returned from England bringing me a personal letter from the Archbishop dated July 26. It describes the close call Lambeth Palace has had from the flying bombs and the savage destruction produced by the blasts from nearby hits. He is pleased I am tackling the Lent book and thanks me for sending him the volume *Anglican Evangelicalism* with two Essays by myself. The last sentence reads: "I keenly look forward to the time when it may be possible to meet again." This was really my great Friend's last personal message to me. The Letter closes as nearly always, "With best love Yours v. affectly William Cantuar:"

This was Letter #29 and the last one, #30, dated October 12, 1944 (two weeks exactly before William's death) is written by a secretary, Dorothy Howell-Thomas, on behalf of the Archbishop to say that he and Canon Baker both think the outline of my proposed book exactly meets the case but want me to remember that it must not exceed 40,000 words.

This book was picked up for separate publication in the Unites States by the Presiding Bishop of the Episcopal Church, Dr. H. St. George Tucker, as his Lent book. It is the only example, I believe, of such a high-level joint selection.

I dedicated the English edition of the book to the Memory of my Father, Charles Wesley Lowry and of William Temple — Philosopher, Archbishop, Father-in-God and Friend. It shows at several points the latter's influence. It enjoyed in Great Britain and the British Commonwealth a comparative large and long-continued sale — in contrast to the United States.

I do not know what William Cantuar. would have thought of a cardinal position which it develops, namely, that man is first and foremost an appetitive creature, a being whose essence it is to desire and love — and then reason. I think that my position here coheres with the Archbishop's in *Nature, Man and God* though any resemblance was indeliberate on my part. Several English reviewers did treat my work as Augustinian in basic trend, as contrasted with the more reason-centered Thomistic position.

There is a passage dealing with devotion and what it is, deeply regarded. I wrote:

Devotion is above all devotedness of self. It is feeling within one's being the reality and knowing within one's will the force of
that devotedness, in short,
Which I account the ultimate in man;
and it is the perpetual direction and offering of this devotedness to God.

That, in actuality, is a description of the heart and soul of William Ebor. et Cantuar. Love and devotion were the mainspring of his being. True, strong, enduring devotion must flow out of Love. William's life and extraordinary career exemplify this from start to finish.

Has there been any other apostle and theologian in our time or any time who was more dominated by the conviction that God's sovereignty is the sovereignty of Love? Have we seen any more loving person?

Doubtless there could be debate and differences of opinion as to the answer to the last question. William himself, for all the consistency of the integration of his life and being around the Love of God, had a keen sense of Sin. His analysis of Sin is sharp and penetrating — also illuminating. It will stand as one of his most brilliant contributions to theology. I believe that he was essentially a once-born soul and to a marked extent throughout his pilgrimage pure and single-minded. He was pure in the sense of the Beatitude: "Blessed are the pure in heart, for they shall see God," with all the implications and ramifications of that saying.

Accordingly it is not possible to know certainly how much William learned about Sin from experience and how much his knowledge came — as one feels so often in reading Thomas Aquinas — from intuition and observation. (Thomas of course threw it all into deductive and syllogistic form, as William deliberately did not. But the kinship is there.) I must rest in the opinion the William knew Sin much less from "the bondage of corruption" than most of us, and I suspect that this was notably so in the complex territory of sex and sexuality.

In any event, there can be no question that William was a man of deep and strong affection. He was very loving, as was bound to be the case with one whose deepest soul was given in continual worship of a God who is Eternal Love. Such Love could not but permeate the whole being of the man and the person. This I believe was the key to "the emotional side of his nature." To think of this aspect of William as an almost intellectual quality uniformly bestowed is nonsense, and to suppose that he was underdeveloped emotionally shows a grave lack of insight. I do agree with his biographer the Dean that he was and remained inappropriable — if he had friends shallow enough to have undertaken such appropriation.

Finally, William was a masterful person, when all was said and done. He had been thwarted very little in his life. He had his preferences, as there must be in friendship, for man is finite. I believe that the Archbishop had some strong preferences, and that he was entitled to them.

But in concluding, as one is almost loath to do, let me invoke and bestow on him the accolade of the Masters of Friendship.

Emerson the American is the simplest, but he had the faculty of going to the heart of a thing. He says at the end of his stirring Essay on Friendship: "To have a friend is to be one." That certainly was William Temple.

Proverbs in the Old Testament has it that "there is a friend that sitcketh closer than a brother." (18:24) William certainly stuck close to his older brother Frederick; and there must have been a great love between them. At the same time, I can truthfully say that my great and beautiful Friend stuck closer to me over a period of many years, and under adverse circumstances, than most brothers.

In the First Book of Samuel we read: "Then Jonathan and David made a covenant, because he loved him as his own soul." (18:3) This covenant held despite the opportunity for jealousy on Jonathan's part. At his end, in death, David lamented him in words that are immortal:

How are the mighty fallen in the midst of the battle! O Jonathan, thou was slain in thy high places.

I am distressed for thee, my brother Jonathan: very pleasant hast thou been to me: thy love to me was wonderful, passing the love of women. (II Samuel 1: 25, 26.)

The love of women has been too meaningful in my life, and too surpassingly transcendental as well as permeable into all sides and aspects of the human nature which God has made, for me to quite echo this lovely lament. But the love that God gave me through and in William Ebor. et Cantuar. was wonderful and a holy thing. In many respects the relationship we had, and which up to the end of his life was in no way diminished, remains the great romance of a long life and a rich and varied experience.

Finally, there is a definition in Aristotle's consummate discussion of Friendship in his *Nicomachean Ethics* which is very apposite and which I believe William knew and would delight in were he able to speak. He might even have quoted it in Greek.

There is, Aristotle says, a friendship for the sake of pleasure, and there is also a friendship for the sake of utility. For these ends "even bad men may be friends of each other, or good men of bad, or one who is neither good nor bad may be a friend of any sort of person, but for their own sake clearly only good men can be friends...The truest friendship then is that of the good...for that which is without qualification good or pleasant seems to be lovable and desirable, and for each person that which is good or pleasant to him...and in loving a friend men love what is good for themselves; for the good man in becoming a friend becomes a good to his friend."

APPENDIX

A Temple Treasury:
Stories, Anecdotes, Epigrams

STORIES AND ANECDOTES

One of the Best of All the Temple Anecdotes

The occasion was a lecture to the York clergy by Dr. Bernard Clements, with the Archbishop in the Chair. After the lecture an elderly clergyman, the Rev. Mr. Shaw, proposed a vote of thanks to the lecturer and then, noting the Archbishop and perhaps carried away by his eloquence, went on thus:

"This is St. William's Day — St. William of York.
I have known four Archbishops of York named William.
There was William Thomas, some of whose descendants
are living among us. There was William Magee, who said
he would rather see England free that England sober, Then
there was William Dalrymple Maclagan, my cousin, who
ordained me. And the last and greatest and simplest of
all is William Temple."
The Archbishop arose and to everyone's delight replied,
without batting an eye: "God, who made me simple, make
me simpler yet."

1935-36 In the USA

The Archbishop related that one day as he was walking down a London Street he passed a second-hand book shop where in a window he saw in large letters this sign:

NATURE MAN and GOD
Slightly spoiled
By William Temple

When Temple told this his laugh was the loudest of all.

Temple was asked by a member of his all-star Conference of younger Priests and Theologians at the College of Preachers what he thought about the Virgin Birth.

To this query he replied, "I am the only person of my acquaintance who has no difficulty whatever with the doctrine of the Virgin Birth!" Followed by explosive laughter — his own.

In Chicago or Evanston at a large private Dinner in the home of George Craig Stewart, Bishop of Chicago and a Highland Scot by birth. (Once I met him on Prince's Street, Edinburgh, and he had just come from the haunts of his forbears. His father was a first cousin of John Brown.)

Temple was at one end of the table, Stewart at the other. Among the guests was Bishop Keeler of Minesota (who related this story to me en route to General Convention in San Francisco in 1949). Stewart got the attention of the whole table. "Your Grace," he called out, "Bishop Keeler here is quite a Victorian. He won't believe that Queen Victoria actually married John Brown."

"Bishop Stewart," replied Temple evenly and in a normal voice, "you don't seem to realize that conceivably there is an Aristotelian mean between Balmoral and immoral."

The Archbishop told on himself the oft-repeated anecdote respecting his Episcopal chimere — the white under-dress with ruffled sleeves. It was soiled and had to be sent out to be laundered. It came back, with a bill attached which read under Items:

One Bell Tent

King George V gave his usual Christmas broadcast over radio in 1935. I heard it and somewhere picked up this story. An Englishman was anxious to have an American friend hear the King. Finally he induced the American to listen with him. The latter listened intently for two or three minutes, then said, "The King! The King of England. It isn't possible. This fellow talks just like an American." I repeated this to the Archbishop in one of the first letters I wrote him, soon after the King's broadcast, which proved to be his last, as he died within the month after making it. However, William Ebor. wrote me that he had sent the story to Lord Wigram, the King's Secretary, who had replied to tell the Archbishop that he had relayed his story to His Majesty, and he had hugely enjoyed it. I was gratified to think that my joke was possibly one of the last good King George V heard.

The Archbishop was very generous, while proceeding on his American tour, about bestowing praise on me as a talented and promising theologian. Some encomiums one heard had obviously been added to in the telling. This one had the earmarks of an authentic Temple remark: "You know Charles Lowry wrote his doctoral dissertation at Oxford on the Doctrine of the Trinity. Now a man who would do that is either a genius or a fool."

1937

At Bishopthorpe soon after my arrival on Friday, July 30th. (His Grace had apparently been at Cambridge recently).

"Charles, have you heard the Cambridge version of the Commandments?"

"No, your Grace, I haven't."

"It goes this way, 'Thou shalt love the Lord thy *Dodd* with heart, soul, mind and strength; and thou shalt love thy *Niebuhr* as thyself.' "

As we were walking toward the Palace from the great Gateway: "They say here in England that I am becoming more and more an Anglo-Catholic; but the spikes, they don't say so."

At tea on the eve of the Edinburgh Conference, at Cowan House, just the Archbishop and myself. (By this time he was dieting: for breakfast coffee and fruit only; for tea, only tea.)

Looking at the cake, William said, "Well Charles, in honor of the occasion, I think I'll break over and have a piece."

At the Edinburgh Conference neared the end, when the snarl over the Ministry became grave and threatened to disrupt the harmony required for a *nemine contradicente* vote, Professor Angus Dun (later Bishop of Washington) made an effective speech which changed the whole atmosphere. The Archbishop, who had been gallantly presiding through this ordeal, referred to Dun later as "Horatio at the Bridge."

Various Stories

Temple was basically a patient man and appeared to suffer bores and fools gladly. Once when asked how he managed to be so patient with such folk, he replied, "By prolonged bouts of inattention."

One of his clergy, according to Dean Iremonger, said of Temple that "he had the punch, but no man ever used it so sparingly." On one occasion there was a speaker who refused to give way and Temple then a Bishop had to cut him down. "But your revered father said," persisted this speaker. "I do not know," replied Temple, "whether my revered father said it or not, but if he did I disagree with what my revered father said."

This evoked loud applause, and the speaker sat down.

A Story Temple used in more than one book to illustrate different points.

An Englishman traveling in Ireland asked of a bystander the way to Roscommon. "Is it Roscommon you want to go to?" asked the Irishman. "Yes", said the Englishman; "that's why I asked the way." "Well," replied the Irishman, "if I wanted to go to Roscommon, I wouldn't be starting from here."

At Manchester on "Christianity and War"

At the beginning of the war I went to hear Dean Wace on this subject. I did not find him helpful. On my return I consulted the *Summa.* I thought that St. Thomas might be more illuminating than Dean Wace...He was.

When Temple succeeded Dr. Cosmo Lang as Archbishop of York, he said that he had two advantages over his distinguished predecessor: he was married, and he was an Englishman!

You might go the length and breadth of Europe and not find another man like the Archbishop. There's only one thing he cannot do: he can't tick you off properly.

(Verdict of Temple's Chauffeur)

I believe he must have learnt very young what some people never learn — that if you are sure of yourself, it does not matter whether or not you are sure of what you are going to meet around the corner.

(Lionel Smith, a long-time friend, of Temple)

To a man of my generation an Archbishop of Temple's enlightenment was a realized impossibility.

(Bernard Shaw on Temple)

Lord Hailsham, Lord Chancellor of Great Britain, told me at tea in the House of Lords in 1979 of hearing Temple preach at Eton while he was an Upper boy there. He went around afterward and talked with the preacher: about the sermon and some problems he had.

Many years after Hailsham had entered Parliament he met Temple now a Prelate. Temple not only recalled meeting him at Eton but remembered what they had talked about, greatly impressing Hailsham.

Temple's favorite poet to the end of his life, was Browning and his favorite poem was *A Death in the Desert,* which he considered the best commentary on St. John. As Headmaster of Repton he gave every boy who reached the Upper Sixth a complete Browning as a present.

Temple's favorite Artist was Botticelli.

A Duke of Wellington Story
(Used frequently by Temple to illustrate the point that all events
are not equally revelatory of the divine character.)

There was great expectation when a hotel waiter undertook to describe the great Duke eating his figs, but the result was an anticlimax. It turned out that the Duke's way of eating them was in no way extraordinary: it was simply quadrisection down the stalk and then four licks.

William lived at Oxford (he was there nine years) with his mother, as his father Frederick had lived with his at Rugby. Neither man married until after his mother's death.

At the Oxford house a number of young men were wont to gather around William and his mother. Bishop Beverly Tucker, who went over in 1905 as a Rhodes Scholar (the second contingent), remembered these occasions and the manner in which William aired freely his opinions on many things. But on one occasion, he was interrupted by his mother who said, "Willie, you know more than I do, but I know best."

On Charles Gore
The two men came out of a difficult Committee meeting and walked together. Gore had lost his temper in the meeting and was brooding

over it. A bad temper, he said, is a terrible thing. Then looking at the beaming, unruffled countenance of Temple, he said: But it's not as bad as having a good temper!

On another occasion Temple met Gore coming out of the London Zoo. The latter was in an upset state of mind. Every time I go to the Zoo, he fumed, it threatens to make an atheist of me. Temple confessed to an opposite feeling.

On his last holiday on top of the Quantock moors looking across the Bristol Channel to Wales — a favorite spot — he talked as always intimately with his wife. This year (1944) the talk turned to plans for the future. Some day he must retire. You must not leave it too late, urged Mrs. Temple. Yes, he replied, and I must give up in time to let Geoffrey (Dr. Fisher) have his whack.

Corrigendum

According to the *Oxford Dictionary of Quotations,* 3rd ed., 1979, Oxford University Press, William Temple is credited with replying to a query about providential interference, "Can't tell; didn't know your aunt."

This is a first-class blooper, as the reference cited for this quotation, Sandford, *Memoirs of Archbishop Temple,* is a work about Frederick Temple; and Frederick Temple is mentioned and quoted on the same page in the Oxford Dictionary. William admired and revered his father to an extreme degree, but their temperaments were quite different. Frederick was a graduate of the University of Hard Knocks, coincidentally with Balliol, Oxford, whereas William was born to the purple and had never known adversity in the slightest degree.

Father and Son were both explosive laughers and had a highly developed sense of humor, but Frederick, a personality described as "granite on fire" was marked by brusqueness and acerbity, in contrast to William.

Temple's Laughter

William from his school and college days was famous for his laughter. "It was laughter," wrote the renowned scientist Julian Huxley, "in the grand manner and on the largest scale, earth-shaking laughter that shook the laugher too. While it infected everybody who heard it with cheerfulness, it was a potent disinfectant against all meanness, prurience, and petty-mindedness. It was the intensely valuable complement of Temple's seriousness."

It is a great mistake to suppose that God is only, or even chiefly, concerned with religion.

Christianity...is the most avowedly materialistic of all the great religions.
> (*Nature, Man and God* p. 478. The same idea phrased in a
> less guarded form appears in *Readings in St. John's Gospel*, I,
> p.xx and is quoted in this form in *The Oxford Dictionary of
> Quotations.*)

A strong case could be made for the contention that on the whole Religion, up to date, had done more harm than good.

Thus for a Christian the Nicene Creed is not an object of faith, but a formulation of a faith of which the object is God revealed in Christ.

The Nazis...believe with great fervor; and we are not going to extirpate their belief by a mild haze of cautiously held opinions.

The best thing is for the Conservatives to do the right things.
> (In conversation July 1939 on the Boat Train to the
> Hook of Holland — the last time I saw W.T.)

The art of government in fact is the art of so ordering life that self-interest prompts what justice demands.

If the aim of the last war was to make the world safe for democracy and freedom, our aim in this war must be to make freedom and democracy safe for the world.

On freedom all spiritual life depends...But man is a self-centered creature. He can be trusted to abuse his freedom.

Nothing is a thing which it is always wrong to have done.

What wears one out is not what one does but what one doesn't do.

Christian character consists of a balance of many virtues, any one of which is comparatively easy to achieve without the others.

On the Americans and the British

We are made for friendship, both in the bewildering differences which so surprise us when we assume similarity, and the equally perplexing similarity which comes to contradict us if we assume that we are different.
> (At Pilgrim Dinner, New York: Jan. 1936)

I am always suspicious of the dilemma in connection with spiritual realities. It is almost inevitable that its crude dichotomy should do violence to the complex delicacy of spiritual relationships.

(To Upper House of Convocation, Canterbury: Jan. 1944)

Let it then be frankly and fully recognized that there neither is, nor can be, any element in human experience which may claim exemption from examination at the bar of reason.

The first condition of attainment in Science or Art or Religion is not loyalty to self, but forgetfulness of self in concentration on the Object; it is most truly the meek who possess the earth.

The primary assurances of Religion are the ultimate questions of Philosophy.

The most disastrous moment (I am tempted to say) in the history of Europe...was that period of leisure when Rene Descartes, having no claims to meet, remained for a whole day "shut up alone in a stove."

The more completely we include Mind within Nature, the more inexplicable must Nature become except by reference to Mind.

The principle of morality is that we should behave as Persons who are members of a Society of Persons.

Strength of will first shows itself in certain splendid incapacities.

The reverence of persons can be appropriately given only to that which is at least personal.

The main interest alike of philosophy and of religion is with the question whether the Cosmic Mind is truly conceived as personal.

Salvation is the state of him who has ceased to be interested whether he is saved or not, provided that what takes the place of that supreme self-interest is not a lower form of self-interest but the glory of God.

We are clay in the hands of the Potter, and our welfare is to know it.

A Conversation, reported by W.T., between Two Theologians, one an Augustinian, the other a Semi- (or Semi-demi) Pelagian:

S.-P. "No doubt the call is from God, so the initiative is with Him; but whether or not I answer the call depends on myself."

Aug. "I see; so your address to the Almightly is: 'For that thou didst call me of thy grace I thank thee; but for that I answered the call I thank thee not, but rather tender my most respectful congratulations'."

If God did not create He would still exist, for He is not dependent for existence on His creation. But if He did not create, He would not be what He is, for He is the Creator.

142

Man is not in his own nature immortal, but he is *capax immortalitatis*.

In the sacrament then the order of thought is spirit first and spirit last, with matter as the effectual expression or symbolic instrument of spirit.

What is wanted is some ground for belief that the occurrence of the evil is an actual element in the total good.

All Christian thinking, and Christian thinking about society no less than any other, must begin not with man but with God.

For the law, and the social order, is our schoolmaster to bring us to Christ.

This world can be saved from political chaos and collapse by one thing only, and that is worship.

One aspect at least of the Divine glory is the triumphant self-sacrifice of love. This is God's very being — not perhaps its entirety, but truly a part of its essence.

There is no such thing given us as a Christian social ideal. If there were, perhaps it might be free from the difficulties which are aroused in most of our minds by the social ideals drawn by men of limited or no inspiration.

It is always possible to begin behaving as a Christian, or at least more like a true Christian than we have done before.

The story of Christ is the story of love gaining its sovereignty through sacrifice.

What is the principle of our traditional education? It is that real education comes not chiefly through instruction, but chiefly through membership in a society.

The question of disestablishment is one in which the Chrch need take no interest at all. It is a question for the State only.

(Statement made at Manchester in 1925)

War Guilt Clause
One clause there is in the existing treaties which offends in principle the Christian conscience...This is the clause *which affixes to one group of belligerents in the Great War the whole guilt for its occurrence.* (Italics Temple's)

(From a sermon preached in Geneva at the beginning of the Disarmament Conference in 1932)

On Pacifism

Temple was never a Pacifist, but in both Wars he defended and was the friend of non-combatants and conscientious objectors. For example, he and Charles Raven remained fast friends.

I remember William saying to me, probably at Bishopthorpe, "The Pacifists are wrong, but they err on the right side."

Somewhere he wrote — and here we get the scholastic Temple with the power of fantastic recall — "Pacifism is actually a heresy; it partakes of Manicheanism, Marcionism, and Pelagianism."

He also said, "Christianity stands not for the elimination of force, but for its consecration."

On Anglicans and Plato

One evening after he had given a lecture, a lady came up to the Archbishop and said, "Your Grace, the Lutherans have Martin Luther as their founder. The Presbyterians have John Calvin. The Methodists have John Wesley. But the Anglicans — pray, whom do we have?" Temple looked at her a moment, smiled benignly, and replied, "Perhaps Plato."

On Pelagianism

Temple said and wrote repeatedly (and note this was a once-born Christian): "Pelagianism is the only heresy that is truly damnable."

Conclusion

I am entirely convinced that prayer is the chief thing.

(A prayer used by the Archbishop after his first Address to Students at Indianapolis in late December 1935. This Prayer is in the new 1979 American Prayer Book on page 832. It precedes immediately the celebrated "Prayer of St. Francis.")

Almighty and eternal God, so draw our hearts to thee, so guide our minds, so fill our imaginations, so control our wills, that we may be wholly thine, utterly dedicated unto thee; and then use us, we pray thee, as thou wilt, but always to thy glory and the welfare of thy people; through our Lord and Saviour, Jesus Christ. Amen.

Author's note. Most of the above sayings or statements of Temple were uttered or taken from books published in the last ten years of his life. They reflect I believe the great Man in the maturity of his powers.

It was in December 1935 that we first met. He was 54 and had less than nine years in which to live. It seems, looking back, incredible, but that is the matrix given by the Calendar.

ACKNOWLEDGMENTS

The three works which, apart from Temple's own writings, have influenced me most are W.R. Matthews, et al, *William Temple: An Estimate and Appreciation* (1946); F.A. Iremonger, *William Temple, Archbishop of Canterbury* (1948); and Joseph Fletcher, *William Temple, Twentieth-Century Christian* (1963).

My book would not have been possible without the material assembled in these studies and the portraitures which they project of the incomparable Archbishop and Christian thinker and leader which William Temple was.

I owe a particular debt to the Matthews volume. Dean Matthews was a dear friend of mine from Oxford days (1930-32) until his death at 93 in 1973. As a professional theologian, his insights into Temple's contribution, and his queries and criticisms as well, have a special value. As always, Dr. Matthews' essay is splendid in its balance.

Two other essays in this slender, rare volume, published only two years after Temple's death, have been especially helpful to me.

W.G. Peck's presentation of *William Temple as Social Thinker* is magisterial, in my view, and indispensable in providing guidance in the mine-strewn field of the mind of the Archbishop in relation to society. Peck gives in his succinct account of "the growth of (Temple's) dominant ideas" a view which is in some contrast to Fletcher's much more elaborated version.

A.E. Baker, writing on *William Temple - The Man*, gives the most moving and penetrating portrait of the person of the Archbishop to be found so far in Temple literature. It comes the closest to encompassing the man I knew.

Dean Iremonger had the impossible task of being the official biographer of the man who was so many things: philosopher, theologian, prophet, prelate, social and political thinker, ecumenical statesman, and spiritual leader not in one but in two world wars. The Dean wrestled nobly with the enterprise entrusted to him; and no one can work on Temple without standing on the shoulders of this biographer. His voluminous work is a mine of riches.

Fletcher finds "curious lacunae" in Iremonger's biography, which he undertakes in part to supply. Dean Iremonger was himself aware of his inability to deal with his subject in the role of philosopher and philosophic theologian. This part of his task he committed to Miss Dorothy Emmet, another friend of mine from Oxford days and a most competent thinker herself.

Joseph Fletcher is a friend whom I have known over five decades. We have also been ideological adversaries. I believe that in his truly remarkable and indubitably admirable study of Temple, Joe has tried steadfastly to check and curb his prejudices. On the whole, he has succeeded. I am puzzled by his neglect of Peck and tempted to see ideology in it.

The more important issue is Fletcher's perception of the great Archbishop in his totality as a Christian and a person. "The reader will find here not a definitive biography, but a portrait. A portrait is...not a photograph or a facsimile."

145

The odd thing is that for all its care and detail, the portrait which emerges in Fletcher's book is flat and almost impersonal. Some people thought Temple seemed this way; an American bishop I knew well who spent every summer in England thought this. But I knew better, and so did A.E. Baker.

The difficulty may be that what surfaces in the amazing *tour de force* achieved by Fletcher is the sense of the Academician. This author is so thorough and so comprehensive that he misses the charismatic, transcendental, unmistakably spiritual quality of his towering subject.

I think also that Joseph Fletcher was too eager to show the modernity of Temple and that he overdid this very real aspect of the thinker and the man. He failed to take into account sufficiently Temple's universality and ultimate conservatism. He made him out too much of an age and not enough a man for the ages.

Nevertheless, no lover of the great Archbishop and assuredly no laborer in the field of Temple scholarship can ignore Joseph Fletcher or fail to stand in his debt. I spent some hours in the British Museum and I labored manfully over the card catalogue in the Library of Lambeth Palace. I added to this a trip to Manchester University and an examination of the Temple collection in that University Library.

For the record I found 91 entries under Temple in the British Museum and 152 in the Library of Lambeth Palace. The William Temple Collection at Manchester is small by comparison but select; and I was able to examine the more recent Temple anthologies, the Lambeth Letters, and some works about Temple.

By comparison Fletcher has a Bibliography embracing 317 items, 221 by Temple and 96 by others, some of these news accounts and editorials. He estimates that a really exhaustive Temple bibliography could turn up at least 500 items.

Just these notations have a *bibliographical* value. Temple was truly a phenomenon in the range and volume of what he wrote, as well as in the quantity of what he caused to be written about him. One wonders whether in all church history any leader or prelate begins to compare with him in either respect.

At one time I had thoughts of attempting a comprehensive Temple bibliography, but I must leave this to a younger scholar and one with readier access to relevant libraries. It has seemed best for me to content myself with a substantial but select bibliography, concentrating on Temple's most important writings and adding works that have appeared since the publication of Fletcher's book in 1963.

I must express here a special debt of appreciation and gratitude to my wife, Kate Rowe Lowry, for her untiring labor on the manuscript of this book. Thanks to her pride and skill, it was when submitted to the publisher in nearly perfect condition. I dedicated an earlier work *To Pray or not to Pray!: A Handbook on American Church-State Doctrine* to her, But I take this opportunity again to say from my heart, "Thank you!"

BIBLIOGRAPHY

PRINCIPAL WORKS BY WILLIAM TEMPLE

A Selection

Chronologically Arranged

1910 *The Faith and Modern Thought.* Macmillan. 172pp.
(Temple's first book)
1911 *The Nature of Personality.* Macmillan. 120 pp.
(Six Oxford Lectures)
1912 *The Kingdom of God.* Macmillan. 143pp.
Foundations: A Statement of Christian Belief in Terms of Modern Thought. By Seven Oxford Men. Macmillan.
(Two Essays: "The Divinity of Christ" and "The Church" by Temple.)
1915 *Church and Nation.* Macmillan. 204pp.
(Paddock Lectures, General Theological Seminary, New York)
1916 *Plato and Christianity.* Macmillan. 102pp.
1917 *Mens Creatrix*: An Essay. Macmillan. 367pp.
(The first of three major philosophico-theological works.)
1920 *Fellowship with God.* Macmillan. 243pp.
(A collection of miscellaneous, non-academic sermons.)
1924 *Christ the Truth.* Macmillan. New York. 341pp.
(English title: *Christus Veritas.* Second major work.)
1926 *Personal Religion and the Life of Fellowship.* Longmans, Green. 87pp. (Lent Book, The Bishop of London)
1928 *Christianity and the State.* Macmillan. 198pp.
(Henry Scott Holland Memorial Lectures)
1931 *Christian Faith and Life.* SCM 139pp.
(Addresses at the celebrated Oxford Mission)
Thoughts on Some Problems of the Day. Macmillan. 206pp.
(Shows Temple in his prime and getting under way as Archbishop of York)
1934 *Nature, Man and God.* Macmillan. 530pp.
(Gifford Lectures at Glasgow. Temple's *magnum opus* and third major work.)
1936 *The Centrality of Christ.* Morehouse-Gorham, New York. 115pp.
(Title in England: *The Preacher's Theme Today.* College of Preachers lectures, Washington, D.C.)
Basic Convictions. Harper, New York. 81pp.
(Addresses, Student Volunteer Convention, Indianapolis.)
The Church and Its Teaching Today. Macmillan, New York. 49pp.
(William Belden Noble Lectures, Harvard University.)
Christianity in Thought and Practice. Morehouse-Gorham, New York. 112pp.
(Moody Lectures, University of Chicago.)
1938 Chairman's Introduction to *Doctrine in the Church of England.* Macmillan. 1938.
(Famous Commission Report)

1939 *Readings in St. John's Gospel:* First Series, Chapters I-XIII. Macmillan. 204pp.

1940 *Readings in St. John's Gospel:* Second Series, Chapters XIV-XXI. Macmillan. 206pp.

Thoughts in War-Time. Macmillan. 149pp.

The Hope of a New World. Macmillan. 125pp.

(Temple as a spiritual leader at his best.)

1941 *Citizen and Churchman.* Eyre & Spottiswode. 111pp.

(Lent Book, Temple's own series, following *The Two Moralities,* by A.D. Lindsay.)

1942 *Christianity and Social Order.* Penguin Books. 94pp.

(New edition of this classic, Ronald Preston, ed., with Foreword by Edward Heath. Shepheard-Walwyn/SPCK. 1976.)

Palm Sunday to Easter. Broadcast Addresses during Holy Week and Easter. SCM (Morehouse-Gorham, New York). 45pp.

1944 *Thomism and Modern Needs.* Aquinas Society of London, Blackfriars. 14pp.

(A famous *ex tempore* lecture.)

What Christians Stand for in the Secular World. SCM. 16pp.

(Written as a Supplement to the Christian News Letter, December 29, 1943. Widely regarded as one of Temple's most important pronouncements.)

The Church Looks Forward. Macmillan. 193pp.

(The Archbishop's valedictory: 25 addresses on varied subjects posthumously collected and published.)

Baker, A.E. Introduction in *Religious Experience*. James Clarke & Co., London. 1958.

Bell, G.K.A. "William Temple: Memoir" in A.E. Baker's *William Temple and his Message*. Penguin Books. 1946.

Dark, Sidney. *The People's Archbishop*. With an appendix, "Dr. Temple as a Diocesan", by A.E. Baker. James Clarke & Co., London. 1942.

Fletcher, Joseph. Biographical Sketch in *William Temple, Twentieth-Century Christian*. Seabury Press, New York. 1963.

Green, V.H.H. *From St. Augustine to William Temple* (Eight Studies in Christian Leadership). Latimer House, London. 1948.
(Contains a penetrating biographical study of Temple written before Iremonger's Life was published.)

Iremonger, F.A. *William Temple, Archbishop of Canterbury*. Oxford University Press, London. 1948.

Iremonger, F.A. "William Temple (1881-1944)." *Dictionary of National Biography 1941-1950*. Pp. 869-873. Oxford University Press, London. 1959.
(A model of compression.)

Lowry, C.W. "William Temple", Christendom, Winter 1943, 26-41.
(The principal American article on Temple following his Enthronement as Archbishop of Canterbury.)

Matthews, W.R. et al. *William Temple: An Estimate and Appreciation*. James Clarke & Co., London. 1946. (Other contributors: S.C. Carpenter, Carl Heath, F. Harrison, W.G. Peck, A.E. Baker.)

Temple, F.S., Ed. *Some Lambeth Letters*. Oxford University Press, London. 1963. (William was a great letter-writer. From Rugby days he cultivated the habit of writing regularly his older brother Frederick, whom he called 'Old'un'. He wrote Frederick constantly from Lambeth in his last period.)

Anthologies

William Temple and his Message: Selections from his writings arranged by A.E. Baker with memoir by G.K.A. Bell. Penguin Books, 1946.

Daily Readings from William Temple. Compiled by Hugh C. Warner. Hodder & Stoughton, London. 1948.
   (A "nuclear thought for every day in the year chosen by Temple's personal Chaplain for five years.)

The Wisdom of William Temple. An anthology from his writings. Compiled by F.H.C. Tatham. A.R. Mowbray, London. 1949.

William Temple's Teaching. (Selections from his writings.) Edited by A.E. Baker. J. Clarke, London. 1949. (Westminster Press, Philadelphia. 1951.)
   (This is an amplified version of Baker's 1946 Penguin without the Bell memoir.)

Religious Experience, and Other Essays and Addresses. Collected and edited with an introduction by A.E. Baker. J. Clarke, London. 1958.

Lent with William Temple. Selections from his writings. Edited by G.P. Mellick Belshaw. Morehouse-Barlow, New York. 1966.

Monographs and Theses on Temple's Thought

An Era in Anglican Theology: from Gore to Temple. By A.M. Ramsey. Scribner's, New York. 1960.

William Temple's Philosophy of Religion. By O.C. Thomas. Seabury Press, Greenwich. 1961. (SPCK, London.)
   (A doctoral dissertation.)

The Political Thought of William Temple, Archbishop of York and Canterbury. By Edward MacConomy. University Microfilms. 1962.
   (A doctoral dissertaion at the University of Michigan; includes a biographical sketch.)

William Temple, Twentieth-Century Christian, By Joseph Fletcher. Seabury Press, New York. 1963.

Temple's Political Legacy. By J.D. Carmichael & H.S. Goodwin. A.R. Mowbray, London. 1963.

Social Concern in the Thought of William Temple. By Robert Craig. Gollancz, London. 1963.

The Kingdom of God in the Thought of William Temple: The Purpose of God for Mankind. By W.R. Rinne. Abo Akadomi, Abo. 1966.
   (Mr. Rinne is a pupil of the Swedish theologian, Gotthard Nygren.)

A Study of the Relationship of Sin, Evil, Finitude, and Value in Nature, Man and God by William Temple. By Richard Magagna. Madison, New Jersey. 1968. University Microfilms.
> (A Drew University doctoral dissertation.)

The Inter-relation of Sacramental and Ethical Conceptions in the Thought of Frederick D. Maurice, Henry S. Holland, Charles Gore, and William Temple. By R.L. Heaton, University of Edinburgh, 1968.
> (A Thesis: Faculty of Divinity)

The Christian Philosophy of William Temple. By Jack F. Padgett. Martinus Nijhoff, Hague. 1974.
> (Based on an unpublished doctoral dissertation at Boston University, 1959; entitled *The Concept of Personality in William Temple's Philosophy.*)

The Ecumenism of William Temple. By Robert R. O'Connell, D.P., S.T.L. Washington, D.C. 1974.
> (A dissertation for the Laureate at the Pontifical University of St. Thomas in Rome. A useful summary of Temple on the Kingdom of God, the Church, and Ecumenism; disappointing in its cavalier dismissal of his theology including *Nature, Man and God* as "not profound.")

William Temple's Idea of Religious Experience; Seen as a Contribution to the Recent Philosophical Discussion of That Subject. By Joseph Everett Allen. Madison, New Jersey. 1978. University Microfilms.
> (Another Drew University doctoral dissertation.)

The Spirit of Anglicanism: Hooker, Maurice, Temple. Ed., W.J. Wolfe. Morehouse-Barlow, Wilton, Conn. 1979.
> (The Chapter on Temple is by Owen C. Thomas.)

William Temple's Christian Social Ethics: A Study in Method. By Alan M. Suggate. 1980.
> (An unpublished doctoral dissertation at Durham University, England.)